CICERO ON LIFE AND DEATH

MARCUS TULLIUS CICERO (106–43 BC) was the son of a Roman equestrian from Arpinum, some 70 miles south-east of Rome. He rose to prominence through his skill in speaking and his exceptional success in the criminal courts, where he usually spoke for the defence. Although from a family that had never produced a Roman senator, he secured election to all the major political offices at the earliest age permitted by law. His consulship fell in a year (63) in which a dangerous insurrection occurred, the Catilinarian conspiracy; by his persuasive oratory and his controversial execution of five confessed conspirators, he prevented the conspiracy from breaking out at Rome and was hailed as the father of his country. Exiled for the executions by his enemy Clodius in 58 but recalled the following year, he lost his political independence as a result of the domination of politics by the military dynasts Pompey and Caesar. His governorship of Cilicia (51–50) was exemplary in its honesty and fairness. Always a firm Republican, he reluctantly supported Pompey in the civil war, but was pardoned by Caesar. He was not let into the plot against Caesar. After Caesar's assassination (44), Cicero supported the young Octavian (the future emperor Augustus) and led the senate in its operations against Mark Antony. When Octavian and Antony formed the 'Second Triumvirate' with Lepidus in 43, Cicero was their most prominent victim; he met his end with great courage.

Cicero's letters, together with his speeches and his political and philosophical works, form the chief source for the history of the late Republic. His philosophical treatises, written in periods when he was deprived of his political freedom, are the main vehicle by which Hellenistic philosophy was transmitted to the West. His prose style raised the Latin language to an elegance and beauty that was never surpassed.

JOHN DAVIE is former Head of Classics at St Paul's School, London and now a Lecturer in Classics at Trinity College, Oxford. He is the author of a number of articles on classical subjects and has translated the complete surviving plays of Euripides for Penguin Classics (four volumes). For Oxford World's Classics he has translated Seneca's *Dialogues and Essays* and Horace's *Satires and Epistles*.

MIRIAM T. GRIFFIN is Emeritus Fellow of Somerville College at the University of Oxford. After her retirement, she edited for five years the *Classical Quarterly*. She is the author of a number of books on classical subjects including ed. with E. M. Atkins, *Cicero on Duties* for Cambridge University Press and *Seneca on Society: A Guide to De beneficiis* for Oxford University Press.

OXFORD WORLD'S CLASSICS

*For over 100 years Oxford World's Classics have brought
readers closer to the world's great literature. Now with over 700
titles—from the 4,000-year-old myths of Mesopotamia to the
twentieth century's greatest novels—the series makes available
lesser-known as well as celebrated writing.*

*The pocket-sized hardbacks of the early years contained
introductions by Virginia Woolf, T. S. Eliot, Graham Greene,
and other literary figures which enriched the experience of reading.
Today the series is recognized for its fine scholarship and
reliability in texts that span world literature, drama and poetry,
religion, philosophy, and politics. Each edition includes perceptive
commentary and essential background information to meet the
changing needs of readers.*

OXFORD WORLD'S CLASSICS

CICERO

On Life and Death

Translated by
JOHN DAVIE

Edited with an Introduction and Notes by
MIRIAM T. GRIFFIN

OXFORD
UNIVERSITY PRESS

OXFORD

UNIVERSITY PRESS

Great Clarendon Street, Oxford, OX2 6DP
United Kingdom

Oxford University Press is a department of the University of Oxford.
It furthers the University's objective of excellence in research, scholarship,
and education by publishing worldwide. Oxford is a registered trade mark of
Oxford University Press in the UK and in certain other countries

Translation © John Davie 2017
Editorial matter © Miriam T. Griffin 2017

The moral rights of the authors have been asserted

First published as an Oxford World's Classic 2017

Impression: 9

Published in the United States of America by Oxford University Press
198 Madison Avenue, New York, NY 10016, United States of America

British Library Cataloguing in Publication Data
Data available

Library of Congress Control Number: 2016951441

ISBN 978-0-19-964414-8

Printed in Great Britain by
Clays Ltd, Elcograf S.p.A.

CONTENTS

CONTENTS

INTRODUCTION

THE fortunes of Marcus Tullius Cicero, Rome's greatest orator, mirrored those of the city of Rome, which he first celebrated, then lamented. He was born at the end of the second century BC when Rome was a republic already ruling a large empire in the western Mediterranean and rapidly extending her power in the east. His career was one of intense activity in politics, the law courts, and the administration, mostly in Rome. It did, however, include a short period of exile in Macedonia and a spell as governor of the province of Cilicia in modern-day Turkey. He died as a victim of the Triumvirate, a legally constituted body comprising the trio of Octavian, Antony, and Lepidus: these men had defeated the Republican cause in the civil war that followed the death of Julius Caesar. After Cicero's death in 43 BC, the three would fall out with one another and, after the ejection of Lepidus from the coalition, the remaining two would plunge Rome into more civil conflict, from which the Republic would never recover. Instead, the victor, Octavian, the youngest of the Triumvirate, would, as the Emperor Augustus, create the new political system of the Principate and unify the empire by a land route connecting east and west. Augustus was to call Cicero 'a learned man and a lover of his country'.[1]

A New Man in the Senate

For Cicero, Rome was both a magnificent city and a cosmopolitan hub of empire. Still more important for him, it was identified with the Republic, a political system that centred on the senate house and the forum, where political speeches were made and important trials held. Elections and legislative decisions also took place exclusively in Rome, so that the increasing number of Roman citizens in Italy and the provinces were without representation, unless they travelled to the capital. Cicero himself was born on 3 January 106 BC in the town of Arpinum, a citizen community for which he retained considerable affection. He was what the Romans called a 'new man'—that is, the first in his family to achieve high public office—rising through the requisite series of magistracies to the highest, the consulship. His mother, Helvia, came

---

[1] Plutarch, *Cicero* 49.3. The remark is addressed to one of his grandchildren whom Augustus discovered was reading Cicero.

from a family that could boast senatorial office holders early in the previous century. His paternal grandfather had held local office, but his father was not very robust and remained a rather bookish gentleman of leisure. He saw to it that his son had a good education, studying at the house of Lucius Licinius Crassus, one of the great orators and statesmen of the day. Another of the boys to appreciate the tutors gathered there was probably Titus Pomponius Atticus, who remained a close friend of Cicero for life. The two then went on to study law with Quintus Mucius Scaevola Augur, a great jurist. All of this was wonderful preparation for a career in public life, where the two chief means of achieving prominence were oratorical skill and military prowess. It was in the senate house and the forum that the aristocrats of Rome devised and enforced the laws, as well as inculcating in the newcomers their own code of behaviour.

Cicero's Friend Atticus

Atticus was born at the end of 110 BC and was three years older than Cicero. The two had been friends since their schooldays. As a well-connected gentleman of equestrian status, Atticus could probably have embarked on a senatorial career had he wanted to do so. But he chose to remain an *eques*, a gentleman of non-senatorial rank, and did not even participate in the activities of public life for which *equites* were eligible. As his biographer Cornelius Nepos wrote:

He never took part in a public auction of taxes or other state services. . . . the post of prefect, offered him by many consuls and praetors, he accepted on condition that he accompany no one to his province, be content with the honour alone, and despise the profit to his estate; not even with Quintus Cicero (Cicero's younger brother) had he wanted to go to Asia, though he had the chance of a legate's position on his staff, for he said that it was not seemly, when he had refused to hold a praetorship, to be a praetor's assistant.[2]

Cicero and Atticus between them arranged Quintus' marriage to Atticus' sister Pomponia, which turned out to be more convenient for the two friends than happy for the wedded pair.

Atticus spent many years away in Athens, where he became involved in civic affairs, and in 68 BC he acquired an estate at Buthrotum in Epirus, to which he also made frequent visits. To the long separation of the two friends, in fact, we owe the wonderful series of letters that

[2] *Letters to Atticus* 6.4.

Cicero wrote to Atticus. These letters suggest that the emotional balance of the friendship was on Atticus' side: his job was to calm down the volatile Cicero and give him good advice. He also looked after his business and financial affairs, especially when Cicero was out of Rome. From those letters of Cicero that were replies to his friend's missives, we can sometimes infer what Atticus had written to Cicero, given that the letters composed by Atticus are not preserved. That we do not have them seems to fit his reticent personality. He outlived Cicero, and we may surmise that he had his own letters destroyed.

Cicero, by contrast, loved the limelight and was determined from the start to have a public career. His education had prepared him well, and he went on to share and relish the excitement of senatorial debate, popular oratory, and the forensic arena in which his peers played out their rivalries and hostilities. Cicero also went through the standard military training and served in 90 BC under Gnaeus Pompeius Strabo, the father of his contemporary Gnaeus Pompeius Magnus (hereafter 'Pompey'), in the Social War, the conflict in Italy that finally brought Rome to grant its citizenship to most of the Italian peninsula. Thus equipped in youth with the relevant military experience, Cicero later, during his governorship of Cilicia, was to fight several campaigns, and he would probably have earned a triumph, the ambition of all Roman commanders, had the civil war not intervened.

The Senatorial Career

Having pleaded his first public cases in the courts, Cicero spent a year in Athens and Rhodes studying oratory and philosophy, sitting at the feet of Apollonius Molon the rhetorician, the Academic philosopher Antiochus of Ascalon, the Stoic philosopher Posidonius, and the Epicureans Zeno and Phaedrus. Although Cicero regarded history and law as essential parts of the orator's education, it was philosophy that he would later particularly recommend in his theoretical works, not only because of the wisdom it lends to the speaker's subject matter, but because of the training that dialectic offers in argument.

On his return to Rome, Cicero successfully campaigned for his first magistracy, the quaestorship. This office he shared with nineteen other young hopefuls also bent on senatorial careers. As the quaestor at Lilybaeum (now Marsala), he was a subordinate of the governor specifically charged with financial duties. During the year that he spent in Sicily (75 BC), he found or made time to visit the tomb of Archimedes, the great Greek scientist, who was buried at Syracuse. When he returned

to the capital, he realized that no one had noticed his absence, and
he resolved never to leave Rome again, except when necessary.[3] That
promise he largely kept, his principal absences being limited to his exile,
his governorship, and his later service in the civil war between Pompey
and Caesar. Back home again, he pleaded in 70 BC the prosecution case
against Gaius Verres for practising extortion as governor of the province where Cicero had served as quaestor. His opening speech was so
powerful that Verres left the city without waiting for the jury's verdict,
though Cicero was not to be cheated of his glory and published four
more speeches castigating the scoundrel. Next, as aedile in 69, he gave
the expected games, though not on as lavish a scale as some other
aediles did. Expensive as this office was, it was preferable for someone
of Cicero's political convictions to that of tribune of the plebs, the other
office leading to the praetorship, for, as tribune, he would have been
forced to choose between demagogic prominence and conservative insignificance. Next, duly elected top of the poll as praetor for 66 BC, he
chaired the extortion court, where corrupt governors like Verres were
brought to trial. He also delivered his first political speech in public.
This was in support of a tribunician bill, the Lex Manilia, which conferred a command on Pompey, with extensive powers and resources, to
conquer King Mithridates VI Eupator. The enemy was the aggressive
and imperialistic king of Pontus, who had massacred Roman and Italian
merchants and other businessmen in Asia.

By this time Cicero had married Terentia, a wealthy and well-born
woman, and fathered a daughter, Tullia, born in 78 BC, who was to be
his beloved soulmate until she died in childbirth at the age of thirty-
three. His only son was born in the same year as Cicero's praetorship,
66. Young Marcus was to prove a good soldier but not a very good student, though Cicero sent him to Athens in his twenties to study with
the Peripatetic philosopher Cratippus, and tried to present philosophy
to him in the accessible form of the treatise *On Duties*, written in the
Stoic vein. He seems to have become an alcoholic later in life,[4] but lived
to become consul in 30 BC after the victory of Octavian at the Battle of
Actium. That wish of his father, at least, he fulfilled.

The Active Consul

For someone of Cicero's non-senatorial background, reaching the
praetorship was a substantial achievement, but Cicero had his eye on

---

[3] *In Defence of Plancius* 65–6.   [4] Pliny, *Natural History* 14.147.

becoming one of the consuls, the two chief magistrates of Rome. Cicero was the only candidate of the seven standing in 64 BC who was a new man, in the sense mentioned above. Although he had retained contacts with his equestrian peers and had cultivated his new senatorial associates, it was the reputation he had acquired as an orator that must have tipped the balance, and he was elected at the earliest age the law allowed, to serve with C. Antonius, the son of a consul. During his consulship of 63 BC, Cicero first defeated a whole battery of reform bills brought by the tribunes of the plebs, and was then, later in the year, faced with armed insurrection. It was his proudest claim, throughout the rest of his career, that he had saved the Republic from the conspiracy of L. Sergius Catilina, a disgruntled aristocrat whom he had defeated in the consular elections. Cicero's rhetoric on the subject, with which he inundated senate and people, is so copious and powerful that it is difficult to estimate the true size of the threat to Rome, the roots of which lay deep in the eighties BC, in the civil war between Gaius Marius and Lucius Cornelius Sulla. The difficulty is compounded by the fact that our fullest ancient source, the historian Sallust, writing a generation later, clearly accepted Cicero's estimation of the Catilinarian conspiracy, even as he shone a glamorous spotlight on the villain rather than on the consul who defeated him. It is another source who tells us that men could still remember Catiline carrying the head of one of Marius' kinsmen through the streets of Rome to present it, still 'full of life and breath' to the dictator Sulla himself. Now, dispossessed farmers, partisans of the murdered general, joined with the disgruntled veterans of Sulla, who had been settled on their confiscated land, and with spendthrift aristocrats hoping for the cancellation of debts, while slaves naturally took advantage of the resulting chaos to seize their liberty. After two Roman armies had finally repressed the rebellion, Cicero made manifest for the first, but not the last time, the strong view he took of the senate's powers: he used a senatorial decree of emergency, followed by a senatorial vote, to execute the conspirators without trial.

Not everyone agreed that this action was in keeping with the Roman constitution, which was a matter of unwritten custom and tradition and subject to various interpretations. As a result, Cicero found himself driven into exile in 58 BC through the attacks of a tribune of the plebs who disapproved, taking the negative *popularis* (democratic or left-wing) view of his procedure. The tribune was Publius Clodius Pulcher, a member of the ancient Claudian family who had given up his patrician status to become eligible for this plebeian office but had not given up his aristocratic pride along with it. He resented having once been made a fool of on the floor of the senate by Cicero's wit. Cicero in despair left Rome for the east before Clodius passed his measure sending into exile anyone who had put Roman citizens to death without trial. Cicero was devastated but unrepentant. In his absence, his house on the Palatine, a source of great pride to him, was plundered and burned, and a temple of Liberty was built on the site; but he was recalled after a year and a half through Pompey's belated efforts on his behalf. After incompetent tribunician efforts, one of the consuls of 57, Lentulus Spinther, proposed the bill for Cicero's recall to the centuriate assembly, the popular assembly in which wealthier voters had great voting power. Not surprisingly, the bill passed, and Cicero at once set sail, reaching Italy on 4 August to a tumultuous welcome and making a triumphant entry into Rome a month later.

Political Frustration and Philosophy

Cicero's euphoria was short-lived. Roman politics was by now paralysed by the domination of Pompey, Crassus, and Caesar, who, acting in coalition, were passing what legislation they chose and controlling the elections. Cicero, though a senior statesman, struggled to maintain his independence, while on occasion lending reluctant support, through his oratorical talents, to their projects and their associates. He also found himself pleading before members of the priestly colleges for the return of the site of his house, a campaign in which he finally succeeded. It was during these years that, frustrated in public life, he first started to put his excess energy, stylistic brilliance, and superabundant vocabulary into writing works of philosophy, which was a new domain for Latin literature. Cicero naturally turned first to rhetorical and political theory, subjects that were not only congenial to him but likely to find a substantial readership among his peers.

To the Greeks and Romans, philosophy had three divisions: physics, logic, and ethics. Rhetoric came under logic, and political theory under ethics. These were the subject areas to which Cicero turned, for writings on them would not only please his readership, but would keep him before the public as a leading statesman, at a time when political circumstances were restricting the inspiration and leadership that an ex-consul would hope to provide.[5] To this period we owe the monumental treatises

[5] The main thesis of Steel 2005.

in dialogue form, *On the Orator* and *On the Republic*. Cicero was later to list them, in the second book of his *On Divination*, among his philosophical works, though the majority of those, including the works in this volume, were written a decade later. Both *On the Orator* and *On the Republic*, like the somewhat later *On the Laws*,[6] were designed to emulate dialogues of the great Greek philosopher Plato: the former was inspired by Plato's *Gorgias*, the latter by his *Republic*. *On the Laws*, meant to recall Plato's dialogue of that title, was started a few years later and never finished. Despite the Platonic titles of two of these works, however, Cicero's dialogues are very distant from the abstract quality of Platonic thought, since even those set in the past, like *On the Orator* and *On the Republic*, were firmly rooted in contemporary concerns at Rome. Cicero chose to set these in periods that he thought boasted statesmen of the calibre Rome had once had and sorely needed again. Thus he used, as speakers for the work on rhetoric, the great orators of the first century BC Lucius Licinius Crassus and Marcus Antonius and, for the political work, the great second-century statesmen Scipio Aemilianus and Laelius. He had in youth already written one rhetorical treatise, *On Invention* in two books, but these later works were far more ambitious in literary form, for, in attempting to rival Plato, Cicero vividly characterized his speakers and set the dialogues in identifiable places.

As the end of the fifties BC approached, the coalition that had been dominating political life began to crumble. It had been patched up in 56 at a meeting in Lucca, but not long after, in 54, Caesar's daughter Julia, who had been married to Pompey to cement the alliance, died, and in the next year Crassus died fighting the Parthians. There followed the terminal breach in the alliance of Pompey and Caesar. We know a considerable amount about the struggle over Caesar's desire to extend his command, the senate's reluctance to see this happen, and Pompey's characteristic fence-sitting, since not only were Cicero and Atticus apart and communicating by letter, but for the year 51–50 Cicero was governing the province of Cilicia and bombarding his friends with requests for news from home. Both his questions and analyses of the political situation in his letters and some of their replies, notably those of his young friend C. Caelius, survive. These last are particularly valuable for they show how differently an observer as acute and sensitive as Cicero himself could read the political situation.

---

[6] Both *On the Republic* and *On the Laws* are available in the Oxford World's Classics series. For these and other works by Cicero in the series, see the Select Bibliography.

Civil War and Dictatorship

Back in Rome, Cicero did what he could to avert civil war, fearing the cost and the outcome. But when war came, despite his doubts about Pompey, Cicero felt that their long-term relationship and his belief that Pompey's was the 'better cause' (Pompey at least claimed to champion the Republic) meant that he must follow him to the east. After Pompey's defeat at Pharsalus in August of 48 BC, however, Cicero abandoned an active role in the war, and in October he returned to Italy, where he stayed for nearly a year at Brundisium awaiting Caesar's pardon. In September of the next year, he was cordially received by Caesar, when he went to Tarentum to meet him on his return from his victories in the east. Cicero then repaired to his villa at Tusculum. He remained profoundly indifferent to Caesar's reorganization and reforms, believing, of course, that the Roman Republic, as he knew it, was the perfect system of government. He was, however, moved sufficiently by Caesar's clemency towards Marcus Claudius Marcellus, who, as consul in 51 BC, had been one of Caesar's most virulent opponents, to speak with appreciation of the dictator in the senate in the autumn of 46. This intervention he later published as the speech *On Behalf of Marcellus*. Combining flattery with advice and admonition, it is the father of all the later imperial panegyrics and also served Seneca well when he was praising, while advising, Nero in *On Clemency*.

Two other cases of interaction with Caesar show again how the dictator's new position distorted political and social relations with his peers: they also show how ready Cicero was to try to make the best of the new situation. In May 45 BC, he composed a letter of political advice addressed to Caesar. It was modelled on Greeks works by Aristotle and Theopompus, addressed to Alexander. He sent it to Caesar's confidants Oppius and Balbus who made all sorts of suggestions for modifying it, which induced Cicero to withdraw the letter altogether. More successful was Caesar's visit in December of 45 to Cicero's villa at Puteoli, where he came to dine. His immediate entourage needed three other dining rooms to accommodate them, to say nothing of the rooms needed for the humbler freedmen and slaves, who also required feeding. And then there were the two thousand hungry soldiers encamped in an open field. As Cicero writes to Atticus, 'There you are—a visit, or should I call it a billeting, which as I said was troublesome to me but not disagreeable'.[7]

---

[7] *Letters to Atticus* 13.52.2.

After his defeat at Pharsalus, Pompey had fled to Egypt, where he was murdered on the orders of the king, who thought—wrongly—that it would please Caesar. On receipt in Rome of the news of Pompey's death, Caesar had been voted exceptional powers: he was made dictator and consul for five years and could designate senior magistrates and make peace and war on his own initiative. In retrospect, Cicero was to say that 'once a single man came to dominate everything, there was no longer any room for consultation or for personal authority, and finally I lost my allies in preserving the republic, excellent men as they were'.[8] He returned to philosophy, writing copious works in many of which he celebrated those excellent men.

He wrote the *Brutus* on the history of Roman oratory, commemorating his great predecessor and rival as an orator, Quintus Hortensius Hortalus, and, in a work now lost, he celebrated the life and philosophy of the younger Cato, who had committed suicide in April 46, after the Republican forces in Africa were defeated. Then, late in 46, he wrote another work on oratory, titled simply *Orator*, in which he speaks of writing about 'greater and weightier subjects' (148). He probably means the trilogy of works of which the first was named after Hortensius and the other two after his deceased contemporaries Quintus Lutatius Catulus and Lucius Licinius Lucullus, and which are set shortly before the death of Catulus in 61. Here Cicero depicts himself socializing and talking on equal terms with these older leading statesmen in their villas. In the *Hortensius* Cicero exhorts his readers to study philosophy; the other two books are devoted to the philosophical school to which Cicero adhered—the Academy, founded by Plato, and in Cicero's day emerging from a more rigorous sceptical phase into a milder scepticism. The *Catulus* concentrates on the sceptical system of Carneades and expounds the milder version of Philo of Larissa; the *Lucullus* debates the more dogmatic system of Antiochus of Ascalon. In these two essays (comprising the *Academic Books*), and in the final edition in four books and featuring Varro and Cicero, the author is a champion of Philo and the probable.[9] The *Hortensius* was the protreptic that, centuries later, converted St Augustine to spiritual things.[10] It clearly was a great success in its own time, for Cicero says that it was the popularity of that work that led him to write others, notably *On Ends* and the revised edition of the *Academic Books*, both composed between March and May 45 BC.

---

[8] *On Duties* 2.63, composed in the latter part of 44 BC.

[9] For a history of the editions of the *Academic Books*, see Griffin 1997.

[10] Augustine, *Confessions* 3.7.

Although, at the end of the *Lucullus* (147), Cicero had adumbrated later discussions on physics and ethics by the same three speakers (Hortensius, Catulus, and Lucullus), his next work, *On Ends*, featured a different set of participants, including his friend Atticus, his brother Quintus, and his cousin Lucius, and they are shown discussing ethics. Ultimately, however, Cicero did cover the three main branches of philosophy: logic (and epistemology) in the *Academic Books*; ethics in *On Ends*, the *Tusculan Disputations*, and *On Duties*; and physics, or at least the metaphysical part of it, in *On the Nature of the Gods* as well as in two supplementary works, *On Divination* and *On Fate*.

Cicero's Motives in Writing Philosophy

In his preface to the second book of *On Divination*, where he summarizes his ambitious programme of treating all aspects of philosophy (2.1–6), Cicero discusses, as in the prefaces to his other works, the two motives we have already mentioned: the need for a substitute for political activity and service to the Republic, and the intellectual challenge of rendering Greek philosophy in elegant Latin derived from his oratorical training. His response to these needs would lead him, he hoped, to increase the glory of Latin literature himself and to encourage contributions from others, as well as to develop a practical ethics for his peers, especially for the young among them.

In the *Tusculan Disputations* Cicero is more emphatic about his aims than elsewhere.[11] If in his *On Divination* he was to look forward to the Roman people being independent of Greek writers in the study of philosophy (2.5), here he insists on Roman ability to excel the Greeks in philosophy as they have in other branches of literature (1.1), defends the Latin language as an instrument for writing philosophy (2.35), and casts himself in the role of teacher of the young. There is, however, another motive, which Cicero mentions in other works as well, but which dominates this work, albeit in a less explicit way. That is Cicero's recent bereavement. Recently there had been upheavals in his personal life. He divorced his wife Terentia early in 46 and by the end of that year had married again, this time his wealthy ward Publilia, whom he was to divorce the next year owing to Publilia's failure to show sufficient grief over what was Cicero's most crushing disaster. In January 45 BC his beloved only daughter, Tullia, gave birth to a son in Cicero's house in Rome and was then moved to his villa at Tusculum, where, in the

---

[11] See Gildenhard 2007, especially 89–206.

middle of February, she died, apparently of complications in the birth. Her child lived only a few months. The deaths, especially hers, left Cicero devastated. He felt that he had fought bravely against fortune in the past but was now wholly defeated: the attacks of his enemies, his humiliating exile had been easier to bear than this.[12] As he wrote to Atticus, 'For a long time it has been my part to mourn our liberties and I did so, but less intensely because I had a source of comfort'.[13] He read every work on consolation that he and Atticus possessed, but the grief was stronger than any comfort they could offer.[14] And so, in the solitude of his villa at Astura, Cicero began writing his own *Consolation* to himself. He collected examples and other material throughout March 'and threw them into one attempt at consolation; for my soul was in a bruised and swollen state, and I tried every means of curing its condition', as he wrote later in the *Tusculan Disputations* (3.76, cf. 1.76). He knew that he was going against the advice of the Stoic Chrysippus, among others, that one should not try to apply remedies to fresh bruises (4.63). He found writing a distraction but was interrupted by fits of weeping.[15] He insists to Atticus, who agreed with others that he should return to Rome and his old activities, that he needs solitude and that his literary activity should at least count as an attempt to disguise his intense feelings, but that he is a changed person: 'the things you liked in me are gone for good'.[16] The *Consolation* 'reduced the outward show of grief; grief itself I could not reduce, and would not if I could'.[17]

Another, related, project absorbed him even while he was engaged on the *Consolation*: this was to deify Tullia by setting up a temple or shrine to her in an accessible place, which Atticus was to find and purchase, though he was unsympathetic to the scheme. Cicero regarded himself as bound by a pledge or a vow, and, as time passed, he urged fulfilment of the vow by the summer.[18] The shrine was to serve as a memorial to Tullia and her exceptional qualities. As he wrote in the *Consolation*, 'And you, the best and most learned of all, placed with the approval of the immortal gods themselves in their company, I shall consecrate in the eyes of all mortals'.[19] Cicero's insistence on this project until July 45 BC is remarkable. He seems to have given it up only when he heard of Caesar's plans to extend the city, which might

---

[12] Lactantius, *Inst.* 3.28.9–10 = frag. 3, *Cicero: Consolationis fragmenta*, ed. C. Vitelli (1979). [13] *Letters to Atticus* 12.28.2. [14] Ibid. 12.14.3.
[15] Ibid. 12.14; 12.15. [16] Ibid. 12.20.1; 12.14.3.
[17] Ibid. 12.28.2. [18] Ibid. 12.41.4.
[19] Lactantius *Inst.* 1.15.16–20 = frag. 23, *Cicero: Consolationis fragmenta*, ed. Vitelli.

interfere with the plot of land he had targeted.[20] He may also have realized the justice of Atticus' objection that some might think he was exploiting Tullia's death to gain glory for himself.[21] The *Consolation* would have to be her memorial.[22]

That was not the end of the healing process. Cicero was to re-use much of the material of the *Consolation* in the *Tusculan Disputations*, written after the shrine project was abandoned. He explicitly notes the overlap of the *Consolation* with Book 3 on distress (*aegritudo*), implying that it was in a calmer mood that the later work was composed, the earlier being written 'in the midst of mourning and grief, for I was no Wise Man' (4.63). The right time to write about these things, he now accepted (see above, p. xvii), was after the first flush of grief was over and one could write less personally and more objectively about immortality and about grief.[23] The theme of Book 1 on immortality was to surface again in his work *On Old Age*.

The Works in this Volume

The *Tusculan Disputations* did not use the format of Cicero's other dialogues, with a proper setting in time and place and carefully characterized speakers.[24] This feature can be related to the emotional crisis Cicero had experienced. The most inspiring source for talking about immortality was the *Phaedo* of Plato, the dialogue that is perhaps the most vivid and dramatic of all of Plato's dialogues, with the condemned Socrates leading the discussion and then drinking the lethal hemlock. Given Roman conventions, Cicero could not bring Tullia, dead or alive, on stage to talk about her fate, as he had Scipio Aemilianus in the dream of Scipio at the end of *On the Republic*. Nor would he have been able to bear making historical contemporary speakers conduct a dialogue about his beloved daughter. On the other hand, a straightforward presentation of arguments, like a teacher or sophist, could not be addressed to his peers.[25] However, he had given instruction to his son in a short work *On the Classification of Rhetoric* and would do so later in the more substantial treatise *On Duties*. The person addressed in the *Tusculan*

---

[20] *Letters to Atticus* 13.33a.1.   [21] See the sensitive discussion in Testard 2002.

[22] See now on Cicero's method of consolation, Baltussen 2013, 76, 81–2.

[23] See Lefèvre 2008, 318–19.

[24] For an analysis of the work see Douglas 1990, 152–3. His notes on 5.70 and 71 draw attention to its awareness of the connection of physics and ethics and of the three areas of ethics. Douglas (162) notes the 'calculated moderation' with which Epicureanism is treated in this work as opposed to *On Ends*.   [25] As he notes in *On Ends* 3.6.

Disputations, though not his daughter or his son, is clearly a young person, eager to learn but troubled, to whom Cicero can represent himself as teaching wisdom and removing anxieties about death and pain in a paternal mode.

The peculiarities of the format have recently received a political explanation: that Cicero was in deep despair about the dictatorship.[26] That is not incompatible with the more personal explanation here given. The result was unique among Cicero's writings, the austerity of the presentation matching the bleakness of his mood. It has been suggested that Cicero treated Epicureanism rather generously in this work because of Caesar's sympathy for the philosophy,[27] but that makes its harsh treatment in *On Ends* in the same year more puzzling.

The works in this volume all put forward clear views held by the author, unlike *On Ends*, the *Academic Books*, and *On the Nature of the Gods*, in all of which the project is to present at length opposing views of different philosophical schools so as to enable the reader to choose for himself. This balanced argumentation was particularly appropriate for someone like Cicero who was a sceptical Academic and believed that the probable view could best emerge from argument on both sides. Cicero himself describes the *Tusculan Disputations* in the preface to Book 2 of *On Divination* (see above, p. xvi) as making plain the means to a happy life, whereas *On Ends* made the conflicting views of different philosophers known. But Cicero always retained his identity as a moderate sceptic[28] and insists that the views he advances as his own here are only 'probable', with the pupil being led on by argument to agree with him (1.16–17, 23, 78; 2.4; 4.7; 5.32–3).[29]

In that same preface Cicero puts *Cato: On Old Age* in the same category as his *Consolation*, in that it shows the beneficial practical results of applied philosophy. With this work Cicero reverted to characterization of his speakers, or at least of the main speaker. But Cicero does not show us the curmudgeonly Elder Cato known from Plutarch and Cicero's letters. This is a genial, intellectual Cato, who expresses a liking for Greek literature, notably Plato and Xenophon, Homer and Hesiod. Cicero also makes him encouraging to the young, and sensitively aware of such characteristics of old age as a liking for reminiscence, boasting,

---

[26] Douglas, 1985, 17; Gildenhard 2007, 4.   [27] Fuhrmann 1992, 151.

[28] Some scholars, notably Glucker (1988), have suggested that Cicero abandoned Philo's scepticism in the 50s, when he was writing *On the Republic* and *On the Laws*, reverting to it in 45 BC, but I find myself in agreement with Görler 1995 and Woolf 2015, who argue for Cicero's continuous adherence to scepticism.

[29] See n. to 2.5, *without loss of temper.*

and a tendency to loquaciousness (¶¶31, 82, 55). Fear of not being in control of one's household (¶37), anxiety about losing the thread of one's discourse (¶56), and awareness of the passing of contemporaries are all demonstrated by Cato, and unpleasant traits often associated with old age, like being fretful and hard to please, and, more seriously, miserliness, are carefully explained away by him as faults of character, not of age (¶65). The choice of Cato as principal speaker was probably influenced not only, as Cicero said, by his actual attainment of old age and by his flourishing as an old man (*On Friendship* ¶4), but also, we may surmise, by his bearing with courage the loss of a child, to which Cicero alludes several times in works of this period (see n. to ¶12, *he endured the death of his son*). The sympathy with which Cato is portrayed must surely be explained to some extent by the similar suffering that Cicero felt they both shared.

On the Orator is set in 91 BC, the year of Lucius Licinius Crassus' death, and *On the Republic* is set in 129, the year of Scipio's death. Similarly, *On Old Age* is set in 150, a year before the main speaker died. *On Friendship*, too, is set in the year before the death of one of the main speakers, Quintus Mucius Scaevola, who recalls a conversation in the year of Scipio's death (5–6). Cicero regarded these two works as companion pieces, composed as they were in the same year, 44 BC, and both dedicated to Atticus. *On Glory*, which shared both that date of composition and the dedicatee, is unfortunately lost. Cicero's close relationship to his elderly, life-long friend Atticus, is spelled out by Cicero in the work on friendship, as he looks back on the first of the trilogy: 'But as on that occasion I wrote on old age as one old man to another, so in this book I have written on friendship as a most affectionate friend to another' (*On Friendship* ¶5). As a friend to a friend: in keeping with this conception of his subject matter, Cicero concentrates there almost exclusively on friendship between two people (*On Friendship* ¶81). He also reveals in that work one of the strong reasons for his friendships with non-senators like Atticus, Gaius Marius, and Papirius Paetus, when he writes (64) that 'true friendships are very hard to discover among those who occupy positions of power and engage in public life. For where would you find a man who would be happy for a friend to gain political office in place of himself?'

The works on old age and on friendship are closely linked, not just in date of composition. The second work mentions Cato several times (*On Friendship* ¶¶4–6, 9–12) even alluding to Cato's discussion with Scipio and Laelius on old age, treated in the first work. The two essays present similar views on the afterlife (*On Old Age*, passim; *On Friendship* ¶14).

Between these two works Caesar was killed and, though more writings followed, notably *On Duties*, Cicero was now active in politics again, defending the 'liberators', attacking Antony, and ultimately supporting Caesar's heir, Gaius Octavius, the future Emperor Augustus, whom he wrongly thought he could use in the service of the Republic. It was not to be. The *Philippics*, those insulting speeches that have coloured the reputation of Antony forever more, ensured that Cicero was put on the proscription list. He was murdered on 7 December 43 BC. He showed great courage in the face of death, as befitted a philosopher and a Roman. All three works of practical ethics—*On Old Age, On Friendship,* and *On Glory*—were to preserve their popularity in the Middle Ages and the Renaissance.

NOTE ON THE TEXT

THE critical editions used as a basis for the translation of the texts in this volume are, for the *Tusculan Disputations*, the edition by A. E. Douglas, *Tusculan Disputations*, 2 vols (Aris & Phillips, 1985–90); for *On Old Age* and *On Friendship*, the Oxford Classical Texts edition by J. G. F. Powell, *De re publica; . . . Cato Maior De senectute; Laelius De amicitia* (2006); and for the two 'Letters to Friends', W. S. Watt's edition *M. Tulli Ciceronis epistulae*, vol. 1: *Epistulae ad familiares*, Scriptorum Classicorum Bibliotheca Oxonienses (1982).

Each of the texts in this edition is preceded by an editorial synopsis of its contents. In the case of the *Tusculan Disputations*, Books 3 and 4 are represented only by Cicero's prefaces, but a full synopsis is given for both books.

SELECT BIBLIOGRAPHY

Life, Works, and Intellectual Context

Baltussen, H., ed. (2013). *Greek and Roman Consolations*, Swansea, Classical Press of Wales.

Barnes, J., and Griffin, M., eds (1997). *Philosophia Togata II*, Oxford, Clarendon Press.

Blom, H. van der (2003). '*Officium* and *Res Publica*: Cicero's Political Role after the Ides of March', *Classica et Mediaevalia* 54: 287–319.

Blom, H. van der (2010). *Cicero's Role Models*, Oxford, Oxford University Press.

Douglas, A. E. (1985). *Cicero Tusculan Disputations I*, Warminster, Aris & Phillips.

Douglas, A. E. (1990). *Tusculan Disputations II & V, with a Summary of III & IV*, Warminster, Aris & Phillips.

Fuhrmann, M. (1993). *Cicero and the Roman Republic*, trans. W. E. Yuill, Oxford, Blackwell.

Gardner, J. F. (1993). *Being a Roman Citizen*, London, Routledge.

Gildenhard, I. (2007). *Paideia Romana: Cicero's Tusculan Disputations*, Cambridge, Cambridge Philological Society.

Glucker, J. (1988). 'Cicero's Philosophical Affiliations', in J. Dillon and A. A. Long (eds.), *The Question of 'Eclecticism'*, Berkeley, University of California Press: 34–69.

Görler, W. (1995). 'Silencing the Troublemaker: *De legibus I.39* and the Continuity of Cicero's scepticism', in J. G. F. Powell (ed.), *Cicero the Philosopher*, Oxford, Oxford University Press: 85–113.

Griffin, M. T. (1997). 'The Composition of the *Academica*: Motives and Versions', in B. Inwood and J. Mansfeld (eds.), *Assent and Argument, Studies in Cicero's Academic Books*, Leiden and New York, Brill: 1–35.

Lefèvre, E. (2008). *Philosophie unter der Tyrannis: Ciceros Tusculanae Disputationes*, Heidelberg, Universitätsverlag.

Lintott, A. W. (2008). *Cicero as Evidence*, Oxford, Oxford University Press.

Mitchell, T. N. (1991). *Cicero, the Senior Statesman*, New Haven and London, Yale University Press.

Powell, J. G. F., ed. (1988). *Cicero: Cato Maior, De senectute*, Cambridge, Cambridge University Press.

Rawson, E. (1985). *Intellectual Life in the Late Roman Republic*, London, Duckworth.

Sedley, D. (2007). *Creationism and its Critics in Antiquity*, Berkeley and Los Angeles, University of California Press.

Steel, C. (2005). *Reading Cicero*, London, Duckworth.

Strasburger, H. (1990). *Ciceros philosophisches Spätwerk als Aufruf gegen die Herrschaft Caesars*, ed. G. Strasburger, Spudasmata 45, vol. 3 of

W. Schmitthenner and R. Zoepffel (eds.), *Studien zur alten Geschichte*, Hildesheim, Olms: 407–98.

Syme, R. (1938). 'Caesar, the Senate, and Italy', *Papers of the British School at Rome* 14: 1–31; repr. in *Roman Papers* 1, ed. E. Badian, Oxford, Clarendon Press, 1979: 88–119.

Testard, M. (2002). 'Observations sur la pensée de Cicéron, IV: La Consolation', *Revue des Études Latines* 80: 95–114.

Treggiari, S. (2005). 'Putting the Family Across: Cicero on Natural Affection', in M. George (ed.), *The Roman Family in the Empire: Rome, Italy, and Beyond*, Oxford, Oxford University Press.

Treggiari, S. (2007). *Terentia, Tullia and Publilia*, London and New York, Routledge.

Woolf, Raphael (2015). *Cicero: The Philosophy of a Roman Sceptic*, London and New York, Routledge.

Oxford World's Classics Editions

Defence Speeches, trans. and ed. D. H. Berry, Oxford, Oxford University Press, 2008.

The Nature of the Gods, trans. and ed. P. G. Walsh, Oxford, Oxford University Press, 1998.

On Obligations, trans. and ed. P. G. Walsh, Oxford, Oxford University Press, 2008.

Political Speeches, trans. and ed. D. H. Berry, Oxford, Oxford University Press, 2008.

The Republic and The Laws, trans. N. Rudd, ed. J. Powell and N. Rudd, Oxford, Oxford University Press, 1998.

Selected Letters, trans. and ed. P. G. Walsh, Oxford, Oxford University Press, 2008.

A CHRONOLOGY OF CICERO

Some minor undatable works are omitted. Lost works are marked with a dagger (†).

Date (BC)	Historical Events	Life of Cicero	Philosophical Works
110	Birth of Atticus.		
106	Birth of Pompey.	(3 Jan.) Birth in Arpinum.	
102		Birth of Quintus Cicero.	
100	Birth of Julius Caesar.		
95	Consulship of L. Licinius Crassus and Q. Mucius Scaevola the Pontifex.	Cicero and Atticus study at house of Crassus.	
91–88	Social War between Rome and her Italian allies, who are defeated but receive citizenship.	Death of L. Crassus (91).	
90		Assumes the *toga virilis*. Serves under Pompey's father in the Social War.	(after 91) *On Invention*.
89		Studying law with Q. Mucius Scaevola Augur.	
88	L. Sulla marches on Rome and goes east. Reforming tribune P. Sulpicius dies.	Hears Philo of Larissa in Rome.	
87	Marius occupies Rome. Posidonius comes to Rome on an embassy.	Studying rhetoric with Apollonius Molon. Studying law with Q. Mucius Scaevola Pontifex.	
83–81	Sulla returns to Rome. Proscriptions. Becomes dictator.	Delivers first published speech, in private case for Quinctius.	
82	Q. Mucius Scaevola Pontifex murdered.		
80	Sulla consul.	Delivers first public speech, defending Sextus Roscius, and then other cases (or 79). Marries Terentia.	

Date (BC)	Historical Events	Life of Cicero	Philosophical Works
79–78	Sulla in retirement and dies.	Studying oratory and philosophy in Athens and Rhodes; hears the rhetorician Apollonius Molon, the Academic Antiochus of Ascalon, the Stoic Posidonius, and the Epicureans Zeno and Phaedrus. (78) Daughter Tullia born.	
77		Returns to Rome.	
75		Quaestor at Lilybaeum (Marsala) in Sicily.	
70	First consulship of Pompey and Crassus.	Prosecutes Verres for extortion in Sicily.	
69		Plebeian aedile: gives games.	
67	Pompey's command against the pirates.	Tullia engaged to C. Calpurnius Piso Frugi. (or 66) Nephew Quintus Cicero born.	
66	Pompey given command against Mithridates.	Praetor, in charge of extortion court. Supports Lex Manilia, which gives Pompey command.	
65		Birth of his son Marcus. Quintus plebeian aedile.	
63	Catilinarian conspiracy exposed.	Consul with C. Antonius. Executes conspirators without trial. Tullia marries C. Piso Frugi.	
62	(Dec.) Pompey returns to Rome.	Buys house on Palatine. Defends P. Sulla. Quintus Cicero praetor.	
61–58		Quintus Cicero governing Asia.	†Memoir in Greek and †Latin poem on his consulship.
60	Pompey, Caesar and Crassus form the 'First Triumvirate'.		
59	Consulship of C. Julius Caesar and M. Calpurnius Bibulus.		

Date (BC)	Historical Events	Life of Cicero	Philosophical Works
58	Tribunate of P. Clodius Pulcher. Caesar campaigns in Gaul.	(Mar.) Driven into exile.	
57	Pompey put in charge of the corn supply.	(Sept.) Returns from exile. Quintus serving as legate to Pompey. Death of Tullia's husband.	
56	Renewal of 'First Triumvirate' at Lucca.	Speeches in support of triumvirs. Tullia engaged to Furius Crassipes; Atticus marries Pilia.	
55	Second consulship of Pompey and Crassus.		*On the Orator* begun.
54		Quintus serving as legate to Caesar.	*On the Republic* begun.
53	M. Crassus dies in Syria.	Elected augur in place of M. Crassus.	
52	Pompey elected sole consul.		*On the Laws* begun. *On the Orator* finished.
51–50		Governor of Cilicia; Quintus on his staff. Tullia marries P. Cornelius Dolabella.	*On the Republic* finished.
49	Caesar invades Italy and becomes dictator. Pompey leaves for the east.	Continues peace efforts, but then joins Pompey.	
48	(Aug.) Pompey defeated at Pharsalus and (Sept.) murdered in Egypt.	(Oct.) Returns to Brundisium and awaits Caesar's pardon.	
47	(Sept.) Caesar returns to Rome.	Pardoned by Caesar, with Quintus and his son.	
46	(Apr.) Caesar defeats Republicans in Africa. (Apr.) Suicide of M. Porcius Cato the younger.	Divorces Terentia. Tullia divorces Dolabella. Delivers *On Behalf of Marcellus* praising Caesar's clemency. Marries Publilia.	*Paradoxes of the Stoics.* †*Eulogy of Cato. Brutus. Orator. On the Classification of Rhetoric.*

Date (BC)	Historical Events	Life of Cicero	Philosophical Works
45	Caesar defeats the Republicans in Spain.	(mid-Feb.) Tullia dies after childbirth. Cicero's son goes to Athens to study. Divorces Publilia.	†*Consolation to Himself.* †*Hortensius. Academic Books. On Ends. Tusculan Disputations. On the Nature of the Gods.*
44	Caesar named *dictator perpetuus.* (15 Mar.) Assassination of Caesar. Antony as consul takes control. (Apr.) Octavian lands in Italy. Brutus and Cassius leave for provinces.	(mid-July) Leaves for Greece but returns to Italy (mid-Aug.) and to Rome. (2 Sept.) Delivers *First Philippic.* (Oct.–Dec.) Visiting his villas.	*Cato the Elder: On Old Age.* Publication of *On Divination. On Fate. Laelius: On Friendship.* †*On Glory. Topics. On Duties.*
43	(Apr.) Battle of Mutina; both consuls die. (Aug.) Octavian seizes the consulship. (Nov.) Triumvirate of Octavia, Antony, and Lepidus. Proscriptions instituted.	Delivers 5–14 *Philippic.* Proscribed. (7 Dec.) killed.	

TUSCULAN
DISPUTATIONS

SYNOPSIS

BOOK 1

1–8 **Introduction**.

Cicero intends to publish five days of discussions combining philosophy and rhetoric, presented as debates and serving as his declamation of old age.

9–15 Proof that death is not an evil for the dead, who are not wretched.

16–25 Proof that death is not an evil for those who are alive and will die.

17–24 Continuous speech by Cicero, summarizing opinions on the nature of death and of the soul, in order to find a probable—not certain—view of them; these opinions are that the soul perishes with the body, or leaves the body, to return to heaven.

26 The interlocutor asks for a demonstration that the soul survives death or that death is free from evil even if the soul perishes and one expects loss of sensation.

27–81 The case for the immortality of the soul.

27–35 Our care for what happens after our death shows that belief in survival is natural.

36–7 Irrationality invented the underworld.

38–49 The nature of the soul shows that its real home is not the body.

50 Philosophers who think otherwise than Socrates and Plato fail to understand the nature of the soul and its relation to the body.

82–111 If the soul perishes, death is not an evil.

83–6 This can free us from present and future evils.

87–8 The dead do not miss the comforts of life.

89–91 Some men have given up their lives out of patriotism.

92–102 Since life is short, living well is more important than longevity.

102–9 Treatment of the corpse is unimportant, as it deals only with the body.

110–11 As life fades, there is solace in a good reputation.

112–19 **Epilogue**.

The gods regard death as a good; the best men have often sought it.

BOOK 2

66 Pain is either not an evil, or is so insignificant an evil as to be eclipsed by virtue.

67 We have a refuge from unendurable pain.

BOOK 3

BOOK 4

BOOK 5

TUSCULAN DISPUTATIONS

BOOK 1

[1] When at last I had gained freedom completely, or largely, from the demanding role of advocacy and my senatorial duties,* I turned again, on your recommendation, Brutus,* to those studies especially which had stayed in my mind but which circumstances had caused me to relinquish.* I now have revived them after a long interval of neglect. Since the systematic study of all the arts which relate to the right way of living is bound up in the pursuit of wisdom, or 'philosophy', as it is called,* I thought I should elucidate this in the Latin language; not that philosophy cannot be understood through Greek writings and instructors,* but my conviction has always been that our forefathers have shown more wisdom than the Greeks, either in making their own discoveries, or in improving upon what they took from them, at least in those areas of expertise they had judged worthy of their serious efforts.*

[2] Morality, rules of life, matters to do with family and household are surely maintained by us in a better and more refined manner, and, when it comes to regulating public affairs, our ancestors certainly used superior practices and laws. What shall I say of military matters? Not only in their bravery have our troops won distinction but also, to an even greater extent, in their training. Again, in the matter of natural gifts as opposed to skills acquired from books, they are beyond comparison with the Greeks or any other nation. In what other people would we find such seriousness, determination, magnanimity, honesty, and integrity, or such moral excellence in every sphere that they could stand comparison with our forbears?*

[3] In learning and in every branch of literature Greece was our superior, and this was an easy victory when we offered no competition. Among the Greeks, it was poets who formed the most ancient literary class. Homer and Hesiod lived before Rome was founded, and Archilochus during the reign of Romulus,* so we came to poetry at a later stage. About five hundred and ten years after Rome's foundation Livius produced a play in the consulships of Gaius Claudius, son of Caecus, and Marcus Tuditanus, in the year before the birth of Ennius, who was older than Plautus and Naevius.* It was at a late date, then, that poets were acknowledged or welcomed by our forbears. It is stated

in the *Origines* that guests at banquets were accustomed to sing of the merits of famous men to the accompaniment of a piper,* but none-theless it is made clear that poetic writing was not held in honour by a speech of Cato, in which he censured Marcus Nobilior for having taken poets to his province. Now, we know that Nobilior in his consul-ship had taken Ennius to Aetolia.* Accordingly the less honour poets received, the less interest there was in poetry, and yet whenever men did emerge with great abilities in this sphere, they did not fail to match the fame of the Greeks.

[4] Or do we think that if Fabius Pictor, a man of true aristocracy, had been accorded honour for his painting, there would not have been among us also many a Polyclitus and Parrhasius?* It is esteem that nourishes the arts, and the thought of fame that kindles all men's enthusiasm for study. All that meets with men's disapproval always lies neglected. It was the view of the Greeks that the highest culture existed in the voice and in the music of strings. So it is said that Epaminondas, the foremost man in Greek history in my judgement, sang remarkably well to the lyre, whereas Themistocles, several years earlier, refused to take up the lyre at banquets and was considered deficient in culture.* Musicians, therefore, flourished in Greece; everyone learned music, and anyone ignorant of it was regarded as lacking in education.

[5] Among them geometry was accorded the greatest respect, so that mathematicians were held in the highest honour. But we have restricted this art to the practical business of measuring and calculating. But on the other hand we were swift to welcome the orator, not at first the learned one* but the one capable in speech, and, at a later stage, the learned one. For tradition tells us that Galba, Africanus and Laelius were learned men, while Cato, their predecessor, was a devoted student. After them came Lepidus, Carbo and the Gracchi, and then such great orators down to our own day that we have yielded little or no ground at all to Greece. Philosophy has lain neglected to our own day and has been denied any illumination in Latin literature.* It is for me to cast this light and to raise it up, so that any service I may have rendered my countrymen in my active life I may also extend to them, if I can, now that I am at leisure.*

[6] In this task I must work all the harder because there are now, they say, many books in Latin written by men who certainly possess merit but have insufficient education. It is possible for a man to hold the right views but to be incapable of expressing these with any elegance; but that anyone should entrust his thoughts to writing, without the ability to arrange them or to express them with clarity, or to attract the reader

by affording him some pleasure, is characteristic of a man who is making an ill-disciplined misuse of both leisure and writing. The result is that these fellows read their own books to their own circle and no one touches them except those who wish to be permitted the same freedom in writing.* Accordingly, if through my own application I have gained any measure of fame as an orator, I will with far greater enthusiasm lay bare the springs of philosophy, the source from which those efforts of mine flowed.

[7] Aristotle, a man of the highest intellect, knowledge and fluency, was put out by the fame of the orator Isocrates, and so began also to instruct young men in speaking and to combine wisdom and eloquence.* In similar fashion I have decided to engage in this greater and more fruitful art,* without abandoning my early devotion to oratory. I have always judged the perfect form of philosophy to be that which can treat the most important problems in a full and rich style. I devoted myself to this practice with such zeal that I even ventured to give set discourses in the manner of the Greeks.* Recently, for example, after your departure, when several friends were staying at my villa in Tusculum, I tried out what I could do in that vein. Just as in the past I would declaim speeches for the courts, spending more time on this than anyone had ever done, so this is now the declamation of my old age.* I would invite friends to propose any subject they wished to hear discussed, and then I debated it, either sitting down or walking about.

[8] Consequently I have put together into so many books the discourses, as the Greeks call them, of five days. The procedure was that, after the man who wanted to hear me had expressed his view, I would speak against it. This is, as you know, the old Socratic method of arguing against another person's view.* In this way, Socrates thought, the probable truth could most easily be discovered. But to make our discussions unfold more conveniently, I will set them out in the form, not of a narrative, but of a dramatic exchange.* This, then, will be how they begin:

[9] A. I regard death as an evil. M.* For those who are dead, or for those who have yet to die? A. For both. M. It is a wretched thing, then, since it is evil. A. Certainly. M. Therefore both those whose lot it is to have died already and those whose lot it is to be are wretched?* A. That is my opinion. M. No one, then, is not wretched. A. Absolutely no one. M. And indeed, if you wish to be consistent, everyone who has been born or will be born, is not only wretched but also wretched for ever. For if you meant that only those who had to die were wretched, you would not be making an exception of any living person—for all must die—but there would be an end to wretchedness in death. Yet, since the dead as

well are wretched, we are born into a wretchedness that is everlasting.
It must follow that those who died a hundred thousand years earlier are
wretched, or rather all those who were ever born. A. That is my view
precisely.

[10] M. Please tell me. You're not frightened, are you, by the stories of three-headed Cerberus in the underworld, the roar of Cocytus,
the crossing of Acheron, and 'Tantalus, worn out with thirst, his chin
touching the water's surface'? Then there's the tale of Sisyphus, 'sweat-
ing and struggling as he rolls the rock but advances not a jot'. Perhaps
you fear as well the implacable judges Minos and Rhadamanthus?*
Before them you will not be defended by Lucius Crassus or Marcus
Antonius,* nor, as your case will be heard before Greek judges, will you
be able to use Demosthenes' services. You yourself will have to plead
your own case before a vast crowd of listeners. This is the fate, perhaps,
that makes you afraid, and this is why you consider death an everlasting
evil. A. Do you think me so deranged as to believe such things? M. You
don't believe they are true? A. Not in the slightest. M. Oh, I'm sorry to
hear that! A. Tell me why. M. Because I could be eloquent in speaking
against such ideas.

[11] A. Anyone could in a case like that. There's no difficulty in
refuting the monstrous inventions of poets and painters. M. And yet
there are fat books written by philosophers who argue against those
very notions.* A. What a fatuous exercise! Who is so stupid as to be
influenced by these stories? M. If, then, there are no wretched people
in the underworld, no one at all can exist in the underworld. A. My
view exactly. M. Then where are they, the people you call wretched, or
what place do they inhabit? If they exist, they must be somewhere.
A. But I think they are nowhere. A. So they have no existence either?
M. Exactly as you say, but I consider them wretched for the simple reason that they don't exist at all.

[12] A. Now I should have preferred you to tremble at Cerberus than
to have made such a thoughtless remark. A. What *do* you mean? M. You
are saying that one and the same man exists and does not exist. Where
is your sharp intelligence? When you say he is wretched, you are saying
that the man who doesn't exist does exist. A. I'm not so dull-witted as
to say that! M. What are you saying, then? A. I say that Marcus Crassus,
for example, is wretched because he lost his famous fortune by his
death, as is Gnaeus Pompey, who was deprived of such great fame,* in
a word as all men are who have quit the light of day. M. You are back
where you started. If they are wretched, they must be.* But a moment
ago you said the dead do not exist. Well, if they don't exist, they cannot

be anything. So they can't be wretched either. A. I'm not perhaps expressing quite what I mean. It is that very state of non-existence once a person has existed that I consider most wretched.

[13] M. What? More wretched than never to have existed at all? So those not yet born are wretched now because they do not exist, and we, if we are to be wretched after death, have been wretched before we were born? Now, I have no recollection of being wretched before I was born. If your memory is better, I'd like to know if there's anything you remember about yourself. A. You are making fun of me, as if I were saying that those not yet born are wretched, rather than those who are dead. M. You say, then, that they exist. A. No, I say they are wretched because they have lost the existence that once was theirs. M. Don't you see that what you are saying is self-contradictory? What can be more of a contradiction than saying that someone who does not exist not only *is* wretched but *is* anything at all? When you come out of the Capenan Gate and see the tombs of Calatinus, the Scipios, the Servilii, the Metelli,* do you consider those men wretched? A. Since you put me under pressure on a matter of wording, from now on I will not say that they *are* wretched but only call them wretched, for the simple reason that they are without existence. M. So you do not say 'Marcus Crassus is wretched' but merely 'wretched Marcus Crassus'.* A. That's right.

[14] M. As if anything put forward as a proposition in that way must not of necessity either be or not be. Haven't you received even an elementary introduction to logic? For this is one of the first principles: every 'proposition'—this is how it occurs to me at present to translate *axioma*: I'll adopt another term later if I find a better one—a proposition, then, is a statement that is true or false. When, therefore, you say 'wretched Marcus Crassus', either you say 'Marcus Crassus is wretched', so that it can be determined if this is true or false, or you say nothing at all. A. Well, I now grant that the dead are not wretched, since you have wrung from me the admission that those who have no existence whatever cannot have a wretched existence either. But aren't we who are living wretched as we have to die? What delight can there be in life when day and night we must reflect that any time now we must die?

[15] M. I wonder if you realize what a weight of misery you have taken from the human condition? A. How so? M. Because, if dying was wretched for the dead as well, we should have an unlimited and everlasting evil in life: but now I see a finishing-line, and once we have gained it, there is nothing beyond it to make us afraid. But I fancy you are following the saying of Epicharmus,* a man of perception and perspicacity, as one would expect of a Sicilian. A. Which saying? I don't

know it. M. I'll give it in Latin, if I can. You know it's not my habit
to speak Greek in a Latin discourse any more than it is to speak Latin
in a Greek one.* A. Quite right too. But do say what this saying of
Epicharmus is. M. 'I don't want to die but being dead doesn't worry me
at all.' A. Now I recognize the Greek. But since you have forced me to
concede that the dead are not wretched, proceed to convince me, if you
can, that not having to die is not wretched either.

[16] Oh, there's no difficulty in that; I have a more ambitious project.*
A. How is there no difficulty in this, and just what is this more ambitious
project you have? M. Because, since there is no evil after death, death
is not an evil either, as the time closest to death is that which succeeds
it, and you grant there is no evil in death. It follows that having to die is
no evil either, for it means arriving at a state which we admit is no evil.
A. Explain that more fully, please. What you have just said is somewhat
thorny* and compels me to agree before I am convinced.* What is this
'more ambitious' project you speak of? M. To demonstrate, if I can,
that so far from being evil, death is actually good. A. I don't ask that
much, but at the same time I'm all ears to hear it. For though you may
fail in your desire, you will still succeed in showing that death is no evil.
No, I'll not interrupt you; I'd rather listen to a continuous speech.*

[17] M. Really? If I ask you a question, will you not reply? A. That
would be discourteous, but I'd prefer you not to ask any questions,
unless it's really necessary. M. I will humour you and elucidate the subject you wish to the best of my ability, but not in the manner of Pythian
Apollo, so that my utterances are certain and unalterable, but as one
poor mortal out of many trying to discover what is probable by trial and
error. To get further than seeing what resembles the truth is beyond my
capabilities.* Certainties will be spoken by those who say such things
can be known for certain and who lay claim to being wise.* A. Proceed
as you think best: I am ready to listen.

[18] We must, then, consider first what death, which seems to be a very
familiar thing, actually is. There are those who regard death as the soul's
departure from the body: some think that no departure takes place, but
that the soul and the body perish together and the soul dies in the body.
Of those who believe in the soul's departure, some hold that it is immediately broken up, others that it continues to exist for a long time, others
that it survives for ever. Moreover, what the soul is, where it is located
and from where it comes is the subject of considerable dispute.* Some
consider the soul is the actual heart [cor], which gives rise to the words
'without heart' [excordes], 'in need of heart' [vecordes], and 'of one heart'
[concordes] being applied to people, and the wise Nasica, twice consul,

got the name 'Little heart' [*Corculum*] and there was 'the man of outstanding heart [*egregie cordatus*], shrewd Aelius Sextus'.*

[19] Empedocles' view* is that the soul is blood permeating the heart. Others have thought that some part of the brain has dominance as the soul. Others, again, hold that neither the heart itself nor some part of the brain is the soul, but some of these have said that the soul's residence and location is the heart and others the brain. Others identify soul [*animus*] and breath [*anima*], as we Romans mainly do: the word makes this clear, for we say *agere animam*, giving up the ghost, and *efflare*, breathing one's last, and *animosos*, spirited, and *bene animatos*, of good spirit, and *ex animi sententia*, in accordance with my intention; *animus* itself has derived its name from *anima*. The Stoic Zeno believed that the soul is fire.* But the opinions I have mentioned, that the soul is heart, brain, breath and fire are widely held: the remaining views are, as a rule, maintained by individuals, for example the early philosophers of long ago, but in most recent times Aristoxenus,* a musician as well as a philosopher. He took the soul to be a kind of tension of the body itself: on the analogy of what is termed 'harmonia'* in singing and stringed instruments, from the natural conformation of the whole body are produced vibrations of different kinds which correspond to notes in music.

[20] This man may not have moved beyond the confines of his own art but he has nonetheless said something, whose exact meaning had been stated and made clear far earlier by Plato.* Xenocrates denied any physical form to the soul, claiming that it was number, whose power, as had been the view of Pythagoras in much earlier times, was the greatest in nature. His teacher Plato imagined the soul to be tripartite,* and placed its sovereign part, that is, reason, in the head as the citadel; the other two parts, passion and desire, he wished to be subordinate to the first, assigning each its place, passion in the breast and desire under the diaphragm.

[21] But Dicaearchus* in three books gave an account of a discussion whose scene is laid in Corinth, and in the first book he introduces as speakers many of the learned men who engaged in the debate; in the other two he shows us Pherecrates, an elderly resident of Phthiotis and descendant, he says, of Deucalion,* arguing that the soul has no existence at all, that the word has no content whatever, and that there is no point in referring to 'animal' or 'animate creatures'; neither in man nor in beast is there *animus* or *anima*, all the power enabling us to feel or do anything is uniformly spread through all living bodies and cannot be separated from the body as it has no separate existence, and there is nothing apart from the body, one and single, composed in such a way

that its activity and power of sensation depend on a natural combination of the parts.

[22] Aristotle, who far surpasses all others, always excepting Plato, in intellect and industry, acknowledged the four well-known elements* from which all things take their origin, and held that a fifth nature* exists from which comes the mind. Thought and foresight, learning and teaching, the making of any discoveries and memory, and so many other things: love and hatred, desire and fear, feeling pain and delight—these and similar emotions, he considers, are not to be found in any of these four elements. He introduces a fifth type which has no name and so he calls the soul itself by a new name, *endelecheia,** by which he means a sort of uninterrupted and perpetual movement. Unless I happen to have left out any, these are effectively all the views held about the soul. There is, indeed, Democritus* but we can dispense with him; great man though he undoubtedly was, he made out that the soul was formed from small smooth round particles through some sort of random collision. There is nothing which thinkers of his school cannot produce out of a bunch of atoms.

[23] Which of these views is the true one let some god decide; which is the most likely to be true* is a large question. So is it our preference to form a verdict on these contradictory views or to return to the subject we first put forward? A. My wish would be for both, if possible, but it is difficult to combine the two. And so, if we are able to free ourselves from the fear of death without discussing these other questions, let's make this our task. But if this cannot be done without unravelling this problem to do with the soul, let's start with this question, if you agree, and tackle the other one at another stage. M. The course I understand you to be proposing strikes me as the more convenient one. Whichever of the views I have set out is the true one, a rational enquiry will reveal that death is either not an evil or that it is in fact a good thing.

[24] For if the soul is the heart or blood or brain, then without doubt, being material, it will perish along with the rest of the body; if it is breath, perhaps it will disperse; if it is fire, it will be put out; if it is the harmony of Aristoxenus, it will be destroyed. What am I to say of Dicaearchus, who says the soul does not exist at all? According to all these views nothing can have an affect on anyone after death. Sensation is lost along with life. If a being is without sensation nothing can affect that being to any extent. The views of the others offer the hope, should this make you glad, that once souls quit the body they are able to reach heaven, as if returning to their home.* A. It does bring me happiness, and most of all I would like this to be true; my second preference would

be to be persuaded that this is so, even if it were not true.* M. What need do you have, then, of my help? I can't excel Plato in eloquence, can I? Read with attention that book of his on the soul:* nothing more will you need. A. I have done so, let me assure you, and often as well. But somehow, while I am reading, I am convinced, but once I've put the book aside and begun to reflect in my own mind on the immortality of souls, all that conviction slips away.

[25] M. Why is this? Do you grant that souls either survive after death, or they perish at death itself? A. I do grant this. M. Well, what if they survive? A. I allow that they are happy. M. But should they perish? A. I grant that they are not wretched, since they do not even exist. I made this admission a short time earlier when you compelled me to it.* M. How, then, or why do you say that death seems an evil to you, when it will either make us happy as our souls survive or not wretched as we no longer have sensation?

[26] A. Show clearly, therefore, if it's not too much trouble, first, if possible, that souls survive after death; then, if you do not succeed in this—for it is difficult—your task is to prove that death is free from any evil.* For the particular thing I fear may be an evil is not to lack sensation but to have to lack sensation.* M. As for authorities for that view which you wish to be upheld, we can make use of the finest, something which should and usually does have the greatest weight* in all cases, and this is, in the first instance, all antiquity, which perhaps had a better perception of the truth, inasmuch as it was closer to its origin and divine ancestry.

[27] Accordingly we find implanted in those men of old, whom Ennius calls *casci*,* the one conviction that there is sensation in death, and a human being at the time of quitting life is not so completely wiped out as to perish entirely. One may understand this not only from many other examples but also from pontifical law and the rites of burial.* These would not have been observed so scrupulously by men endowed with such powerful intellects, nor would their violation have been forbidden under penalty of guilt which could in no way be atoned for, were it not a deep-rooted conviction of these men that death was not a passing away that destroyed and did away with all things, but a kind of migration and changing of life that functioned for men and women of distinction as a guide to heaven but for all other humans it* was held down to ground level,* but even so remained constant.

[28] This is why we Romans hold the belief that 'Romulus passes his days in heaven in the company of the gods', as Ennius said in agreement with tradition, and among the Greeks, from where he passed on

to us and as far as Ocean, Hercules is thought of as so great and so helpful a god. This is why Liber, son of Semele, is so regarded, and the brothers who are Tyndareus' sons enjoy by tradition the same renown. Of
them the story goes that they not only assisted the Romans to victory in
battle but also delivered the news of it. Again, is not Ino, the daughter
of Cadmus, whom the Greeks call *Leucothea*, identified by our countrymen with the goddess Matuta? Furthermore, isn't almost the whole of
heaven, to give no more instances, filled up with the human race?*

[29] Indeed, were I to attempt to investigate old records and to
extract from them the examples provided by writers of Greece, it will
be found that even those gods reckoned to be of the highest standing*
set out on their journey to heaven from here. Inquire whose tombs* are
pointed out in Greece, recollect, as you have been initiated, the revelations you received in the mysteries,* and then you will understand how
widely this belief extends. In fact, since they had not yet studied the
natural philosophy which first began to be taken up many years later,
men had only such convictions as they had gained from the instruction
of nature;* they had no grasp of the reasons and causes of things, and
were often influenced by visions,* particularly those at night, with the
result that they thought that those who had quit life still lived.

[30] Moreover, just as it seems to be advanced as the strongest argument for believing in the existence of gods that there is no race so savage, no one in the world so uncivilized, that his mind has no trace of a
belief in the gods—many have misguided ideas about the gods, which
usually results from corrupt convention, but all think that a divine
power and divine nature exist, and that this is not due to human confer-
ence or discussion, nor is the belief established by regulations or laws;
in every instance the agreement of all peoples must be regarded as a law
of nature*—is there anyone, then, who does not grieve at the death of
loved ones primarily because he thinks they have been deprived of life's
comforts? Put an end to this belief and you will have put an end to grief.
No one sheds tears at his own misfortune: it may be, one feels sorrow
or pain, but the familiar mournful lamentation and melancholy weeping arise from our belief that the loved one has been deprived of life's
comforts and is aware of this.* And this feeling we have is not the product of any reasoning or learning but because we are guided by nature.

[31] But the overriding proof that nature itself makes a silent judgement about the immortality of souls is that all men feel anxiety,* indeed
the greatest anxiety, about what will happen after death. 'He plants trees
to be of service to the next generation', says a character in the *Synephebi**—
with what in mind if not that future generations also matter to him?

Will, then, the careful farmer plant trees of which he himself will never see one berry, but a great man not plant laws, regulations, the state itself? The procreation of children, the continuation of a name, the adoption of sons,* the careful preparation of wills, the very inscriptions on tombs and epitaphs—what meaning do they all have except that the future too is in our thoughts?*

[32] Again, you cannot doubt that our ideal of human nature should properly be formed from that nature at its best. Then what better type of nature can we find in the human race than that of those who consider they were born to help, protect and safeguard their fellow men? Hercules has gone to join the gods; never would he have done so, if he had not built that road for himself while he lived among men. Such things are now old stories, hallowed by the religious feeling of every-one. Further, in this commonwealth of ours, with what thought in their minds do we imagine so many eminent men lost their lives for their country?* Was it so that their name might be confined within the same limits as their lives? No one would ever offer himself up to death on his country's behalf if he did not have a high hope of immortality.

[33] Themistocles* might have enjoyed a life of leisure, as might Epaminondas,* as might I myself,* not to cite old examples from the history of other lands. But somehow or other there is fixed in the minds of men a sort of prophetic vision of future ages, and this presentiment is strongest and most apparent in men of the greatest genius and lofti-est spirit. Remove this feeling and who would be so insane as to live his life in constant toil and danger?

[34] I speak of statesmen, but what of poets? Do they not wish for fame after death? How else should we understand these lines:

> 'Look, fellow citizens, on old Ennius' sculptured face:
> he told of the mighty deeds of your forefathers.'

He demands the reward of fame from those whose fathers he had made famous, and he wrote besides: 'Let no one [honour] me with tears, [nor hold my funeral with weeping]. Why so? Living, I pass from mouth to mouth of men.'* But why speak of poets? Artists have the wish to be famous after death. Why else did Phidias insert his own likeness on the shield of Minerva,* not having permission to inscribe his name? Then there are our philosophers. Do they not inscribe their names on the very books they write on the subject of despising fame?

[35] But if universal agreement is the voice of nature, and all men the world over agree that there is something which affects those who have departed from life, then we too are obliged to think the same. If it is our

belief that those whose soul excels in intelligence or virtue have the high-est perception of nature's essence, since they have the finest natures, then, as all the best men serve posterity as well as they can, it is probable that there exists something of which they will have awareness after death.

[36] But just as it is nature that determines our belief in the gods' existence, but reason our understanding of their nature, so it is the agreement of all races that underpins our belief that souls survive, but reason by which we must learn their place of dwelling and what they are like. It is ignorance of this that has created the world below and those terrors which you seemed to have good reason for holding in contempt. Bodies fall into the ground and are covered with earth, *humus*, from which is derived our word to be buried, *humari*. This led men to believe that the rest of the life of the dead was passed beneath the earth. This view held by them created serious misconceptions, which were made worse by the poets.*

[37] The audience that fills the theatre, which includes foolish women and children, is moved when it hears the impressive verses:

> Here am I; from Acheron I come by steep and wearisome road
> through caverns built of rough rocks piled high, vast in size, where
> the darkness of the underworld, thick, impenetrable, endures.*

So strong was this misconception, now, to my way of thinking, dispensed with,* that, although they knew the corpses had been cremated, they still imagined that things took place in the world below which cannot occur or be understood without bodies. They were incapable of grasp-ing the conception that souls have an independent life, and tried to discover for them some shape or form. This is the basis for Homer's entire *Nekuia*,* for the *nekuiomanteia* that my friend Appius* practised, and for Lake Avernus* in our neighbourhood,

> Whence souls are raised, revealed from the gloomy darkness,
> through deep Acheron's open mouth by means of salt blood,
> the phantoms of the dead.

They want these phantoms to speak, something that cannot be done without tongue or palate or the shape and working of throat, chest and lungs. They were unable to perceive anything with their minds, and so they referred everything to the test of eyesight.

[38] Now, it requires considerable intelligence to separate the mind from the senses and to divide thought from mere habit.* So there must in my belief have been other thinkers across the many centuries but, as far as literature tells us, Pherecydes of Syros was the first to say that

men's souls are everlasting, and he is certainly of some antiquity, as he lived when my kinsman was king. This view received the strongest support from his pupil Pythagoras.* When this man came to Italy in the reign of Tarquin the Proud,* he made a strong impact on what we call Magna Graecia* both through the high regard for his instruction and also the force of his influence. For many generations afterwards the name of Pythagoras was so highly regarded that no other teachers were thought of as learned.* But I return to the first Pythagoreans. They would give virtually no reasoned argument to support their view apart from what was to be explained by numbers or figures in geometry.

[39] The story goes that Plato came to Italy* in order to study the Pythagoreans and learned all the Pythagorean doctrines, and was the first not only to hold the same view as Pythagoras about the immortality of souls but also to have furnished reasons. But unless you object, let us pass over this proof and abandon this entire hope of immortality. A. Are you leaving me in the lurch, after creating the highest expectations in me? Believe me, I'd rather go wrong in the company of Plato—I know how much you esteem him and my admiration for him is due to your own commendation—than hold the right views with his opponents.

[40] M. Bravo! I should be happy myself to go wrong with that same thinker.* Surely we have no doubt, as we have in most matters—but certainly not this, since the mathematicians are persuasive—that the earth is placed in the centre of the universe and in comparison with the compass of the entire heavens it occupies a space equivalent to the point that mathematicians call the *kentron*.* Moreover, we don't doubt that the nature of the four elements which produce all things is such that, as though they had shared out and apportioned the possibilities of motion, the earthy and moist are carried perpendicularly into land and sea by their own inclination and mass, while the two remaining parts, one fiery, the other airy, just as those just mentioned are carried into the centre of the universe by their own mass and weight, so these conversely fly vertically upwards to the heavenly region, whether their own nature tends towards what is higher, or because bodies lighter by nature are driven away from ones that are heavier. As this is established, it ought to be clear enough that souls, once they have left the body, whether they are airy, that is composed of breath, or fiery, are carried up on high.*

[41] But if the soul is a kind of number, a suggestion more subtle than clear, or that fifth nature, which is not named rather than not understood, then they are even more uncorrupted and pure so that they transport themselves far away from earth. The soul, then, must be one of these, if the nimble human mind is not to lie submerged in the

heart or the brain, or in the blood, as Empedocles maintained. As for Dicaearchus together with Aristoxenus, his contemporary and fellow pupil, let us not concern ourselves with them, despite their undoubted learning. The one, it seems, never even felt upset at not realizing that he possessed a soul, while the other is so charmed by his own music that he tries to import it also into this problem. Now we are able to recognize a *harmonia* that is created from musical intervals, and the different combinations of these again produces further *harmoniai*. But how a *harmonia* can be created by the position of limbs and the attitude of the body when it lacks a soul, I fail to see. No, let this man of music, for all his learning that cannot be doubted, leave this question to his master Aristotle, and himself teach singing. It is a good piece of instruction laid down in the Greek proverb: 'Let each man practise the art he knows'.*

[42] As to that notion of the chance encounter of indivisible bodies that are smooth and round, which Democritus holds to be heated and formed from breath, that is to say, airy, let us reject it completely. If the soul belongs to those four elements of which, they say, all things consist, it consists of heated breath, the view, I see, which Panaetius favours in particular: it must, then, always seek the higher regions. For there is no downward tendency in these two elements, and always they aspire to what is higher. Accordingly, if they dispersed in space, that occurs at a great distance from earth, or, if they survive and preserve their quality, then all the more must we infer that they are carried up to heaven and that this thick and compact air which is nearest to earth* is broken through and parted by them. For the soul contains more heat, or rather burns with greater intensity than our own air, which I have just described as being thick and compact. We can deduce this from the fact that our bodies are fashioned from the earthy type of elements and derive their heat from the burning of the soul.

[43] There is the further point that the soul finds it easier to escape from this air of ours, as I regularly call it, and to burst through it, because nothing is swifter than the soul: no kind of speed exists that can match the speed of the soul. If it survives uncorrupted and unchanged in its nature, it must follow that it is carried away in such a way that it pierces and parts asunder all this sky above us, in which clouds, storms and winds gather due to the moisture and mist caused by the earth's evaporation. When the soul has traversed this region and reached and recognized a nature like itself, where the flames from the thin air and the modified heat of the sun combine, it comes to a stop and brings to an end its soaring ascent. When it attains a state of lightness and heat equal to its own, as if balanced by equal weights it becomes quite motionless,

then and only then finding its natural place of rest once it has made its way through to conditions resembling its own. Here it is in need of nothing, and will be nourished and sustained by the same things which give sustenance and nourishment to the stars.

[44] Since it is the firebrands in our bodies* which generally fire us with virtually all our desires, and we are the more inflamed by our jealousy of those who possess what we long to have, we will assuredly be blessed once we have left our bodies behind and are free of desires and jealousies. And what we do now, when anxious thoughts cease to trouble us, that is, we wish to study and investigate something, we shall then do with far greater freedom, devoting ourselves entirely to contemplation and examination, because there exists naturally in our minds a positively insatiable longing to discover the truth.* The easier it is made for us to discover heavenly things merely by the borders of that land to which we have come, the keener will be the desire for that discovery that they implant in us.

[45] For it was this beauty even here on earth that aroused that philosophy, on fire with desire for knowledge, which Theophrastus* terms the philosophy 'of our fathers and forefathers'. It will give enjoyment above all to those who, even when they inhabited the earth surrounded by gloom, still longed to pierce it with the sharp edge of their minds. Men now think it a particular achievement if they have seen the entrance to the Pontus and those narrows through which passed the vessel named 'Argo, as chosen Argive warriors on board her voyaged in quest of the ram's gilded fleece' or those who saw the famous straits of Ocean 'where the hungry wave parts Europe and Libya'.* So just what manner of sight* do we suppose it will be when we are at liberty to survey the entire earth, its position, shape and outline, and to discern both the regions that are habitable and those again whose intensity of cold or heat makes them lack all cultivation?

[46] For even now it is not our eyes that enable us to perceive what we see: the body has no power of sensation, but as we are told, both by natural philosophers and by men of medicine, who have seen these things opened up and disclosed, there are pathways bored from the seat of the soul to the eyes, ears and nostrils.* Many times, therefore, we are impeded by absorption in thought or some attack of disease, and we fail to see or hear, despite having eyes and ears that are open and unimpaired. From this it can easily be understood that it is the soul which both sees and hears, not those organs that are, so to speak, the windows of the soul, and which nonetheless do not enable the mind to perceive anything, unless it is attentive and actively engaged. Moreover, it is with

the selfsame mind that we grasp things as completely different as colour, taste, warmth, smell and sound. The soul could never recognize these through its five messengers, were it not that everything was referred to it and it was the only judge of everything. And without doubt they will be perceived in much more pure and more transparent form on the day when the soul arrives free where nature leads it.

[47] For as things are, those passages which are open from the body to the soul have been fashioned by nature with workmanship of the greatest skill but they are, in a way of speaking, fenced in* with solid earthy bodies. However, when there will be soul and nothing else, there will be no impediment to prevent it from perceiving what kind of thing each thing is. If the occasion demanded, I could describe at any length you liked the number, variety and greatness of the sights the soul is going to have in the heavenly places.

[48] Indeed when I give thought to this, I am often astonished at the preposterous behaviour of some philosophers who regard natural science with amazement, bestowing thanks on its discoverer and founder and showing him reverence as if he were a god.* They say that, thanks to him, they have been freed from tyrannous masters,* everlasting dread and fear by day and night. What dread? What fear?* What old woman is so deranged as to fear the things *you* would apparently have been afraid of, had you not been instructed in science, 'Hell's lofty sanctuaries of Acheron, Death's pallid regions, veiled in murky cloud'?* Does it not make a philosopher ashamed to boast of not fearing such things and having discovered their falsity? One can deduce the sharpness of their wits from this: they would have believed this if they had not been *instructed* otherwise.

[49] But they have achieved something impressive: they have learned that when death's time has come, they will perish utterly. Granting this—I make no objection—what grounds for happiness or boasting lie in this? Really no reason occurs to me why the view of Plato and of Pythagoras should not be true. Even had Plato not brought forward a single argument—notice what a tribute I pay the man—he would vanquish me simply by his authority. But in fact he has produced so many arguments that he seems to want to persuade other men, and certainly to have persuaded himself.

[50] But there are a great many thinkers who oppose this belief and mete out the punishment of death to souls by a sort of capital sentence. Yet there is no reason why they should regard the soul's immortality as incredible apart from their inability to comprehend and grasp mentally the notion of soul without body.* As if they had any understanding of

its nature, shape, size or location when it is actually in the body! But if all the things that are now hidden from view in the human body could be seen, is it likely that the soul would come into sight or that it would be of such fine substance that it would evade the eye?

[51] Let those who say they cannot understand soul without body ponder this, and they will appreciate what their understanding of it is while it actually resides in the body.* For my part, when I contemplate the nature of the soul, the notion of what the soul is like when it occupies the body, in a house, so to speak, that is not its own, comes as a much more difficult and intricate thing than what it is like once it has made its departure and arrived in the free heaven, as if it were its true home. Unless it is the case that we cannot understand the nature of something we have never seen, then certainly we can form a conception of God himself and of a divine soul set free from the body. I grant that Dicaearchus and Aristoxenus,* due to the difficulty of comprehending what the soul is or what it is like, said that it had no existence at all.

[52] The crucial point to grasp is that the soul sees by means of the soul and beyond question this is the meaning of Apollo's injunction counselling each man to know himself.* He is not, I take it, directing us to know our own limbs or height or shape. We are not bodies, and when I say this to you, I am not speaking to your body. So when the god says, 'Know thy self', his meaning is 'Know thy soul.' For the body is a kind of vessel or receptacle for the soul. Whatever is done by your soul is done by you. Unless it was godlike for the soul to have this knowledge, this instruction, the product of some penetrating intelligence, would not have been attributed to the god.

[53] But if the soul itself proves to lack knowledge of its own nature, tell me, please, will it not even know that it exists, not even know that it moves? This is the foundation of Plato's argument set forth by Socrates in the *Phaedrus* and put by me in the sixth book of my *Republic*.

What always moves is eternal. What causes motion in something else and is itself set in motion by an outside agency, when it ceases to move must also cease to live. Accordingly only what is the cause of its own motion, because it never is abandoned by itself, never ceases to move either. On the contrary, this is also the source and origin of motion in all things that move. [54] But an origin has no beginning; for all things have an origin but this origin itself cannot be born from anything else. Whatever is produced from something else would not be an origin.* But if it never arises, it never perishes either; for once an origin is destroyed, it will not itself be reborn from anything else, nor will it create anything from itself, since all things must arise from an origin. As a consequence the origin of motion derives from what is self-moving, and this can neither be born nor die, or else the entire heavens must fall and all nature come to a halt, through not finding any power from which to receive a primary impulse causing movement. As it is evident, then, that whatever moves itself is eternal, what man would deny that souls have been assigned this quality? For everything which is set in motion by an external impulse is inanimate; a living creature moves through its own movement from within. This is the specific essence and character of the soul. If it is the one thing of all that is self-moving, it has certainly not been born and is eternal.

[55] Though all of the ten-a-penny philosophers put their heads together— I regard this as a fair description of those who disagree with Plato and Socrates* and that school—not only will they never expound anything with such elegance but they won't comprehend either the exactness of the argument that has produced this conclusion. The soul, then, is aware that it moves, and with this awareness comes also the realization that its own and not an external force is the cause of its motion, and that it is impossible for it ever to be deserted by itself. This constitutes the proof of its immortality, unless you have anything to put forward in response. A. I am perfectly happy that no objection should even have entered my head, so much do I support the view you have expressed.

[56] M. Well, are you any the less impressed by those arguments that show there exist some divine elements in human souls? If I could discern how these elements could come into being, I should see also how they cease to be. For in the case of blood, bile, phlegm,* bones, sinews, veins, in short the total formation of the limbs and the entire body, I think I can say from what they are compounded and how they are made. In the case of the soul itself,* if there were nothing in it except the fact that by means of it we live, I would believe that nature sustained the life of men as much as the life of a vine or tree; we say that these things also 'live'. Again, if the soul of man had no characteristic other than that of desire or rejection, that also it would share with the beasts.

[57] First of all, the soul has memory, and one, moreover, without limit, that embraces things without number. Plato maintains that this is recollection of a previous life. In the book called *Meno* Socrates asks a small boy certain geometrical questions to do with the dimensions of a square. He answers these as a boy would, and yet so easy are the questions that, as he answers step by step, he arrives at the same conclusion as he would have done if he had learned geometry. Socrates claims it follows from this that learning is nothing other than recollection.* This topic he develops in much fuller detail in that discussion which he held on the very day he departed this life.* He teaches that anyone, even someone who seems to be totally ignorant, in answer to skilful questioning shows that he is not learning things at that moment but is recognizing

them through recollection, and that it would be quite impossible for us to possess from childhood so many 'notions' (which they call *ennoiai*) of so many important things, implanted and, as it were, stamped on our souls, had not the soul actively engaged in acquiring knowledge before it entered the body.

[58] And since there is no real existence in anything, as Plato argues throughout his writings—he thinks nothing that comes into being and perishes has real existence—and only that exists which always remains the same in character—what he calls *idea* and we 'idea': the soul could not become acquainted with them when it was imprisoned in the body; it brings them with it as things known already. It follows that there is no need for us to be surprised at knowledge of so many things. But these are things the soul cannot see clearly when it suddenly finds itself in such an unfamiliar and disordered dwelling-place. But once it has composed itself and recovered, then it becomes acquainted with those things by remembering them. So learning is quite simply recollection.

[59] But in my case there is something perhaps even more extraordinary about memory.* What is it that causes us to remember, or what is its essence and what is the source of that? I am not inquiring into the powers of memory Simonides* reputedly had, or Theodectes,* or Cineas,* who was sent as an envoy to the senate by Pyrrhus, or, in recent times, Charmadas,* or Metrodorus of Scepsis* who died quite lately, or our own Hortensius.* I speak of the memory of men in general and particularly of those who are engaged in some higher branch of study and art, whose mental powers it is difficult to estimate—so much do they remember.

[60] To what conclusion, then, does my discourse lead? I think it must by now be obvious what that power is and what is its source. Certainly it is not related to the heart, the blood, the brain or atoms. Whether it is of breath or fire I do not know, and unlike those others, I am not ashamed to admit to my ignorance where I am ignorant. This point I should swear, if I could maintain anything else on this difficult subject, that, whether the soul is breath or fire, it is divine. Think it over, please, can you really think that the impressive power of memory could derive from or be compounded from earth with its cloudy murky atmosphere? If you do not see this particular point, at least you see the nature of the problem underlying it, or, if not even that, you surely see its significance.

[61] Well, then. Is it our belief that there is a kind of spaciousness in the soul into which what we remember is poured, as if into a vessel? That would be ridiculous. It is impossible to conceive of any kind of bottom or such shape for the soul, or of any such great 'spaciousness'. Or do we

suppose that the soul resembles wax and that memory consists of the traces of things stamped on the mind? What traces of words or actual objects can be left, and besides what of such boundless size could there be that was capable of reproducing so much material? Again, what, finally, I inquire, is the power which explores what is hidden and goes by the name of discovery and research?*

[62] Do you think it was formed from this earthy, mortal and perishable nature? Take, for example, the man who first supplied all things with names,* something which Pythagoras thought required supreme wisdom, or who first gathered together mankind, scattered up to that time, calling it to a fellowship of life, or who used a few written characters* to define the meaning of the sounds of the voice in their apparently endless variety, or who marked down the courses of the wandering stars, the way they passed in front of each other and came to rest? They were great men, all of them, as also were those who earlier discovered crops, clothing, places to dwell, a civilized life, means of protection against wild animals, men whose civilizing and domesticating influence upon us was the cause of our passing from the necessary arts to the finer ones. Great pleasure for our ears has been gained by the discovery and regulation of sounds of diverse quality, and we have looked up at the stars, both those which are fixed in specific spots and those which are described erroneously as 'wandering'.* The man who observed their revolutions and all their movements with his soul showed that his own soul resembled the soul which had created these things in the heavens.

[63] For when Archimedes* fastened on a globe the movements of the moon, sun and the five wandering stars, he imitated Plato's god who fashioned the world in the *Timaeus** in making a single revolution regulate movements which in slowness and speed were completely dissimilar. If that cannot take place in the universe without a god's intervention, neither could Archimedes have reproduced those same motions on a sphere without a god's intelligence.

[64] In my view even more eminent and distinguished fields of activity are not uninfluenced by a divine power, or allow me to think that the poet pours forth his grand, resounding verses without some heavenly stimulation of the mind, or that eloquence flows with a tide of echoing words without the aid of some greater power.* In the case of philosophy, mother of all the arts, this is quite simply, as Plato holds,* the gift, or, as I do, the discovery of the gods. It instructed us first in the worship of them, then in justice among men, which has its basis in the fellowship of the human race, then to self-control and greatness of soul. It also drove from our minds as from our eyes the darkness,* so that

we saw all things above and below, the first and the last and what lay between.

[65] A power which is capable of achieving so many great things seems to me to be wholly divine. For what is the memory of facts and words? What, further, is discovery? There is surely no greater thing that can be conceived even in a god. The merriment of the gods was not caused by ambrosia, I think, or by nectar, or by having their drinks served by the goddess of Youth, and I do not listen to Homer when he says that Ganymede was snatched by the gods because of his good looks, to serve as Jupiter's cup-bearer. There was no just cause why such great wrong should be suffered by Laomedon. This was imagined by Homer and he transferred to the gods the characteristics of men: I would have preferred him to transfer divine characteristics to us.* But what divine qualities? Vitality, wisdom, discovery, memory. Accordingly the soul is, as I say, divine, as Euripides boldly says, a god; and indeed, if god is breath or fire, so also is the soul of man; for just as the heavenly nature is free from earth and moisture,* so the human soul is devoid of both these elements. But if there exists a fifth sort of nature, which Aristotle first mooted,* this is the nature both of gods and souls. In accordance with this view I have given the following statement of it in my *Consolation*, using these precise words:

[66] No origin of souls can be found on earth, as nothing mixed and compounded resides in souls, nothing that seems to be born or fashioned from earth, nothing even that is either moist or airy or fiery. For in these elements there is nothing which can possess the power of memory, thought, reflection, nothing that can retain the past, foresee the future and embrace the present. These powers belong to the gods alone, and never will there be found any source from which they can come to a man except from god. The soul's essential character is, then, entirely unique, distinct from those elements that are everyday and familiar. Accordingly whatever it is that has consciousness, life and activity must be heavenly and divine, and for that reason eternal. Indeed god himself, who is comprehended by us, can be comprehended in no other way than as some mind unfettered and free, separated from all mortal ingredients, conscious of and moving all things, and itself endowed with everlasting motion.*

[67] Of this kind and of the same nature is the human mind.—Then where is that mind you speak of and what is its nature?—Where is yours and what is its nature? Are you able to say? Or if I do not possess all the faculties needed for comprehension I would like, will you not permit me to use even those I possess?—The only power the soul lacks is that of seeing itself. But the soul resembles the eye in that, while not seeing itself, it perceives other things. It is unable to see, what is of least

importance, its own form, though, it may be, that too it can see, but let us not follow up the point—it sees for certain its power, perspicacity, memory, motion, swiftness. These attributes are considerable, divine, everlasting. What it looks like or where it dwells are questions we need not even ask.

[68] First we see the beauty and brightness of the sky, next the way it revolves at a speed greater than our thought can grasp, then the way night and day alternate and the seasons interchange in divisions of four to suit the ripening of crops and keeping our bodies well adjusted. We see their controller and guide, the sun, and the moon, marking and indicating the days as if in a calendar by the waxing and waning of its light; then in the same sphere with its twelve divisions* move five stars, keeping the same courses with perfect consistency, despite differing from one another in their movements; then there is the aspect of the sky at night, everywhere adorned by stars, and the earth's sphere rising from the sea and fixed in the centre of the whole universe, habitable and cultivated in two quite distinct zones. Of these the one in which we dwell is 'set beneath the pole, towards the seven stars, whence the dread howling of the North wind piles up the freezing snows',* the other is the southern one, which is unknown to us and called by the Greeks *antichthon*.*

[69] The other parts are uncultivated, because, it is thought, they are frozen with cold or parched with heat. But here, where we dwell, never ceases in due season

the sky to shine, the trees to put forth leaves, the joy-giving vines to burgeon with tendrils, the branches to be weighed down by their abundance of olives, the cornfields to bestow their grain, all things to flourish, the streams from fountains to ripple on their way, the meadows to be clothed in grasses.*

We see then the great number of animals, some for eating, some for tilling the fields, some for riding, some for clothing us, and man himself, the observer of the heavens and worshipper of the gods, his requirements served by all the fields and seas.

[70] When, therefore, we see these and countless other things, can we doubt that there stands over them in authority either a creator, as Plato believes, or if these have always existed, as Aristotle thinks, a controller of so mighty a work of construction?* It is the same with the mind of man: although you do not see it, as you do not see god, nonetheless, as you recognize god from his works, so from memory, discovery and the swiftness of movement and all the loveliness of virtue you must acknowledge the divine power of the mind.

Where, then, does it reside? My belief is, in the head,* and I can provide reasons for my belief. But the soul's location I shall discuss at
another time; without doubt it is in you. What is its nature? One special
to it, I think, and its very own. But suppose it is composed of fire or of
air—that has no bearing on the present matter in hand. Be aware of
this point alone, that, as you know god, despite not knowing his location and appearance, so your own soul should be known to you, even if
you do not know its location and shape.

[71] In inquiring about the soul we cannot doubt, unless we are utterly
obtuse in science, that in souls there is no admixture, no compounding,
no combination, no mortising, no complexity. This being the case,
there is no possibility of its being separated off or split up or taken apart
or torn to pieces; so there is no possibility of it perishing either, for perishing is a sort of separation and parting and divorcing of those parts
which before destruction were held together by some kind of combination. These and similar reasons prompted Socrates not to seek out any
advocate when on trial for his life, nor did he throw himself on the
jury's mercy but showed a noble obstinacy that derived from greatness
of soul, not from arrogance, and on the last day of his life this was the
very subject on which he discoursed at length. And although a few days
earlier he could easily have been delivered from prison, he refused.*
Then when he was almost holding in his hand the cup that would bring
him death, he spoke such words that it seemed he was not being thrust
towards death but ascending to the heavens.

[72] The tenor of his belief and substance of his discourse* were
that two paths exist, twofold courses for souls when they quit the body.
Those who had polluted themselves with the vices of men and given
themselves up entirely to their lusts, and under their blinding influence
had defiled themselves by private vices and acts of wickedness or
through outrageous public conduct had perpetrated crimes beyond
divine forgiveness, faced, in his view, a pathway apart, which separated
them from the society of the gods. But those who had kept themselves
pure and chaste, who had kept the smallest contact with the body, had
constantly set themselves apart from it, and in their human bodies had
followed as their example the life of the gods, enjoyed before them, so
he maintained, the prospect of an easy return to those from whom they
had come.

[73] And so he relates that, just as the swans* that are dedicated to
Apollo—and this is with good reason, as they appear to have from him
the power of prophecy, that enables them to foresee the good that is in
death, and die singing and with joy—so should all good and learned

men conduct themselves. Indeed, doubt on this point would be impossible for anyone, did we not have the same experience in focusing our thoughts on the soul as frequently befalls those who gaze intently at the sun in eclipse, namely that they lose their sight entirely. Similarly, the mind's sight, once it turns its gaze on itself, sometimes grows dim, and for that reason we abandon careful scrutiny. And so, doubting, watching on all sides, hesitating, in dread of adversity in its many forms, our discourse drives ahead as if in a skiff on a vast sea.

[74] But this is ancient material, and Greek at that. Cato, now, when he departed from this life, rejoiced at having found a reason for dying. The god who exercises rule within us forbids us to quit this world without his instruction. But when the god himself provides a just cause, as he did once in Socrates' case, and does now in Cato's,* and often to many others, I assure you most certainly that with joy the wise man will depart from this darkness into that light. Nonetheless he will not break the fetters of his prison—the laws forbid it—but will take his leave once summoned and released by the god as though by a magistrate or some lawful authority. 'The entire life of philosophers', as the same sage puts it, 'is a careful preparation for death.'*

[75] For what else are we doing when we remove the soul from pleasure, that is, from the body, from our private means, which are the handmaid and servant of that body, from public affairs, from business of any kind: what, I say, are we doing then except summoning the soul to its own presence, compelling it to have its own companionship and withdrawing it completely from the body? Is separating the soul from the body anything other than learning how to die? Let us therefore practise this, believe me, and cut ourselves off from our bodies, that is, let us accustom ourselves to dying. This will resemble that heavenly life even while we are on earth, and, at the same time, when we are released from our chains here and carried to that place, the progress of our souls will be less retarded. For those who have always spent their lives in the body's shackles, even when they gain release, advance more slowly, like men who have spent many years bound in chains. And when we have come to that place, then at last shall we know life; for this life is a death, and did you wish it, I could lament over it.

[76] A. You have lamented sufficiently in your *Consolatio.* When I read it, I wish for nothing more than to quit this world, and all the more so after what I have just heard.* M. The time will come, and quickly too, whether you draw back or make haste: life wings on its way. But so misguided is the notion that death is an evil, as you thought not long ago, that I incline to the thought that for a human being everything

else is evil, or, at least, that no other good thing is to be preferred, if indeed we are going either to become gods ourselves* or to share the gods' company.* A. What difference does it make? M. There are some here who do not approve of that conclusion, and in this discussion of ours I shall never let you get away with thinking that on any reasoned basis death is an evil.

[77] A. How can it be, now that I have come to know your views? M. You ask how it can be? Crowds of opponents advance on us, not just Epicureans, whom I do not personally despise, but somehow or other they win few plaudits from all the most learned, but my beloved Dicaearchus has argued most critically against the soul's immortality. He wrote three books which are called 'The Lesbian Dialogues' because the discussion takes place in Mytilene,* and in these his aim is to show that souls are mortal. The Stoics, however, bestow on us a generous lease of life, as if to make us crows: they declare that our souls will last a long time but not for ever.* You are not then unwilling, surely, to hear why, even if this view is true, death still does not belong in the category of evils? A. As you like, but no one will drive me away from my belief in immortality.

[78] M. I approve of that, but we should never be over-confident in any matter. Frequently some clever line of argument influences us, so that we waver and change our view even in questions that are comparatively clear*—in the present question there is a measure of obscurity. So if that occurs, let us be armed against it. A. Agreed, but I'll take care it does not. M. Is there any reason then why we don't bid our friends the Stoics farewell? I mean those who declare that, once they have left the body, souls do survive, but not for ever. A. Yes, bid *them* farewell, as they maintain what is most difficult in the whole issue, namely that the soul can continue to exist without a body. But they do not acknowledge the further point, which not only is easy to believe but, once their own point is granted, becomes its logical consequence, that is, that the soul, having survived a long time, does not perish. M. A good criticism,* and that is just how things stand.

[79] Should we then believe Panaetius when he disagrees with Plato, his master? He calls him everywhere in his writings divine, most wise, most holy, the Homer of philosophers, but this one view of his, that the soul is immortal, he rejects.* His position is one that no one denies, that whatever is born also dies. Souls, he says, are born, as is shown by the likeness of children to their parents, something which is apparent not only in bodies but in mental qualities as well. He brings forward a second argument, that nothing which feels pain cannot also be ill;

what can fall ill will also perish; now souls experience pain, therefore they also perish.

[80] It is possible to refute these arguments. They are made by a man who does not know that, when immortality of souls is spoken of, it is the mind that is spoken of, which is always free from every disorderly emotion, not those parts of us subject to attacks of anxiety, anger and lust, those parts that Plato, whom he criticizes here, regards as separated and isolated from the mind.* As to the question of likeness, it is more evident in animals, whose souls lack reason. In the case of humans, the likeness is more in the form of the body, and it makes a great difference in what kind of body the souls themselves are placed. Many conditions of the body have the effect of sharpening the mind, and many of blunting it. Indeed Aristotle says* that all men of intellect are melancholic, so it does not bother me that I am rather slow on the uptake. He gives a long list of examples, and, as if the point were accepted, he provides a reason why this is the case. Now if such an influence on the mind's condition is exerted by things engendered in the body—whatever they are, it is such things that cause the likeness—likeness does not provide any necessary reason why souls are born.

[81] I make no comment on cases where there is no likeness to be seen. I wish Panaetius could be here—he and Africanus were close friends: I would ask him which member of his family Africanus' great nephew had looked like—in his features he resembled, perhaps, his father, but in his way of life he was so like all vile persons that he was easily the worst.* I would ask also which one the grandson of Publius Crassus,* a wise, eloquent and distinguished man, had resembled, and the grandsons and sons of many other famous men, whom there is no point in my naming. But what are we about? Have we forgotten that the present subject of our enquiry is that, after we had adequately discussed immortality, there was no evil in death even if souls perished? A. Well, I did remember but I was perfectly happy to let you stray from the subject when you were talking about immortality.

[82] M. I see that your sights are set high and your wish is to make the move to heaven. I hope that may be our lot. But suppose, as those other thinkers argue, that souls do not survive after death. I see that, if this is true, we are deprived of the hope of a happier life. But what evil is implied by such a view? For suppose that the soul perishes as does the body; is there then any pain or the slightest sensation in the body after death?* I think not. No one says that there is, although Democritus* is charged with this by Epicurus but Democritus' followers deny it. Accordingly there is no sensation left in the soul either, for the soul is

nowhere. Where then is the evil, since no third possibility exists? Or is it that pain must inevitably accompany the actual separation of soul from body? Granting my belief in the truth of this, how slight a thing it is! But I consider it false, and the fact is that generally the separation occurs without sensation, sometimes even with pleasure. But the whole matter is insignificant, whatever its nature, for it is over in a moment.

[83] What does cause distress, or rather torture, is the departure from all the good things in life. However it would, perhaps, be more accurate to say 'from the bad things'. Why should I now grieve for the life of man? I could do so, with truth and justice. But when it is my aim to avoid the notion that we shall be wretched after death, what need is there to make life as well more wretched by lamentation? I did that in the book in which I did my utmost to bring myself consolation.* So it is from bad things, not good, that death removes us, if we seek the truth. Indeed this was argued by Hegesias of Cyrene* with such eloquence that it is said he was prevented from lecturing on the subject in his classes by King Ptolemy* because many of those who heard his words took their own lives.

[84] There is an epigram of Callimachus* on Cleombrotus of Ambracia who, he says, despite having suffered no misfortune, flung himself from the city wall into the sea after reading Plato's book. There is a book by the man I mentioned earlier, Hegesias, his *Apokarteron*,* in which a man who is dying from starvation is called back by his friends, and, in replying to them, he details the discomforts of human life. I could do the same, even though less positively than he, for his view is that absolutely no one derives benefit from living. I pass over other cases: is it in fact of benefit to *me*? I had been stripped of all the things that confer comfort and distinction both in family life and in a public career, and assuredly, had I died before this happened, death would have taken me away from bad things, not from good.*

[85] Let us imagine there is a man whose life is unmarked by suffering, who has received no wound from fortune. The famous Metellus had four distinguished sons,* but Priam had fifty,* of whom seventeen were born to him by his rightful wife. Over both men fortune had the same power but exercised it in the case of only one. Metellus was laid on his pyre by many sons and daughters, grandsons and granddaughters, but Priam was bereft of all that offspring and, after seeking refuge at the altar, was cut down by the hand of the enemy. Had he died with his sons alive and his kingdom unharmed, 'with barbaric riches around, and fretted roofs, richly carved'*—would he then have taken leave of things good or bad? At the time his belief would certainly have been,

from things good. Certainly it would have been a better fate for him, and no such tearful dirge as this would have been sung: 'All things I saw wrapped in flame, Priam's life by force undone, Jupiter's altar befouled with blood'. As if in that hour anything better than that violence could have befallen him! But if he had met an earlier end, he would have wholly escaped such an outcome; at the actual time of his death what he escaped was the awareness of suffering.

[86] My friend Pompey was afflicted by a serious illness at Naples,* but he regained his health. The townsfolk put garlands on their heads, as indeed did the people of Puteoli. There was a steady stream of public congratulations from the towns. It was foolish enough behaviour and worthy of Greeks, but still it served to indicate good fortune. If his life had terminated then, would he have departed from good things or bad? Certainly he would have escaped wretchedness. He would not have waged war against his father-in-law, would not have taken up arms when he was unprepared, would not have left his home behind, would not have fled from Italy, would not have lost his army and fallen, defenceless, to bands of armed slaves.* His pitiable children and his wealth would not have become the property of his conquerors. If he had met his death before all this, he would have died at the height of his prosperity, but by the prolongation of his life how many grim disasters of unbelievable force did he experience to the full! These things are avoided by death because, even if they haven't happened, they *might* happen. But men do not entertain the thought that those things can happen to them. Each of us hopes to enjoy for himself the good fortune of Metellus, just as if either there exist more lucky people than unlucky, or any certainty existed in human affairs, or it is more sensible to hope than to fear.

[87] But let us make this concession, that men are deprived by death of good things: are we then bound to concede that the dead lack the blessings of life, and that this is a wretched state? Certainly this is what they must say. Or is it possible for a man who does not exist to lack anything? 'Lack' is in itself a gloomy word, implying as it does this sense: 'he had once, he doesn't have now, he misses, looks for, feels the need of'. These are the troubles, I think, that burden one who lacks: he lacks eyes, blindness is hateful; he lacks children, childlessness is hateful. This holds for the living, but as regards the dead, none of them lacks the comforts of life, nor even life itself. I am speaking of the dead, who have no existence whatever: do we, who exist, lack either horns or feathers? I think not. Would anyone say so? Undoubtedly no one. Why so? Because when you don't have a thing for which you are unsuited by

nature or usage, you wouldn't 'lack' it, even if you were aware of not having it.

[88] This is an argument on which we must insist repeatedly, having established the point on which we can have no doubt if souls are mortal, namely that the destruction involved in death is so total that not even the slightest hint of sensation is left. So, now that this has been properly established and confirmed, we must investigate thoroughly, so as to be sure of it, what we mean by 'to lack', so that no misconception remains in our use of the expression. 'To lack', then, means not to have what you would wish to have; in 'lacking' there is a notion of 'wishing', except when another meaning attaches to the word, as in the case of a fever. For there is another sense in which 'to lack' is used, when you do not have something and are aware that you do not have it, even if this is not a matter of great regret to you. The expression 'to lack' is not used in the case of death: for that would not be an occasion for grief; we use it of lacking something good, and that lack is bad. But not even a man who is living 'lacks' a good thing if he does not feel the want of it. In the case of a living man it is, however, an intelligible thing to say that you 'lack' monarchy—though this cannot be said quite accurately of you, yet it could of Tarquin* after he had been forced to abandon his monarchy—but in the case of a dead man it is not even intelligible: 'to lack' is pertinent to one who has sensation, and one who is dead has no sensation; 'lacking' is, therefore, not found in the dead either.

[89] And yet what need have we to philosophize over this, when we see the question does not to any great extent require philosophy? How often have not only our commanders but also their entire armies rushed to certain death! If death was indeed their fear, Lucius Brutus would not have fallen in battle preventing the return of the tyrant he himself had driven out, nor would the elder Decius doing battle with the Latins, his son with the Etruscans, his grandson with Pyrrhus have exposed themselves to the weapons of the enemy.* Spain would not have witnessed the Scipios dying for their country in the selfsame war, Cannae would not have witnessed the fall of Paulus and Geminus, Venusia of Marcellus, Litana of Albinus and Lucania of Gracchus.* Not one of these men can be wretched today. Not even on the day they drew their last breath, for no one can be wretched when sensation has been lost.

[90] But, you may say, the very absence of sensation is loathsome. Loathsome, yes, if this absence involved 'lacking'. But since it is quite clear that nothing can exist in a man who has no personal existence, what that is loathsome can exist in one who neither lacks nor has sensation? All too frequently, it is true, this belief persists, but this is because

it harbours within it all the soul's shrinking from the fear of death. For once a person has realized what is clearer than the light of day, namely that when soul and body are done away and the entire living being destroyed and total annihilation has occurred, the creature which existed has become nothing, he will plainly perceive that no difference exists between a Hippocentaur, that never had any existence, and King Agamemnon, and that Marcus Camillus is no more concerned with the present civil war than I was with Rome's capture in that man's lifetime.* So why would Camillus have been pained at the thought that these events would take place some three hundred and fifty years after his lifetime, and why would I feel pain at the thought that some city would conquer our own in ten thousand years' time? Because love of one's country is so strong that we measure it, not by what we feel, but by its own safety.

[91] And so, while death presents a daily threat because of the uncertainties of chance, and while it can never be far away because of the shortness of life, it does not deter the wise man from taking thought for his country and his loved ones for all time. His view is that posterity itself, of which he is bound to have no awareness, is yet his concern. Accordingly even the man who judges that the soul is mortal may still attempt deeds that will not die, not from a desire for fame, which he is not going to be aware of, but from a desire for virtue, which inevitably ensures fame for a man, even if he does not pursue it.* If it is a condition of nature that, just as our birth brings the beginning of all things, so our death brings the end of all, then just as nothing affected us before birth, so nothing will affect us after death. What evil can there be in this, considering that neither the living nor the dead are affected by death? The latter have no existence, the former it will not touch.

[92] Those who minimize its importance represent it as being very like sleep, as if anyone would wish to live for ninety years with the condition that, once he had completed sixty, he should sleep for the remainder.* Not only would this be against the wishes of the man himself, not even his relatives would wish it. Endymion, if we are willing to listen to legends, fell asleep once upon a time on Latmus, a mountain in Caria, and has not yet woken up, I imagine. Surely you don't think he troubles himself over the 'difficulties' of the moon, by whom he is supposed to have been lulled to sleep so that she might kiss him as he slept? Why should he be troubled, when he doesn't have even any sensation? You have sleep, death's counterfeit, and every day you put it on like clothing, and you doubt the fact that there is no sensation in death, despite seeing that in its counterfeit there is no sensation?

[93] So let such follies, almost old wives' tales, claiming that it is wretched to die before our time, be rejected. What is this 'time', I ask? Nature's? But it is nature that has made a loan of life, like one of money, with no fixed day of repayment. What grounds, then, do you have for complaint, if nature calls in this loan whenever it wants? Those were the terms on which you had taken the loan. The same people think that if a small child dies, this must be borne calmly, and if it is an infant in the cradle, that should not even occasion a lament. And yet in the latter case nature has shown more cruelty in calling in what it had given. 'Not yet,' they say 'had the infant tasted the sweetness of life: the other was already hoping for great things, which he was beginning to enjoy.' But in all other matters it is held to be better to get some part rather than none: why should it be otherwise in life? However, Callimachus put it well when he said that Priam shed tears far more often than Troilus.* Yet we praise the luck of those who die at a ripe old age.

[94] Why should this be? Because, I suppose, none of them would find a longer life more agreeable, if it were granted to them. For without doubt a man finds nothing more pleasurable than wisdom, and this is certainly conferred by old age, though it takes away everything else. But what life is long? For a human being is anything at all long? Is it not true that old age 'follows hard now on children, now on youths as they run, and catches them unawares'? But because we have nothing beyond, we call this 'long'. All such things are described as either long or short relatively to the amount allotted to each object. On the river Hypanis which flows from part of Europe into the Black Sea, Aristotle says that little creatures are born which live for a single day.* One of them, therefore, that has died at the eighth hour of the day has died at an advanced age; one that has died at sunset is senile, and all the more so if this occurs at the summer solstice. Compare our longest lifetime with eternity: we shall be found to be virtually as short-lived as those little creatures.

[95] Let us, then, treat with contempt all follies—what gentler name can I give to such trifling?—and locate the entire essence of living well in energy and greatness of soul, in disdain and scorn for all things human, and in every form of virtue. As things are, we are unmanned by mawkish thoughts, so that, if death arrives before we have realized the promises of the Chaldaeans,* we regard ourselves as robbed of some great blessings, as cheated and left destitute.

[96] But if suspense, anguish and torment afflict us in our expectation and longing, then, heavens above, how delightful must be that journey at whose completion we will have no further care and no anxiety!

How I admire Theramenes! What a noble spirit he has! Although to read of his end costs us tears, still there is no cause for pity in the death of so great a man. He was thrown into prison by order of the thirty tyrants and, when he had swallowed the poison as a thirsty man might, he tossed the remnants out of the cup to make a splash and, with a smile at the sound it made, said, 'This I drink to the health of the fair Critias', the man who had treated him so abominably. The Greeks have a custom at parties of naming the guest to whom they are about to pass the cup.* With his last breath this splendid man made a joke, although he had already absorbed death and was grasping it in his innards, and for the man he had toasted in poison he made a true prophecy of the death which shortly overtook him.

[97] Who would praise this calmness in a mighty soul at the moment he was facing death, if he judged death to be an evil? Into the same prison and to the same cup in a few years time came Socrates, condemned by a jury* that showed no less criminal behaviour than the tyrants who found Theramenes guilty. What, then, is that man's speech that Plato makes him give before the judges when sentence of death has already been passed on him?*

I am extremely hopeful, gentlemen of the jury, that my being sent to my death is fortunate for me; for one of two consequences must ensue, either that death takes away completely all sensation, or that death involves a departure from these regions to some other place. And so, if sensation is annulled and death resembles that sleep which sometimes brings the most tranquil repose without even the appearances of dreams, then good gods, what gain it is to die! How many days can be found worth preferring to such a night? If time to come for all eternity is like this, who is more fortunate than I? [98] But if there is truth in what is said, that death is a passage to those shores inhabited by the dead and departed, that is much happier still. To think that, once you have escaped from those who want to be considered judges, you enter the presence of those who are truly called judges, Minos, Rhadamanthus,* Aeacus, Triptolemus, and meet those who lived their lives with justice and good faith—can you regard this journey you have made as an ordinary one? What value, I ask, can you put on being allowed to hold conversation with Orpheus, Musaeus, Homer and Hesiod? For my part I would wish to die many times, if it were possible, to have the privilege of discovering the things I am describing. What delight would be mine if I met Palamedes, Ajax and the other men overthrown by a verdict that was unjust!* I should put to the test the wisdom of the supreme king* who led a mighty army to Troy, and the wisdom of Ulysses and Sisyphus, and when I made these enquiries, as I have done here, I would not for that reason be condemned to death. So I ask you members of the jury who have voted for my acquittal not to fear death. [99] For nothing evil can befall a good man either in life or death, never will his welfare be ignored by the immortal gods, nor has this happened to me as a result of mere chance. Indeed I have no grounds for anger against my accusers or those who have condemned me except that they have formed the belief that they are doing me harm.

This is what he spoke and to this effect, but there is nothing to surpass his final words:* 'Well, it is now the time', he said, 'to leave this place, for me to die, for you to live. Which is the better is known to the gods: it is known, I think, to no man.'

Truly, I should prefer greatly to have this frame of mind rather than the fortunes of all those men who passed judgement on him. He himself knows what he says no one knows, apart from the gods—which is the better fate—for he has just said it, but still at the end he maintains his well-known position of declaring nothing to be certain.*

[100] Let us maintain the view that nothing which has been given to us by nature is evil, and let us understand that, if death is an evil, it is an everlasting evil. For death is seen as the end of a wretched life; if death is wretched, there can be no end. But why do I speak of Socrates or Theramenes, men pre-eminently famous for virtue and wisdom? A certain man of Sparta, not even his name has been handed down to us, showed such disdain for death that, after the ephors had condemned him and he was being led out to execution, his face wore a happy and cheerful expression. Someone, an enemy of his, said, 'Do you despise the laws of Lycurgus?' 'No,' he replied, 'I am deeply grateful to him for inflicting on me a penalty I don't need a loan or a mortgage to pay.' A man Sparta might be proud of!* In my own eyes a man of such great spirit was innocent, despite being found guilty.

[101] Similar examples have been produced beyond number by our own country. But why should I cite commanders and leaders, when Cato* writes that the legions often marched eagerly to a position from which they did not think they would return? With a courage like this the Spartans met their deaths at Thermopylae, earning these lines of Simonides: 'Tell Sparta, wayfarer, that you saw us lying here, obeying the sacred laws of our country.' What does the general Leonidas say? 'Set forth with a valiant heart, Spartans. This day, perhaps, we shall take dinner with the dead.' That was a bold race of men, while Lycurgus' laws were held in respect. When a Persian enemy said boastfully in conversation, 'You will not see the sun because our spears and arrows are so numerous', one of these men said in reply, 'Why, then, we will be fighting in the shade!'*

[102] I speak of their men—of what nature was the Spartan woman? When she had sent a son into battle and heard of his death, she said, 'That is why I gave birth to him, to be a man who would not hesitate to meet death for his country.' Granted, the Spartans were brave and hardy—there is much effectiveness in their state's system of training. But do we not also admire Theodorus of Cyrene, a philosopher not to be despised? When King Lysimachus was threatening him with the cross,* he said, 'Threaten these nobles of yours with such fearful things: it makes no difference to Theodorus whether he rots on the ground or in the air.' This saying of his reminds me that I should say something about burial and interment—not a problematic matter, especially as we have discovered what was said a little earlier on the subject of lack of sensation. Socrates' view on this is stated clearly in the book* in which he meets his death, of which we have spoken already at some length.

[103] When he had discussed the immortality of souls and the time of his death was now pressing, he said in reply to Crito's question how he wished to be buried, 'I have expended much effort for nothing, my friends; I have not succeeded in persuading my friend Crito that I will fly away from here and leave behind nothing of myself. But just the same, Crito, if you are able to catch me or come upon me anywhere, then bury me as you see fit. But believe me, not one of you will catch me when I leave this place.' He spoke admirably there, for he gave his friend a free hand and also showed that the whole topic caused him not the slightest anxiety.

[104] Diogenes showed less humanity; his opinion was the same but, being a Cynic, he expressed himself more harshly, instructing that he be thrown out unburied.* Then his friends said, 'To the birds and beasts?' 'Certainly not,' came the reply, 'but put a stick near me so I can drive them away.' 'How will you be able to,' they said, 'for you will not be aware of them?' 'How then will the mauling of beasts affect me when I am not aware of them?' Anaxagoras made an impressive remark when he was dying at Lampsacus and his friends asked him if he wanted to be taken to his home-town of Clazomenae, if anything happened to him. 'No need for that at all,' he said: 'it's the same length of journey to the underworld wherever you start from.'* As regards the whole issue of burial, there is one principle to be maintained—it is the body it has to do with, whether the soul has perished or still has its strength; it is obvious that in the body no sensation survives, whether the soul has perished or has slipped away.

[105] But everywhere misconceptions abound. Achilles ties Hector to his chariot and drags him along, thinking, I suppose, that Hector is

being mangled and is aware of it. He is therefore exacting vengeance, or so it seems to him—but the poor woman laments as she would over an act of great cruelty: 'I have seen what it cost me the greatest sorrow to see, Hector swept along by the chariot with its team of four.'* What Hector? How long will he be Hector? A better way of putting it is found in Accius when he makes Achilles, finally restored to good sense, say, 'No, in truth I restored to Priam the corpse, Hector I have taken away.'* So it was not Hector you dragged but a body which had belonged to Hector.

[106] Look, another rises up from the earth, to stop his mother sleeping: 'Mother, it is you I call on, you who relieve your care, suspending it in sleep, and have no pity for me, arise and give your son burial.'* When words like these are chanted in impressive and doleful strains, such that fill entire theatres with sadness, it is difficult to avoid the judgement that the unburied are wretched—'before wild beasts and birds . . .'—he fears his use of his limbs will be less effective if they are mangled, but has no dread of this if they are consumed in fire—'and do not allow my remains, half-eaten and with bones exposed, to be foully scattered, stained with gore, across the earth'.

[107] I do not see what his fear is, as he pours out such fine seven-footers to the accompaniment of the flute. We must, then, adhere to the point that after death nothing should cause us concern, when many men punish their enemies even when they are dead. Quite superb are the verses in which Ennius has his Thyestes utter curses. His first prayer is that Atreus may perish by shipwreck—a harsh fate, to be sure, as such an end is not without painful consciousness. But what follows is meaningless: 'Himself transfixed on the top of rugged rocks, disembowelled and hanging by his side as he spatters the rocks with filth, with gore and black blood.' Not even the rocks will be more free of all sensation than will Atreus, 'hanging by his side', on whom Thyestes imagines he is invoking torture. They would have been cruel if he had sensation, without any they are nothing. But the following lines are completely without meaning: 'Nor let him have a tomb to withdraw to, a haven for his body, where with human life resigned, his body may find respite from ills.' You see how seriously mistaken this is: he supposes there is a haven for the body and the dead man finds rest in his tomb. Pelops is much at fault for not educating his son* and instructing him in the limits of concern in each particular situation.

[108] But why should I take note of the opinions of individual men, when we may observe the different misconceptions of nations? The Egyptians embalm their dead and keep them in the house;* the Persians even smear them with wax before burial, so that the bodies may last as

long a time as possible; the Magi* have the custom of giving the bodies
of their people burial only when they have been mangled by wild beasts;
in Hyrcania the common folk breed dogs for the community's use, the
nobility for private use. We know that this is a noble breed of dog, but
each man procures the creatures to mangle him, spending as much
as his resources permit, and this they regard as the finest way of giving
a man burial. Many other examples are collected by Chrysippus*—
in every enquiry he is punctilious—but some are so disgusting that
speech shuns and shudders at them. We must, then, give no respect to
this entire subject as regards ourselves, while not disregarding it in the
case of those near to us, provided that we who are alive are aware that
the bodies of the dead have no awareness.

[109] Let the living attend to how much they should concede to the
demands of custom and their own good name, so long as they recognize
that it has no bearing at all on the dead. But without doubt death is
faced with the greatest acceptance when the life that is passing can console itself with its own distinctions. No one has lived too short a life
who has discharged the perfect duties of perfect virtue. In my own life
there have been many occasions when death would have been oppor-
tune, and I wish I could have met it. No further goal was being achieved,
life's duties had been performed in full, and there only remained the
conflict with fortune. Accordingly, if reason alone does not make us
able to disregard death, nonetheless the life I have led would enable me
to take the view that I have lived enough and to spare. For although
consciousness will not be there, yet the dead do not lack their own
peculiar blessings of praise and glory. Even if glory has nothing in it to
justify our seeking it, yet it follows virtue like a shadow.*

[110] If ever the judgement of the people about good men is sound,
it is something to be applauded rather than a cause of happiness to those
men. But I cannot say, however this will be received, that Lycurgus
and Solon lack the glory due to legislation and political organization,*
or Themistocles and Epaminondas that due to military excellence.*
Salamis itself will be swamped by Neptune sooner than the memory of
the victory at Salamis, and Leuctra will be destroyed sooner than the
fame of the battle of Leuctra. Far more slowly will glory abandon Curius,
Fabricius, Calatinus,* the two Scipios, the two Africani, Maximus,
Marcellus, Paullus, Cato, Laelius, and countless others.* The man who
lays claim to some resemblance to these, measuring it not by popular
repute but by the infallible commendation of good men, will advance,
if so it is to be, with confident heart to meet death, in which we have
found there is either the greatest good or no evil. Even when prosperity

smiles on him he will wish to die; no accumulation of good things can cause so much joy as their loss can cause vexation.*

[111] This appears to be the meaning of the well-known remark of the Spartan who, when Diagoras of Rhodes, a celebrated Olympian victor, had seen in a single day his two sons victorious at Olympia, went up to the old man with these words of congratulation: 'Die now, Diagoras— your destiny is not to ascend to heaven.'* Such feats the Greeks regard highly—perhaps too highly—or rather they used to view them like this, and the man who said this to Diagoras thought it magnificent that three Olympic victors came from a single household and thought the father would gain no advantage by lingering longer in life as a target for fortune. Now I had already given you in a few words what I regarded as an adequate reply. You had granted that the dead are in no evil, but my object in proceeding to speak further is that this concession provides the greatest solace in times of longing and grief. Grief that is our own or felt on our account we should bear with restraint, in case we are thought to be indulging in self-love. It is a suspicion that tortures us with unendurable grief if we suppose that the loved ones we have lost exist with some consciousness in those ills imagined in popular belief. My wish has been to root that view out of *myself* completely,* and for that reason, it may be, I have been too lengthy.

[112] A. You, too lengthy? Not *my* impression. The first part of your discourse made me long for death, but the effect of the latter part was that sometimes I was not unwilling, sometimes not troubled. Your discourse as a whole, however, certainly had the effect of making me not regard death as among evils. M. Then I take it we have no need of a peroration such as rhetoric would prescribe? Or is it now the time for us to abandon this art entirely?* A. No, do not abandon the art to which you have always brought distinction, and with good reason—for that is the art, if we wish to speak the truth, that had brought you distinction. But just what is this peroration you have in mind? I am eager to hear it, whatever it is.

[113] In the schools of rhetoric it is customary to cite the judgements of the immortal gods on death. They do not invent these themselves, but have regard to the authority of Herodotus and many other writers. The story first to be related is that of Cleobis and Biton, the sons of the priestess of Argos. It is a well-known tale: it was ordained that she should ride in a chariot to a customary appointed sacrifice, to a shrine some distance from the town. When the animals pulling her were making slow progress, then those young men whose names I have just stated stripped off, anointed themselves with oil, and took their place at the

yoke. In this way the priestess was conveyed to the shrine, and since her chariot had been drawn by her sons, it is said that she asked the goddess in prayer to give them the greatest reward for piety that a god can bestow on a mortal. Later the young men feasted with their mother and then they went to sleep. In the morning they were discovered dead.

[114] A similar prayer, it is said, was offered by Trophonius and Agamedes. After they had completed the building of the temple to Apollo at Delphi, they worshipped the god and asked for a reward for their effort and its fine result, no slight reward, certainly, but nothing definite and what was best for a man. Apollo revealed to them that he would grant their prayer on the third day after that one, and when it dawned, they were found dead. They say that the god gave his judgement and he was indeed the god to whom the rest of the gods had granted the power of prophecy beyond all others. A further story is told about Silenus, who had been taken prisoner by Midas and granted his captor this gift, as it is written, in exchange for his release: he told the king that by far the best thing for man was not to be born, but the next best thing was to die as soon as possible.*

[115] This thought was used by Euripides in his *Cresphontes*:* 'For it was fitting that we gather in throngs and mourn, where someone has been born to the light of day, reflecting upon the various ills of human life. But the man who by his death had brought to an end his grievous toils his friends should bear to his grave with all praise and happiness.' Something similar exists in the *Consolation* of Crantor.* He says that a certain Elysius of Terina* was in profound grief for the death of his son and, coming to a place where spirits are called up, he asked what had caused so great a calamity. Three verses of the following sort were given to him on tablets: 'In life men wander with ignorant minds. By the power of the fates Euthynous has won death. So to reach his end brought him more benefit, as it did you.'

[116] With reference to these and similar authorities they maintain that the immortal gods have by means of facts settled the case. Certainly Alcidimas, the pre-eminently famous rhetorician* of olden times, actually wrote a work in praise of death, which consists of a list of the evils that afflict mankind. He failed to supply those subtle arguments deduced by the philosophers but he was not failing in richness of expression. Famous deaths met for one's country are not only treated by rhetoricians as glorious but also as fortunate. They go back to Erechtheus, whose daughters eagerly sought to save their fellow citizens' lives by sacrificing their own.* Then there is Codrus, who dressed himself as a slave to avoid being identified, as he would have been in the clothes of a king,

and plunged into the midst of the enemy, because an oracle had been given that if the king was killed, Athens would be victorious.* The example of Menoeceus is not ignored, who likewise shed his blood freely for his country when an oracle was delivered.* Iphigenia ordered that she should be led to be sacrificed at Aulis, 'so that by her blood the enemy's blood should be drawn'.* They pass from these to more recent events. Often on their lips are Harmodius and Aristogiton; the Spartan Leonidas and the Theban Epaminondas* are frequently cited. Our own Roman examples are not familiar to them, and it would be a sizeable undertaking to reckon up that tally of names: so numerous are the men we see who set their hearts on death with glory.

[117] In view of this we must still draw upon great eloquence and address the populace as if from a platform, so that mankind may begin either to wish for death or at any rate to cease fearing it. For if that final day brings not annihilation but a change of abode, what more can be wished for? But if it destroys and wipes us out completely, what is better than to fall asleep in the midst of the toils of life and, closing our eyes, to be lulled into everlasting sleep? If this were to happen, Ennius expresses himself better than Solon. For our poet says, 'Let no one honour me with tears, nor hold my funeral with weeping.'* But here we have the wise Solon: 'Let my death not lack tears: let us leave sorrow to friends that they may celebrate my funeral with sounds of mourning.'

[118] As regards ourselves, if anything should happen such as to suggest a sentence passed by the god* that we should leave life, let us obey with feelings of joy and gratitude, and regard ourselves as being released from imprisonment and relieved of our chains, in order that we may move on to an eternal home that is clearly ours or else lose all sensation and vexation. But if no sentence is delivered, let us still frame our thoughts so that we regard that day, so fearful to others, as propitious to us, and count nothing evil which is appointed by the immortal gods or by nature, the mother of all. It is not at random or through mere chance that we have been begotten and created, but without doubt there has existed some power to take thought for the human race and not give birth or nurture to something which should first suffer the manifold burdens of hardship then fall into an eternal evil of death. Let us think of it rather as a haven and place of refuge that has been prepared for us.

[119] Oh, if only we might be carried there under full sail! But if we are cast back by contrary winds, we must still be brought back to the same point a little later. And can one individual find wretched what is necessary for all? There you have the peroration, in case you think

that anything has been neglected or omitted. A. Indeed I do have it, and I assure you this peroration of yours has really strengthened me. M. Excellent, I call that. But now let us make some concession to our health. Tomorrow, and for as many days as we are here at Tusculum, let us examine these matters and especially those which provide relief from anxieties, fears and desires.* This is the richest reward that all philosophy offers.

BOOK 2

[1] Neoptolemus in Ennius' play* says that he must engage in philosophy but only in a few particulars, for complete commitment to it is not to his liking. But for my part, Brutus, I consider that I must engage in philosophy—for how can I better employ myself, especially now that I have no kind of employment? But not in a few particulars, like Neoptolemus. For in philosophy it is difficult for a man to know a few things without also knowing either most things or everything. A few things can only be selected from a great many, and someone who has once grasped a few will not fail to pursue the remainder just as eagerly.

[2] But all the same in a busy life, and, as with Neoptolemus at that time, a soldier's life, even a few things are often of great benefit and bear fruit—if not the full measure to be gained from all of philosophy, yet such as can at times free us to some extent from desire or mental distress or fear. For example the result of that discussion I lately held at my villa at Tusculum appeared to be a considerable contempt for death, and this contributes in no small degree to liberating the mind from fear.* The man who fears what cannot be avoided can in no way live with a mind at peace. But the man who has no fear of death, not only because dying is unavoidable but also because death holds no terrors for him, has gained for himself a potent means of ensuring that his is a life of happiness.

[3] And yet it does not escape me that many will argue passionately against my view—something I could only have avoided by writing nothing at all. If my speeches, which I wanted to win the approval of people in general—it is a popular art, oratory, and eloquence's success consists in the audience's approval—but if a number of critics were found to deny anything praise except what they trusted they themselves could imitate with success, and to rate as the highest flight of eloquence only what they were capable of aspiring to, and when they were submerged in a flood of ideas and words, to say they preferred to a style of rich abundance one that was lean and impoverished, from which the 'Attic style' had arisen,* something quite unknown to those very people who claimed to follow it and have now fallen quite dumb, laughed to scorn, we might say, by the forum itself—what do we imagine will happen now, when it is evident that we cannot rely in the slightest on the support of the people, our supporters of old?

[4] Philosophy contents itself with just a few judges, deliberately for its part shunning the people at large, who themselves eye it with suspicion and loathing, so that anyone disposed to attack philosophy in its entirety could depend on the people's support, or if he should try to focus his attack on the particular school of philosophy I follow, he can count on a supply of auxiliary troops from the remaining schools of philosophy to swell his numbers. But I have replied to those who criticize philosophy as a whole in the *Hortensius*, while I have put forward in adequate detail the arguments to be made on behalf of the Academy in the four books of the *Academics*.* However, I am so little opposed to receiving criticism that it is something I welcome with open arms, for in Greece itself philosophy would never have been so highly honoured if it had not flourished because of the rivalries and disagreements of men of great learning.

[5] Accordingly, I encourage all who are able to do this to grasp distinction in this field also from the now failing hand of Greece and to transfer it to this city, just as our forefathers by their energy and application transferred here all the remaining forms of distinction, at least those that were desirable.* And distinction in oratory indeed was in this way brought from a low point and reached a peak, so that now, as is nature's way with virtually everything, it begins to decline and seems likely in a short time to dwindle to nothing, whereas out of these times,* as far as Latin literature is concerned, philosophy is being born, and we are helping this process and allowing ourselves to be contradicted and refuted. This is something resented by those who are, so to speak, enslaved and dedicated to certain definite and fixed views, and have their hands so tied by necessity that they are forced to defend for consistency's sake even propositions that normally earn their disapproval. But we, who follow probability and cannot advance further than what presents itself as likely, are prepared both to refute without rudeness and to be refuted without loss of temper.*

[6] If, then, these studies are brought over to ourselves, we shall not even require Greek libraries, which contain an endless number of books due to the great number of their writers. The same things are said by many writers, and so they have stuffed the world with books. The same thing will happen to the Romans as well, if these studies attract a greater tide of writers. But if it is in our power, let us stimulate those who practise philosophy in a reasoned and methodical way, as they have benefited from a liberal education and apply a correct manner of discourse.

[7] There exists a class of men who lay claim to the title of philosophers and are said to be the authors of a great many books in Latin. These

I personally do not despise, for the reason that I have never read them;
but as the writers of these books on their own admission avoid in what
they write a systematic approach, due subdivision, correctness or a polished style,* I have no interest in reading what brings no pleasure.
What is said and what is thought by followers of this school even someone of the slightest education knows. Therefore, since they themselves
take no trouble over how they speak, I do not understand why they ought
to be read, unless it is by those who hold the same views, reading to one
another.

[8] For, just as Plato and the other Socratics,* and then those who
derived from them are read by everyone, even those who either do not
accept their teaching or do not pursue it with the greatest enthusiasm,
whereas Epicurus and Metrodorus* are thumbed by scarcely anyone outside their own adherents, so these Latin writers are read only by those
who think their ideas are right. But my view is that whatever is committed to writing should be deserving of recommendation as reading to
all educated persons; and, if this is something I myself cannot achieve,
I do not feel there is any less obligation for that reason to keep to this
practice.

[9] Accordingly my preference has always been for the practice of
the Peripatetics and the Academy of discussing all subjects from opposite
standpoints, not only because it was the only way of discovering what
was probable in each instance but because it afforded the greatest training in expression.* It was Aristotle who employed this method first, and
then his followers. But in our own day Philo, whose lectures I regularly
attended,* adopted the practice of at one time giving instruction in oratory, at another in philosophy. My friends persuaded me to adopt this
practice in my villa at Tusculum and I have spent the time at my disposal in it. Accordingly, after we had devoted our energies in the morning to oratory, as we had done the day before, we went down into my
Academy* in the afternoon, and there a discussion took place which
I do not set out in narrative form but in virtually the same words used
in the actual discussion.

[10] Well, as we strolled to and fro, this was the way the conversation
began, with this kind of introduction: A. It is impossible to say how much
pleasure or rather comfort I received from your discussion yesterday.
Conscious though I am of never having been excessively devoted to life,
still a kind of fear and pain sometimes crossed my mind when I reflected
that one day would bring an end to the light and the loss of all life's
advantages. I have been so entirely liberated from this kind of distress,
believe me, that I consider nothing worthy of less anxiety.

[11] M. There is nothing to wonder at in this. It is the effect of philosophy. It provides medicine for the soul, takes away futile worries, frees us from desires, banishes fears. But the power it has does not affect everyone to an equal extent. It has a great effect whenever it takes hold of a character that is suitable. Not only fortune 'favours the brave', as in the old proverb, but to a far greater degree reason, which strengthens the power of bravery by, as it were, instructing it. It is obvious that nature has produced in you one who is elevated and lofty, with contempt for human things. A discourse against death, therefore, easily found a home in a gallant spirit. But surely it is not your view that these same arguments carry weight with those very people, except just a handful, by whom they have been devised, discussed and written down. How few philosophers can be found who are so constituted in their character, souls and way of life as reason demands, who regard their own teaching, not as a mere display of learning, but as a rule of life, who listen to their own instructions and obey their own precepts!

[12] Some of them you can see so frivolous and boastful that it would have been better for them not to have been students, others greedy for money, not a few for renown, many the servants of their lusts, so that their language conflicts marvellously with their lifestyle. This strikes me as totally shameful. If someone who claimed to be a teacher of grammar were to speak ungrammatically, or someone who wished to be regarded as a musician were to sing out of tune, this would be the more shameful because he is making mistakes in the very subject he professed to know. Similarly a philosopher who errs in his way of life is liable to the more shame as he falls short in the task of which he aims to be the master and fails in living, though he is a professor in the science of living. A. Surely, then, if matters stand as you say, we should be afraid that you are beautifying philosophy with a glory that is false? What greater proof is there that it confers no benefit than the existence of certain thoroughly trained philosophers who lead shameful lives?

[13] M. But that is really no proof. Just as not all cultivated fields are productive, and Accius' saying* is not true: 'Even if good seeds are sown in inferior soil, yet by their own nature they yield a splendid crop,' so not all cultivated minds yield fruit. And, not to abandon this simile, just as a field, however fertile, cannot be productive without cultivation, so the soul cannot be without teaching. Each is ineffective without the other. Now the cultivation of the soul is philosophy. It pulls out vices by the roots and makes souls ready to receive sowings, entrusting to them and, one may say, sowing within them the kind of seeds that, on attaining full growth, will bear the richest fruits. Let us therefore

proceed as we have begun. Tell me, please, what subject you would have me discuss.

[14] A. I regard pain as the greatest of all evils.* M. Even greater than disgrace? A. I do not venture to assert that, and it makes me ashamed to have been dislodged so swiftly from my position. M. It would involve you in more shame if you persisted in your view. There is nothing more unworthy than for you to think anything worse than disgrace, criminal behaviour and infamous conduct. In order to escape these, any pain is not so much to be rejected, as to be actively sought out, undergone, welcomed. A. That is very much my belief. Accordingly, granting that pain is not the greatest evil, it is certainly an evil. M. Then do you see how much of the fear of pain you have jettisoned as a result of a brief hint?

[15] A. I see clearly, but I desire more. M. I'll indeed try, but it is a major undertaking, and I require a mind that does not resist proof. A. That you will have. I will do as I did yesterday and will now follow the argument wherever it leads me. M. I will begin, then, by speaking of the weak thinking shown by many philosophers of different schools. Foremost among these in authority as well as antiquity is the Socratic Aristippus,* who did not hesitate to say that pain is the greatest evil. The next to show himself a ready adherent of this spineless and effeminate view was Epicurus, followed by Hieronymus of Rhodes, who said freedom from pain was the highest good,* as he held that so much evil resided in pain. The remainder, with the exception of Zeno, Aristo, and Pyrrho,* took much the same view as you recently expressed, that pain is admittedly an evil but other things are worse.

[16] So with regard to this notion promptly rejected by nature itself and a sense of innate nobility, so that you could not assert that pain is the greatest evil, and in the face of disgrace be forced to abandon your view, that rejection has been consistently maintained age after age by our instructress in life, philosophy. What duty, what renown, what glory will be so prized that the man who has convinced himself that pain is the greatest evil will consent to acquire them at the cost of bodily pain? Moreover, what shame, what degradation would a man not endure in order to escape pain, if he had concluded that it was the greatest evil? Again, who will escape misery, not only at the moment of being oppressed by excruciating pain, if this represent the greatest evil, but also when he is aware that such a prospect might await him? And what man lies beyond its reach? The consequence of this is that absolutely no one can be happy.*

[17] Of course, Metrodorus* thinks a man is completely happy if he enjoys a good physical constitution which is assured of always remaining

so. But what man is there who can rely on this assurance? Epicurus in fact says such things that I think he is trying to make us laugh. In one passage he maintains that if the wise man suffers burning or torture—you expect him, perhaps, to continue 'he will endure it, he will bear it to the end, he will not capitulate'—no mean triumph, by Hercules, and worthy of that very Hercules by whom I swore. But this does not satisfy that harsh and inflexible man Epicurus. If he is inside Phalaris' bull,* he will say, 'How sweet this is, how little it troubles me!'* Actually 'sweet'? Isn't it sufficient that it isn't bitter? And yet those very philosophers who deny that pain is an evil are not accustomed to say that it is 'sweet' for anyone to experience torture. They say it is harsh, hard to bear, hateful, contrary to nature, but not an evil. But Epicurus, who says that pain is the only evil* and the worst of all evils, maintains that the philosopher will describe it as 'sweet'.

[18] *I* don't require *you* to describe pain in the same terms as Epicurus used, a man, as you know, devoted to pleasure. Let *him* by all means say the same inside Phalaris' bull as he would if he were in his bed: *I* am not disposed to grant wisdom so much efficacy against pain. If a man shows bravery in enduring it, duty is satisfied. I do not require him to enjoy the experience into the bargain. Pain is a condition that without doubt is sad, harsh, distasteful, at odds with nature, difficult to submit to and to endure.

[19] Look at Philoctetes, whose groans we must forgive. He had seen Hercules himself on Oeta shrieking with the intensity of his pain. So no comfort did this hero have from the arrows he had received from Hercules in those hours when 'the veins of his flesh, tainted with venom from the viper's bite, give rise to foul torments'. And so he cries out as he appeals for aid, desiring death: 'Ah! Who is to commit me to the salt waves from the summit of the lofty crag? Now, now I am being devoured. The power of the wound, the ulcer's fire brings ruin on my soul.'* It seems difficult to say that a man compelled to shout out in this fashion is not involved in an evil, and a considerable one at that.

[20] But let us turn our eyes on Hercules himself, who was broken by pain at the very time when death itself was bringing him to his goal of immortality.* What cries he utters in the *Trachiniae* of Sophocles! When Deianira* had caused him to don the tunic steeped in the Centaur's blood and it had stuck to his flesh, he says:

O many sufferings, harsh to tell of, bitter to endure, that I have known and drained to the dregs in body and soul! Neither Juno's fearful anger implacable, nor grim Eurystheus* brought so much woe upon me as that one mad woman, the daughter of Oeneus. She it was who netted me, all unwitting, in this Fury's shirt, that clings to my side, tears at my flesh with its bite, and pressing hard upon me, drains the breath from my lungs. Now it has sucked out all my discoloured blood. So my frame has been consumed by the ghastly catastrophe and wasted away. Caught in a web of ruin I, yes I, am being slain. No hand of an enemy, nor massive Giants, progeny of Earth, nor Centaur of double form* in his onset has dealt these blows to my body, nor violence of Greeks, nor any barbarian cruelty, nor cruel race banished to the earth's ends, through which I roamed, everywhere driving away all manner of savage beasts, but I, a man, am done to death by a woman's female hand. Son of mine,* for your father's sake be true to this name, and, as I die, do not let your love for your mother defeat me. Seize her with a son's loyal hands and drag her here to me. Then I shall see if I or she has the greater claim on your heart. [21] On your way, be bold, my son! Shed tears at your father's destruction, have pity! Nations will weep for my wretchedness. Ah, that I should utter from these lips the lamentations of a girl, when no man ever saw me groaning at any affliction! My manly heart is crushed, wasted, reduced to a woman's! Approach, my son, stand near, look at your father's piteous body, mangled and torn! Look, all here, and you, father of the gods, I beseech you, hurl upon me the flashing fury of your thunderbolt! Now, ah, now they wrack me, the searing throes of pain, now the fire steals over me. O hands that conquered once, [22] O breast, O back, O sinews of my arms! Was it your strong grip that once made the Nemean lion gasp out his final breath,* gnashing his teeth? Was this the right hand that brought peace to Lerna by slaying the loathsome serpent?* Did this lay low the twin-bodied band?* Did this bring down the beast that laid waste to Erymanthus?* Did this seize in a net and bring up from gloomy Tartarus the triple-headed hound born of the Hydra?* Did this slay the dragon with its many coils that kept close watch over the gold-bearing tree?* Many other trials has this my conquering hand engaged in, and no one has gained the spoils by eclipsing my fame!

Can we think pain so insignificant when we see Hercules himself bearing it with such scant endurance?

[23] Let Aeschylus come forward, not only a poet but a Pythagorean as well,* as we are told. In his play how does Prometheus bear the pain he suffers for his Lemnian theft! 'From here, they say, fire was assigned in secret to mortal men; the wise Prometheus stole it by craft and paid the penalty by fate to Jupiter most high.'* So, as he pays this penalty, nailed to the Caucasus, he says these words:

Titan race, kindred in blood to us, offspring of Heaven, look upon me bound in chains to rugged cliffs, as sailors in fear tie up their ship, dreading night on the loud-roaring sea. Saturn's son, Jupiter, has fixed me here like this, Jupiter's divine power has enrolled the hands of Mulciber.* He has broken through my limbs, driving in these wedges with cruel workmanship. By his skill I have been pierced through and make this Furies' fortress my miserable dwelling. [24] Every other sorrowful day, approaching on baleful wings, Jupiter's servant rends me with his crooked talons and tears my flesh asunder as he makes his

savage meal. Then crammed and fully sated with my rich liver, he gives vent to
a piercing scream and soars into the heights, wiping off my blood with fea-
thered tail. But when the liver he has devoured has grown large and been
renewed, greedily he returns once again to his hideous feasting. Thus I nurture
this guard of my woeful torment, which with misery unending makes me
a thing of ugliness while yet I live. For, as you see, bound by Jupiter's chains
I cannot keep from my breast the bird I dread. [25] So, of myself bereft,
I endure wracking plagues, seeking an end to my torment with longing for
death. But Jupiter's power keeps me far from death. And this lamentable doom,
ancient and heaped up from age to dreadful age, is fastened on my body, from
which fall drops melted by the sun's heat which constantly make wet the rocks
of Caucasus.*

I think we can scarcely say that someone so afflicted is not wretched,
and if we say he is wretched, we are certainly saying that pain is an evil.

[26] A. Up to this point *you* are in fact pleading *my* case, but I'll give
this my attention in a moment. In the meantime where do those verses
come from? I don't recognize them. M. I'll tell you, have no fear; you
are quite right to ask. You see, I take it, that I have no lack of time for
myself? A. What is your point? M. You attended the lectures of philosophers frequently, I believe, when you were in Athens. A. Why, yes,
and it gave me pleasure. M. Well, did you observe that, even if no one
was particularly fluent on those occasions, they nonetheless inserted
verses of poetry into their discourses. A. I did, indeed, and a great
number of verses in the case of Dionysius the Stoic.* M. Quite right.
But he did this in a mechanical fashion, without any proper selection or
appositeness. Philo* would introduce verse excerpts as if they were original, and well-chosen and to the point. And so, now that I have fallen
in love with what I may call this old man's schoolboy exercise, I concentrate for my illustrations on our own poets. But whenever they are lacking, I have translated in addition many passages from the Greek poets,
so that in this kind of discussion Latin discourse should not lack any
embellishment.

[27] But do you see what harm poets cause? They represent men of
heroic temper as weeping, they enervate our spirits and, what's more, they
are so beguiling that they are not only read but learned by heart. So when
to a bad domestic training and a sheltered and finical way of life the
poets are added as well, they constrict all the sinews of manhood. Quite
correctly, then, did Plato banish them from the society which he fashioned
in his search for the best character and the best political constitution.*
But we, taught of course by Greece, read and learn these things from
childhood, regarding this education and instruction as a free man's
right.

[28] But why are we angry with the poets? Those instructors in virtue, the philosophers, have been known to say that pain is the greatest evil. You, however, young man, stated that this was your view a short time ago, but when I asked if it was even greater than dishonour, at a word you abandoned the idea. Put this same question to Epicurus. He will say that moderate pain is a greater evil than the greatest dishonour, as no evil is attendant on dishonour as such unless the consequence is pain. What, then, is the pain that Epicurus feels when he actually states that pain is the greatest evil? I cannot conceive of anything more dishonourable emerging from the lips of a philosopher. Accordingly I was satisfied when you gave me the reply that you regarded dishonour as a greater evil than pain. If you hold fast simply to this view, you will understand how pain must be opposed. We should not so much ask whether pain is an evil as strengthen the soul to endure pain.*

[29] The Stoics produce foolish syllogisms* to prove that pain is no evil, as if the problem is purely linguistic and not factual. Why do you seek to deceive me, Zeno? When you say that what appals me is not an evil at all, I am taken in and desire to know how the thing I regard as the most wretched of all is not even evil. 'Nothing is evil,' he says, 'unless it is base and wicked.' You are resorting to silliness. You're not removing the cause of my distress. I know that pain is not wickedness. Stop proving that to me and prove instead that it makes no difference whether I feel pain or not. 'It never makes any difference,' he says, 'that is, for living a happy life, which is based on virtue alone, but nonetheless it is to be rejected.'* Why? 'It is harsh, contrary to nature, difficult to endure, miserable, troublesome.'

[30] That's an abundance of words to describe something we all call in a single word 'evil'. You provide me with an account of pain but don't get rid of it, when you say it is harsh and contrary to nature, a thing that can hardly be borne or endured, and you do not lie but you should not have given ground on the substance while showing off in your use of vocabulary. 'Nothing is good that is not honourable, nothing evil that is not base.' This is mere wishful thinking, not proof. It would be better and truer to say that all things rejected by nature belong to the category of evils, all things accepted to the category of what is good. Once this is established and the verbal controversy laid to rest, the superiority of what your colleagues correctly hold fast to—what we call honourable, right and fitting, and sometimes also describe by the inclusive term 'virtue'—will still be so pronounced that in comparison all the things regarded as goods of the body and of fortune appear paltry and minute,

and no evil, not even if all of them were concentrated in a single place, is to be compared with the evil of immorality.*

[31] If, then, as you admitted at the outset, immorality is worse than pain, then pain is clearly of no account. As long as you consider it base and unworthy of a man to groan, shriek aloud, lament, to be broken and weakened by pain, as long as a sense of honour, nobility and reputation obtain, as long as you control yourself by keeping your eyes on these things, pain will, I assure you, give way to virtue and lose its strength through the exercise of your mind.* Either no virtue exists or all pain is to be despised. Do you grant the existence of wisdom, without which we are incapable of understanding what any virtue is? In that case will it allow you to do anything that brings you no advantage and involves you in pointless effort? Or will moderation let you do anything in an uncontrolled fashion? Or is it possible for justice to be practised by a man who because of the violence of pain discloses secrets entrusted to him, betrays his accomplices, and reneges on many obligations?

[32] Again, how will you answer the claims of bravery and its companions, greatness of soul, dignity, endurance and disdain for life's vicissitudes? When you are lying prostrate and crushed, lamenting your state in pitiful words, will you hear 'What a man of courage!' said over you? No, if you are reduced to such straits, no one will so much as call you a man. Bravery, then, must be jettisoned or we need to find a grave for pain. Do you, then, not know that, if you lose one of your Corinthian vases,* you can possess the rest of your goods in safety, but that, if you lose one virtue, even if it is impossible for virtue to be lost—yet if you do admit to not possessing one, you will possess none?*

[33] Surely, then, you cannot describe as a brave man, a man of great soul, a man of endurance, a man of dignity, a man who holds human problems in contempt, either the Philoctetes of the play—I prefer not to use you as an example here*—but we can certainly not describe as brave the man who lies prostrate 'in a damp hut that echoes with weeping, complaining, groaning and crying, repeating from its dumb walls tearful sounds'.* It is not my contention that pain is not pain—why else would there be a need for bravery?—but that it is subdued by endurance, provided that such a thing as endurance exists; if it does not, why do we exalt philosophy or take pride in its name? Pain stings, or if you like, strikes deep. If your defences are gone, present your throat.* But if you have Vulcan's armour* to protect you, that is, bravery, resist. If you fail to do this, this guardian of your honour will leave you deserted.

[34] The laws of the Cretans, ratified either by Jupiter or, as the poets say, by Minos* in accordance with Jupiter's wishes, and likewise those of

Lycurgus* educate the youth through toil, hunting, running, endurance of hunger and thirst, exposure to cold and heat. Indeed in Sparta boys are given such a hail of whiplashes at the altar 'that from their flesh the blood flows in streams',* sometimes even, as I heard when I was there,* resulting in death. Not only did none of these boys ever utter a cry but he didn't even utter a groan. Well, then, is this something boys are capable of but men will not be? Where custom has the power will reason lack it?

[35] A particular difference exists between toil and pain. They are beyond question closely related but there is still a particular difference. Toil is the execution of work or duty of undue difficulty on the part of the body or mind, but pain is a disagreeable movement in the body, repugnant to the senses. To these two things one term is applied by our friends the Greeks, whose language is richer than our own. Consequently they call men who work hard devoted to, or rather in love with, *pain*, while we more appropriately call them *toilers*. For it is one thing to toil, but another to feel pain. O Greece, sometimes you are deficient in the words you think you abound in always!* It is, I say, one thing to toil and another to feel pain. When Gaius Marius' varicose veins* were being cut out, he felt pain; when he was leading his troops under a blazing sun, he was undergoing toil. There is, however, a sort of resemblance between the two things: the habit of toil makes the endurance of pain easier.

[36] Accordingly those who gave to Greece the shape of its political institutions wanted the bodies of their young men to be strengthened by toil. This rule was applied by the men of Sparta also to their women, the sex that in all other cities enjoys a pampered existence, 'concealed behind the shade of a house's walls'. Those men wanted nothing of the sort 'in Spartan maidens, whose pursuit is more the wrestling ground, Eurotas,* sun, dust, toil and warfare than barbarian fertility'.* So while pain sometimes intervenes in these exercises involving toil—they are pushed, struck, thrown over and fall—the actual toil covers over with a hard skin, as it were, the pain they feel.

[37] As for military service—I speak here of our own, not that of the Spartans, whose column advances to the musical measure of a pipe, receiving no word of encouragement except the beat of anapaests—you can see, firstly, what gives rise to the name our armies have (*exercitus*), and, secondly, the toil, the considerable toil of the marching troops, carrying more than half a month's rations, carrying whatever utensils they want, carrying a stake. Our soldiers no more number shield, sword and helmet as burdens than they do their own shoulders, arms and hands. Weapons, they say, are the soldier's limbs, and these they carry so close to hand that, should need arise, their burdens are cast aside and they

can fight with weapons as free for employment as their limbs. Again, there is the training of the legions, the double, the charge, the battle-cry—what great toil they all involve! This is the source of that courage in battle that makes them ready to accept wounds. Bring up a body of troops of equal courage but untrained and they will seem like women.

[38] Why does such a difference exist between raw troops and veterans as we have found?* Recruits generally have the advantage in years but, when it comes to enduring toil and despising a wound, habit is the instructor. Again, isn't it true that we see wounded men often being carried off the field of battle, and the raw, untrained soldier giving vent to the most shameful cries of grief, however trifling his wound, whereas the trained veteran, all the braver on that account, only looks for the surgeon to put on a bandage and says,

O Patroclus, I come to you seeking help at your hands before I meet a cruel death bestowed by the enemy's hand (and by no means can the stream of blood be staunched), to see if by some way your wisdom can better frustrate death. For the wounded crowd the entrance ways of the sons of Aesculapius and access is impossible. [PATROCLUS:] Surely this man is Eurypylus.* How fate has tried him!

[39] Where lamentation succeeds lamentation so promptly, observe how devoid of tears is his reply, how he even affords a reason why he should practise endurance with a calm spirit:

[EURYPYLUS:] The man who contrives another's death should know a like end is prepared for him, that he may share an equal fate.

Patroclus will take him away, I believe, to set him down on the bed, to bandage his wound. Yes, if that man had a human nature, but nothing less have I seen. He asks what has taken place:

[PATROCLUS:] Speak, speak, how stands the Greek cause in battle?

[EURYPYLUS:] It is impossible to express in words how much effort supports the mighty deeds.

Then say nothing more and bind up the wound. Even if Eurypylus could do this, Aesopus could not.*

[EURYPYLUS:] When Hector's fortune turned our stalwart line . . .

and the rest of the tale he unfolds in his pain. So beyond control in a man of courage is the soldier's love of renown. Will this, then, be something of which a veteran soldier is capable but not a trained philosopher? No, the latter will be better able, and in no small degree.

[40] But I have been so far speaking of the familiarity bred of training, not yet of reason and wisdom. Old women regularly endure a lack of food for a period of two or three days; take from an athlete his food for a single day and he will appeal to Olympian Jupiter, the very god in whose honour he trains, he will cry out that he can't bear it. The force of habit is considerable. Huntsmen spend the night in snow on the mountains; Indians allow themselves to be burnt;* boxers thrashed by their opponents' gloves* do not even utter a groan.

[41] But why mention those who regard an Olympic victory as equal to the consulship of old?* Consider gladiators, who are either desperadoes or barbarians, and what blows they endure! See how men who have been well trained would rather receive a blow than shamefully avoid it! How often it appears that their dearest wish is to satisfy their owner or the people! Even when exhausted by their wounds they send word to their owners to ask what their wishes are. If they have given satisfaction, they say, they are content to fall. What gladiator of ordinary skill ever uttered a groan or altered his expression? Who brought shame on himself not only when on his feet but even when admitting defeat? Who having stooped in defeat has drawn in his neck at the order to take the fatal sword-thrust? Such is the power of training, practice and habit. Will then,

'the Samnite,* a vile fellow, worthy of that life and place'

be capable of this, but a man born to renown have any part of his soul so enfeebled that he cannot make it strong by means of practice and reason? Many people tend to regard a gladiatorial show as cruel and lacking in humanity, and I am inclined to think it is, as conducted these days.* But in the days when criminals were fighting to the death with the sword, for the ear there could perhaps be many better forms of training to face pain and death, but for the eye there was none.

[42] I have spoken of training, of habit and practice. Come, if you will, and let us turn our attention to reason,* unless there is anything you would like to add to this. A. Are you asking *me* to interrupt *you*? I couldn't even entertain such a wish, so compelling do I find your argument. M. Well, let us leave it to the Stoics to determine whether feeling pain is an evil or not.* They seek to arrive at the conclusion that pain is not an evil by means of some contorted and trivial little syllogisms that make no impression on the feelings. In my own estimate, whatever pain may be, I do not think it as important as it is considered, and I say that people are too deeply affected by its bogus look and appearance, and that all pain can be endured. What, then, shall I take as

my starting-point? Or shall I touch briefly on the very points I raised recently to make it easier for my argument to advance further?

[43] It is, then, a point of general agreement among not just the educated but the uneducated that it is characteristic of men who are brave, great in spirit, enduring and superior to the fortunes that afflict humanity that they endure pain without complaining. And no man has existed who thought that praise should not be bestowed on one who suffered in such a spirit. Accordingly, seeing that this ability is both required of brave men and commended when found, surely it is shameful either to shrink from the coming of pain* or to fail to endure it once it has arrived? And yet it may be true that, while all correct states of mind are called virtues, this is not the appropriate term for them all, and rather they have all been named after the one virtue* which transcended all others. For virtue (*virtus*) derives its name from *vir* (a man), and the defining quality of a man is above all bravery, whose two main functions are disdain for death and disdain for pain. Accordingly these must be employed if we want to be in possession of virtue, or rather if we want to be true men, since the word *virtus* has been borrowed from *vir*. You will, perhaps, ask how, and the question is correct, for it is claimed by philosophy that it possesses such a cure.*

[44] Along comes Epicurus, not a bad fellow at all, rather, a first-rate man: he gives advice in accordance with his intelligence.* 'Pay no attention,' he says, 'to pain.' Who is saying this? The same man who calls pain the greatest evil. These are not quite consistent statements. Let us listen. 'If pain is at the extreme,' he says, 'it must be short.'

'Tell me that once more!'

I fail to understand properly what you mean by 'at the extreme' and 'short'. 'I mean by "at the extreme" something which cannot be exceeded, by "short" something which is shorter than anything else. I hold in contempt a degree of pain from which a short space of time will deliver me almost before it comes.' But what if the pain is as severe as Philoctetes' was? 'I certainly do regard that pain as pretty severe, but still not at the extreme, for the pain was confined to his foot. His eyes are healthy, as are his head, his chest and lungs, everything is healthy. Accordingly, he is far from suffering pain at the extreme. It follows', he says, 'that continuous pain involves more happiness than vexation.'

[45] I cannot say that so eminent a man as this is lacking in sense but I think we are being mocked by him. What *I* say is that the extreme of pain—I say the extreme, even if there is another ten atoms greater*—is

not necessarily short, and I can name many worthy men who for several years have suffered tortures of pain from gout. But the clever fellow never fixes a limit either for the degree or length, to let me know what he means by 'the extreme' in pain or 'short' in time. Let us, then, pass him by as one who says absolutely nothing, and force him to admit that ways of relieving pain are not to be sought from one who has declared that pain is the greatest of evils, even though that same man shows some grit in enduring stomach gripes and difficulty in passing water.* We must seek a cure from another source, therefore, and especially if we are enquiring what is the most consistent belief, we should ask those who regard what is honourable as the greatest good and what is base as the greatest evil.* When you are in their presence you will not dare, believe me, to groan and writhe. Virtue itself will take you to task, speaking through them:

[46] 'When you have seen boys at Sparta, young men at Olympia and barbarians in the arena receiving the most terrible blows and suffering them in silence, will you cry out like a woman if some pain happens to make you twitch, rather than bear it bravely and calmly?' 'It is unbearable. Nature cannot tolerate it.' I see! Boys endure it prompted by glory, others endure it through shame, many through fear, and do we still fear that nature cannot tolerate what is endured by so many people in so many places? Nature in fact not only tolerates but also demands it, for nature thinks nothing more excellent, nothing it would rather seek to possess, than honour, renown, esteem, glory. My wish in using this number of terms is to express a single idea, but I employ more than one of them in order to make my meaning as clear as possible. What I wish to say is that by far the best thing for man is something he should desire to possess in and for itself, that has its source in virtue, or resides in virtue itself, that is of itself praiseworthy, something I would sooner describe as the only good rather than deny it to be the greatest good;* and as these terms I use describe what is honourable, so to describe what is base I must use their opposites—nothing is so loathsome, nothing so contemptible, nothing so unworthy of a human being.

[47] If you are convinced of this—at the outset you said you thought there was more evil in disgrace than in pain—it remains that you should exercise command over yourself. Now I find this statement perplexing, as if we have two personalities, the one issuing orders, the other obeying them, but nonetheless it does not lack sense. For the soul is divided into two parts,* and one of these partakes of reason, while the other does not. Therefore when we receive the instruction to be masters of ourselves, we are being instructed that reason should control

recklessness. Nature has seen to it that there is in the souls of virtually all people an element of softness, of lowliness, of the abject, of, as it were, what is nerveless and feeble. If he possessed nothing beyond this, man would be the most hideous of all creatures; but at his side stands reason, the mistress and queen of all, who through striving by her own strength and forging onward becomes perfected virtue. What a man must look to is that reason commands that part of the soul which ought to obey.'

[48] 'How will this happen?' you will say. Just as the master commands the slave, or the general the soldier, or the parent the son. If that part of the soul which I have described as soft behaves disgracefully, if it submits to lamentation and tears as women might, let it be clapped in irons and tightly confined by the guardianship of friends and relatives;* for many a time we find men broken by a sense of shame who would never be mastered by reason. And so such people we shall have to keep almost in chains and guard closely like slaves, while those of stronger spirit but deficient in vigour we shall have to remind to preserve their honour, like good soldiers recalled to duty. When in *The Bath** that wisest hero of Greece is wounded, he does not complain to excess, rather we should say his words show restraint: 'March slowly onward,' he says, 'and with calm step, for fear a keener pain may seize me from the jolting.'

[49] Here Pacuvius improves on Sophocles.* In that writer Ulysses laments over his wound most tearfully. And yet the very men who carry the wounded man as he groans softly say to him unhesitatingly, with an eye to the dignity of his character,

'You, too, Ulysses, though we see you sorely wounded, show a spirit almost too womanly for one accustomed to spend his life in war.'

The wise poet understands that habit is a teacher not to be despised when it comes to bearing pain.

[50] And the hero for all his great pain keeps himself under control:

'Keep your hold on me! Hold me! My wound overpowers me. Lay it bare. Oh, my suffering! I am being tortured.'

He begins to lose hold of himself. Then at once he stops:

'Cover it up, leave me at once! Leave me alone; you make the fierce pain worse by your touch and shaking.'

Do you see how what has been silenced is not a bodily pain that has been stilled but a mental pain that has been reprimanded? And so at the end of *Niptra* he takes others also to task, and this he says when he is dying:

'It is becoming to complain of adverse fortune, but not to bewail it; this is the duty of a man: weeping was bestowed on a woman's nature.'

That weak part of his soul obeyed reason, just as a conscientious soldier obeys a strict commander.

[51] But the man in whom there shall be perfect wisdom—we, certainly, have not set eyes on any such before now,* but his character, if only he can be discovered, is expressed in the teachings of the philosophers— well then, he, or rather such reason as will exist in him in complete and absolute form, will command that weaker part of his nature, as a just parent commands good children. He will achieve his wish with a nod, with no effort and no unpleasantness; he will rouse, stir and arm himself so that he may face pain as he would the foe. What are the weapons he will take up? Effort, fortifying and engaging himself in private conversation with such words, 'Beware of anything shameful, slack, unbecoming in a man.'

[52] Ideals of honourable conduct should be kept before his eyes. Let him contemplate Zeno of Elea* who endured every torment rather than reveal the names of his accomplices in the plot to overthrow tyranny. He should reflect on Democritus' follower Anaxarchus who fell into the hands of king Timocreon in Cyprus and without begging for mercy rejected no form of torture.* The Indian Callanus, a barbarian without education born in the foothills of the Caucasus,* was burnt alive at his own wish: if we have a sore foot or tooth, or even suppose our whole body hurts, can't we put up with it? There is an opinion, petty and womanish, and just as commonly held in pleasure as in pain; when this causes us to melt and dissolve in feebleness, we are incapable of enduring a bee-sting without shouting.

[53] But in fact Gaius Marius, a man of country origin but certainly a man, when under the surgeon's knife,* as I said before, ordered from the outset that he should not be tied down, and no man before Marius, they say, underwent an operation without such restraint. Why, then, did others afterwards do the same? It was the force of his great example. Do you see, then, that it is belief, not nature,* that creates evil? And yet the same Marius shows that the pain had a fierce bite, for he did not offer his other leg. In this way he both endured pain as a man and was unwilling as a human being to endure greater pain unnecessarily. The entire point, therefore, is to be ruler of one's self. I have now made clear the nature of that rule, and reflecting upon the conduct that is most worthy of endurance, of courage and greatness of soul, not only controls the mind but also makes pain itself in some way easier to bear.

[54] For in battle it happens that the cowardly and faint-hearted soldier throws away his shield the moment he sees the enemy, and runs away as fast as he can, for this reason sometimes forfeiting his life, even with no wound on his body, while no such fate befalls the soldier who has stood his ground. In a similar way those who are unable to bear the sight of pain throw themselves down and lie there, stricken and lifeless, while those who have put up resistance very often leave the battlefield victorious. The soul has certain points of resemblance to the body. Weights are carried more easily when the body is tense but with real difficulty when it is relaxed, and in a way most similar the soul by its own tension* casts off all the pressure of burdens but by relaxing is so weighed down that it cannot raise itself up.

[55] And if it is the truth we seek, the soul must apply tension in the performance of all duties. This is, as it were, the only safeguard for duty. But in the matter of pain the precaution to be observed above all others is that we do nothing despondently, cravenly, idly, nothing as a slave or a woman would, and principally that those outcries of Philoctetes are resisted and rejected. There are occasions, though not many, when it is allowable for a man to groan aloud but this is never true of howling, even in the case of a woman. That, in fact, is the form of keening that the Twelve Tables forbade to be employed at funerals.*

[56] Indeed, never does a brave and wise man so much as groan aloud, unless perhaps in order to tense himself to be steadfast, as runners on the track shout out as loudly as they can. Athletes do the same when they are training, and boxers at the moment of hitting an opponent actually groan aloud as they throw punches, not because they feel pain or are losing heart, but because, when they give vent to this sound, their whole body is tensed and the blow that comes is the more powerful. Again, if men wish to shout louder, they hardly think it sufficient to strain their lungs, throat and tongue, from which we see the sound is extracted and poured forth. The whole body, tooth and nail, as the saying goes, they enlist to serve the effort of the voice.

[57] Why, I have even seen Marcus Antonius* touch the ground with his knee, when he was straining every nerve in conducting his own defence under the Varian law.* Military catapults have weightier discharges of their stones, and the other propulsion-machines of their missiles, the more powerfully they are tightened and drawn back. It is similar with the voice, with running and with the boxer's blow: the greater the tension in the delivery, the more impressive it will be. Since this tension has so powerful an effect, we shall resort to a groan when in pain, if it will serve to boost our morale. But if the groaning is utterly

woeful, weak, despondent, tearful, then I would scarcely describe the one who has succumbed to it as a man. Even if the groaning should bring some measure of relief, we should still consider what was fitting for a man of courage and spirit. As it does nothing to diminish the pain, why do we wish to incur disgrace to no purpose? What brings more disgrace to a man than womanly weeping?

[58] And this rule that is laid down for pain has a wider scope: all things, not just pain, should be resisted with a similar mental tension. Anger blazes up, lust is aroused: we must seek refuge in the same citadel and take up the same weapons. But since it is pain we are discussing, let us leave these examples to one side. Accordingly, to bear pain calmly and quietly, it is of the greatest benefit to consider with all of one's heart, as the saying goes, how honourable it is to do so.* We are by nature, as I have said before—it must be repeated again and again—most enthusiastic devotees of honour, and if we catch a glimpse of its radiance, there is nothing we are not prepared to bear and endure to the end in order to make it our own. It is because of this race, this rush of souls towards true renown and honour that those dangers are faced in battle. Men of courage do not feel wounds in the battle line, or they do feel them but prefer death to being dislodged from that place of honour,* even by a single step.

[59] The gleaming swords of the enemy were seen by the Decii,* as they charged their line of battle. What lessened all fear of wounds for them was the nobility of death and glory. You don't imagine that Epaminondas* groaned aloud, when he felt his life ebbing away together with his blood? The country he had inherited was the servant of the Spartans but he left it their master. These are the consolations, these are the healing balms for the greatest pains.

[60] What, you will say, is there in peacetime, at home, in our beds? You call me back to philosophers, who do not often step forward into the line of battle. One of them, Dionysius of Heraclea,* a most inconstant fellow, had been taught by Zeno to be brave but pain made him forget his lesson. When he was suffering from kidney trouble, even as he howled he kept shouting out that the beliefs he had previously held about pain were untrue. When his fellow student Cleanthes asked what argument could possibly have made him abandon his earlier view, he replied: 'Because if, having studied philosophy so much, I was still unable to bear pain, that would be sufficient proof that pain is an evil. But I have spent very many years on philosophy and I cannot bear pain; so pain is an evil.' Then Cleanthes stamped his foot on the ground and quoted a line, they say, from the Epigoni: 'Do you hear this, Amphiaraus,

hidden beneath the earth?'—he meant Zeno, saddened that Dionysius had so much betrayed the spirit of his master's teaching.*

[61] This was not true of our own Posidonius,* whom I have often seen with my own eyes, and I will tell the story that Pompey was in the habit of relating. On his arrival at Rhodes on his return journey from Syria, he told how he felt a wish to hear a lecture by Posidonius, but on hearing that a bad attack of arthritis was making him seriously unwell, he still wanted to pay the distinguished philosopher a visit.* On seeing him and offering his respects, he paid him distinguished compliments, saying he was put out at not being able to hear him lecture. But Posidonius replied, 'You *can* hear me; I will not let physical pain cause so great a man to have come to see me in vain.' Accordingly Pompey told how that man from his sick-bed gave a weighty and full discourse on this very topic, that there is nothing good which is not honourable, and when spasms of pain scorched him he said repeatedly, 'It's no use, pain! Trouble me as you will, never shall I admit you are an evil.'

[62] In summary, all toils that bring fame and distinction become at once bearable because of the effort they demand. Don't we see that, among those who highly esteem the sports called gymnastics, no pain at all is shunned by the competitors who enter for them? And, in the case of men who value the prestige of hunting and horse-riding, no pain whatever is shunned if they have this aim. What should I say about our ambitions, about desire to enjoy offices of state? When men in earlier days* used to garner these positions a vote at a time, what flame were they not prepared to run through? Accordingly, Africanus always had in his hands Xenophon the follower of Socrates, and he praised him especially for saying that the same hardships in war were not equally arduous for general and soldier, since the general's high rank itself made his hardship easier to bear.*

[63] But all the same, it happens that what holds sway with the common herd of foolish people* is an opinion about honour, since they cannot perceive what the thing itself is. And so they are influenced by reputation and the judgement of the masses, as they suppose honourable anything that wins the approval of the majority. But as for you,* should you find yourself before the eyes of the public, I would not have you depend on their judgement or accept their view of what is most fair. The judgement you must exercise is your own.* If you content yourself in approving what is right, then not only will you win the victory over yourself, as I was prescribing a little earlier, but over all men and all things.

[64] Put this thought before you: that largeness of soul and, so to speak, building it up to the greatest possible height, which is most

clearly apparent when pains are treated with scorn and contempt, is the fairest thing of all, and all the fairer if it has no truck with the people and, without seeking to win their applause, still gives pleasure to itself. Moreover, it is my view that all things seem more praiseworthy which are done without advertisement and the people's witness, not that this is to be avoided—all good deeds wish to have their setting in the light of day—but all the same there can be no more important audience for virtue than a good conscience.

[65] And let us take thought primarily for the question how this endurance of pain, which I have frequently said must be strengthened by a tension of the soul,* should show itself evenly, whatever form the pain takes. Often many men who have bravely received and bravely endured wounds sustained through their passion for victory or for glory, or even to preserve their rights and freedom, have relaxed the tension and prove incapable of bearing the pain of disease. The pain they had endured with ease they had not endured through reason or wisdom but rather because of excitement and ambition. And so some savage barbarians are able to fight with the sword most fiercely but are unable to bear illness as men should. Now Greeks, people who are not particularly courageous but, as human capacity goes, intelligent enough, cannot look an enemy in the face but they bear sickness with patience and as humans ought.* The Cimbri and Celtiberi, however, revel in battles but moan in sickness. Nothing can achieve an even balance if it does not have firm reason as its basis.

[66] But since one sees that men who are led on either by excitement or mere opinion are not broken by pain in the pursuit and realization of their aims, one must think either that pain is not an evil or that, even if it is decided that whatever is unpleasant and at odds with nature should be called evil, nevertheless it is of such insignificance* that it is so eclipsed by virtue as to be seen nowhere. Give thought to this, I beg you, night and day. This question will spread more widely and occupy a field considerably larger than applies to pain alone. For if all our actions have the purpose of avoiding what is morally bad and attaining what is morally good, we shall be free to despise not only the stabs of pain but also the thunderbolts of fortune, particularly as we have the refuge that came out of our discussion yesterday.*

[67] If some god should say to a man who was at sea with pirates in hot pursuit, 'Throw yourself from the ship. You have at hand to catch you either a dolphin, as Arion of Methymna found,* or else the famous horses of Neptune which aided Pelops,* the ones, they say that "swept along the chariot on high above the waves". They will take you up and

carry you to wherever you wish'—he would abandon all fear. So, when harsh and loathsome fears assail you, if they are too great for you to bear, you see the refuge you must seek.* This is virtually what I thought should be said on this occasion. But perhaps you stick by your opinion. A. Far from it. I believe that in two days I have been set free from the fear of two things, which made me seriously afraid. M. Tomorrow, then, it's to the water-clock.* That is what we arranged, and I see this is a debt I cannot leave unpaid to you. A. Absolutely—oratory in the morning, then our discussion at the same time as today. M. So be it; I will be at your service in these interests that do you so much credit.

BOOK 3

Preface

[1] Since we are composed of soul and body, Brutus,* what am I to suppose is the reason why for the care and safeguarding of the body an art has been devised, whose usefulness is such that men have paid it the honour of ascribing its discovery to the immortal gods,* whereas for the soul an art of healing has not been felt so needed before its discovery, nor has it become the object of study after becoming known, nor has it won the respect and approval of so many, indeed a greater number has viewed it with suspicion and hatred. Is it because the soul is our means of judging a feeling of weariness and pain in the body, whereas the body does not help us in realizing the sickness of the soul? From this it follows that the soul forms a judgement on its own condition at the moment when the agent of reaching that judgement is itself sick.

[2] Now if nature had brought us into the world so endowed that we could look at it with insight and understanding, and under its excellent guidance could complete the course of our lives, there would, of course, be no cause for anyone to need philosophical education. But as it is, nature has given us only tiny sparks, which under the corrupting influence of bad customs and beliefs we quickly extinguish so fully that a glimpse of nature is nowhere to be seen. The seeds of virtue are inborn in our characters and, if they were allowed to mature, nature with its own hand* would lead us on to the life of happiness; but as things are, from the moment we enter the light of day and our upbringing begins,* we are at once involved in all manner of wickedness and completely mistaken opinions, so that it seems as if we almost drank in deception with our nurse's milk. But when we have been returned to our parents,* and are next handed over to schoolmasters, that is when we are tainted with such a wealth of different misconceptions that truth gives way to falsehood and nature itself to rooted prejudice.

[3] To this add also the poets,* who, when they hold out the fair prospect of learning and wisdom, are heard, read, learnt by heart and so take deep root in our minds; but when to this are added the people's voice, represented as some sort of finishing master, and all the masses with their combined tendency to follow bad practices, then clearly we are contaminated by vicious beliefs and abandon the teachings of nature, so that we think the best perception of nature's meaning belongs

to those who judge that the best, the most desirable, the most excellent ambition for a man is public office and military commands and glory in the eyes of the people; the very best men among us are swept away towards this, and though they desire to achieve what is truly honourable, the particular object especially of nature's search, they find themselves in the most futile of pursuits and strive to gain not virtue as the rounded work of a sculptor, but a shadowy image of glory. For glory is a thing of genuine substance and clearly defined, not a shadowy image: it is the agreed approval of good men, the incorrupt verdict of jurors who decide correctly the question of outstanding virtue, and it responds to virtue as its echo;* and since it generally accompanies actions rightly performed, it is not to be rejected by good men.

[4] But that glory which claims to be a copy of the true kind, is rash and negligent, and generally gives its approval to errors and faults. It is public acclaim, and by pretending to be honourable it caricatures true glory's fair beauty. This is the influence that makes men blind, so that, despite having ambitions that were even noble, yet, in their failure to understand either where these were to be found or what they really were, some of them bring utter ruin on their own countries and others cause their own ends.* And indeed these men with the best of aims go wrong not wilfully but through taking a wrong turning* in their course. What of others? When men are carried away by desire for money, lust for pleasure, when their souls are in such confusion that they are not far removed from madness,* is there no treatment to be applied to them? Is it because ailments of the soul are less harmful than those of the body, or because the body can be cured that no means exist for curing souls?

[5] But diseases of the soul are both more dangerous and more numerous than those of the body. They are troublesome from the very fact that it is the soul they affect and disturb, and in the words of Ennius,* 'A sick soul goes ever astray; it can neither endure nor hold out, and never ceases to harbour desire.' And to say nothing of others, what diseases in the body can be more serious, I ask, than these two diseases of distress and desire?* How can a view be established which would make it out that the soul cannot heal itself, seeing that the actual means of curing the body have been discovered by the soul, and seeing that the constitution of the body in itself contributes a great deal to the cure of the body, and not all of those who have submitted to being treated immediately regain their health as well, whereas souls that have prepared themselves to be cured and have obeyed the teachings of wise men undoubtedly are restored to health?

[6] There exists assuredly medicine for the soul, and that is philosophy; its aid must be sought not, as in the case of bodily diseases, outside ourselves, and we must exert ourselves with all our resources and forces to have the power to be ourselves physicians to ourselves. However, as regards philosophy in general, enough, I think, has been stated in the *Hortensius** on the importance of making it the subject of earnest study. Again, from that time onwards I have almost uninterruptedly discussed and written on the most weighty subjects.* But in these books there have been set out those discussions held by us with our friends in my villa at Tusculum. But since the two previous days saw us talking about death and pain, the third day of discussion will comprise this third book.

[7] For when we came down into our Academy* after the day had now inclined towards afternoon, I called upon one of those present to put forward a subject for discussion. This is how our business proceeded from that moment.

BOOK 4

Preface

[1] While in many respects, Brutus, I marvel constantly at the talents and virtues of our compatriots, I do so especially in the case of those studies which they embraced at a comparatively late period and transferred to this country of ours from Greece.* For although from the city's first beginnings the auspices, the religious rites, the popular assemblies, appeals to the people, the Council of the Fathers, the disposition of Horse and Foot, and the entire military system had been to a godlike standard established by the practices followed under the kings, and to some extent also by the laws,* later, once the commonwealth had been liberated from the tyranny of kingship, there occurred a marvellous advance towards general excellence at a rate defying belief.* But this is not at all the place for me to discuss the customs and practices of our forefathers or the regulation and balancing of the government; these matters have been described by me in sufficient detail elsewhere, above all in those six books I have written on the commonwealth.*

[2] But now, as my mind is engaged in learned studies, a fair number of reasons present themselves why these also* with their derivation in external sources, appear not only to have become the focus of men's aspirations but also to have been maintained as objects of close study. For almost within sight of our ancestors was that man of outstanding wisdom and fame, Pythagoras,* who lived in Italy at the very time when Lucius Brutus, the renowned founder of your illustrious family, set his country free. Now, as Pythagoras' teaching spread far and wide, it made its way, as I consider, into this community of ours, and this is not only likely from conjecture but also is signified by particular pieces of evidence. For, as Greece was at that time flourishing in Italy in the form of great and powerful cities, shown by the name she was given of 'Great Greece', and in those cities the name of Pythagoras himself and, after him, of the Pythagoreans had such influence, is there anyone who thinks that the ears of our countrymen were closed to the great learning they spoke?

[3] What is more, I think that his admiration for Pythagoras was the reason also why King Numa was considered by later generations to be a Pythagorean. For as men grew acquainted with the instruction and practices of Pythagoras, and heard from their forefathers of that king's

fairness and wisdom but through lapse of time were ignorant of their periods and dates, they formed the view that the man who excelled in wisdom had been a student of Pythagoras.* So far only will we entertain conjecture. Many traces of the Pythagoreans can be brought together, it is true, but nonetheless I will make little use of these, since this is not the subject under discussion at this time. For as we are told it was customary with them to pass on certain teachings with a measure of secrecy through verse and to bring their minds from intense meditation into a state of calmness by singing to the music of the lyre, that writer of great authority, Cato, has said in his *Antiquities** that it was our ancestors' custom at banquets that guests at table should sing one after the other in praise of the virtues of famous men to the accompaniment of the flute. From this it is clear that even in those times there existed poetry and melodies composed in accordance with the notes of the voice.

[4] And yet it is made clear also by the Twelve Tables that by that time the composition of songs was practised on a regular basis, since there it is enacted that this is forbidden if it is prejudicial to another's wellbeing. And indeed we are supplied with a proof of the culture of those times by the fact that stringed instruments strike up a prelude when banquets are served for the gods and feasts for magistrates, which was a particular feature of the Pythagorean training of which I speak. And further it is my own view that the poem of Appius Caecus which receives considerable praise from Panaetius in a letter he wrote to Quintus Tubero is Pythagorean.* In our own practices as well there are many things that have been derived from the Pythagoreans which I pass over in case it should appear that we have learned from other sources knowledge we are thought to have gained by our own efforts.

[5] But to direct our discourse back to the main argument, how short is the time span in which has emerged such a wealth of great poets and, besides, such distinguished orators! This shows that it is readily apparent that our countrymen had the ability to be successful in all spheres as soon as they had formed the wish to be so. But of the studies remaining we shall both speak elsewhere, if the need arises, and have often spoken. The pursuit of wisdom has indeed been long-standing among our countrymen but despite this I do not find men I can identify by name before the days of Laelius and Scipio. When these two were young men, I observe that the Stoic Diogenes and the Academician Carneades were sent by the Athenians as ambassadors to the senate.* Now, as these men had never taken any part in public life, and one of

them was from Cyrene, the other from Babylon,* there is no question of their ever having been summoned from their lecture rooms or selected for that office, if some of the leading Romans of those times had not been familiar with philosophical enquiry. However, though they entrusted other subjects to writing, some the principles of civil law, some the speeches they had made, some the memorials of their forefathers, they pursued in their lives rather than in their writings this most productive of all the arts, instruction in how to live well.

[6] And so, of that true and logically precise philosophy which derived from Socrates and has established itself until now among the Peripatetics (with the same notions being expressed by the Stoics in different languages,* whereas the Academic school* discussed the points of difference between the two of them) there are virtually no, or very few, Latin memorials. This may be due to the Romans' concentrating their attention on great practical enterprises or to their belief that such studies could not be committed to ignorant minds. Meanwhile their silence was replaced by the voice of Gaius Amafinius,* who had plenty to say. The publication of his books created a stir among the general public which flocked to the teaching he singled out for attention. This may have been because it was not difficult to grasp, or they were being tempted by the allurements of beguiling pleasure, or possibly because, in the absence of any better instruction, they clung to what was available.

[7] After Amafinius again many partisans of the same system produced many writings, with which they took all Italy by storm, and, although the greatest proof of the superficial nature of their arguments is that they are so easily grasped and win approval from unlearned people, those fellows regard this as their teaching's main support. But let every man defend the views that he has, for judgement is free. I shall hold on to my rule and, without being tied to the laws of any one school of thought that in philosophy would compel my obedience, I shall always seek to find the most probable solution to every difficulty.* This has been my frequent practice on other occasions and recently, too, in my Tusculan villa I observed this practice carefully. Therefore, now that I have set out in full the discussions of three days, this book comprises the fourth day. For, once we had gone down into the lower gymnasium* as we had done on the earlier days, our business proceeded as follows.

BOOK 5

[1] This fifth day, Brutus, will bring to an end our discussions at Tusculum. That was the day on which we discussed the topic of which you approve more warmly than any other. Not only from that book which you wrote* with such careful argument and dedicated to me but also from our numerous conversations, I have realized the strength of your belief that virtue is self-sufficient for living a happy life. Even if it is difficult to prove this in view of the many diverse agonies I have suffered at fortune's hands, yet such is its importance that every effort must be made to make this proof easier to accept. For of all the subjects treated by philosophy, no theme is more serious or more splendid.

[2] Since those who first devoted themselves to the study of philosophy* were stimulated by their concern to abandon all other considerations and give their undivided attention to searching for the best condition of life, it was undoubtedly their hope of a happy life that made them invest such considerable care and effort in that pursuit. And so if through their efforts virtue has been discovered and brought to maturity,* and if in virtue there is adequate security for living happily, who would not regard both their laying down of the task of philosophy and our taking it up as admirable? But if, on the other hand, virtue is fortune's slave, subject to diverse and uncertain chances, and lacks the strength to protect itself, then I am afraid that, in hoping to achieve a happy life, it is not so much virtue we should rely on as saying our prayers.*

[3] For my own part, when I reflect on those misfortunes* with which fortune has tried me sorely, I begin at times to lose trust in this belief and to feel alarm at the weakness and frailty of the human race. It is my fear that, in giving us weak bodies and combining with these both incurable diseases and intolerable pains, nature has also given us souls that not only share in the body's pains but also, apart from this, are involved in their own torments and distresses.

[4] But in this attitude I take myself to task for basing my estimation of virtue's strength on the frailty of others and perhaps on my own, not on virtue itself. For virtue, provided any such thing exists—a doubt, Brutus, sent packing by your uncle*—keeps at its own level all things that can befall a man, and, looking down on them, holds in contempt the misfortunes of mankind, and, free as it is from all fault, considers that nothing affects it apart from itself. Our way, however, is to make all

adversities worse by fear as they approach and by grief when they are present, preferring to condemn the nature of things rather than our own errors.

[5] But we must seek from philosophy all correction of this fault, as of all other failings and offences. It was to philosophy's bosom I was driven from my earliest years* by my wishes and interests, and in these dire misfortunes, buffeted by a great storm, I have sought refuge in the same harbour from which I first hoisted sail. O philosophy, guide to life, you who search out virtue and drive out vice! Without you what could not just I but man's life in general have achieved? You created cities, you called together into communal living the scattered tribes of men, you united them firstly in shared habitations, then in marriage, then in the common bonds of writing and speech. You were the discoverer of laws, the teacher of morality and ordered life. In you we sought refuge, from you we asked for help, to you I entrust myself, as once in large measure, so now deeply and entirely. A single day spent well and in accordance with your lessons is to be preferred to an unending life of error. Whose resources, then, are we to employ in preference to yours, who have not only bestowed on us peacefulness of life but have also done away with the fear of death?

[6] And yet, so far is philosophy from receiving the praise its services to human life have deserved that it is ignored by most men and even traduced by many. Does anyone have the temerity to traduce the mother of life and to defile himself with this parricide, showing such wicked ingratitude as to impugn the very one he ought to respect, even if his powers had denied him comprehension? But, in my opinion, this misconception, this darkness has blinded the minds of the uneducated, because they are incapable of looking back sufficiently far into the past, and do not consider that the men who were the first to furnish the life of man with its needs were philosophers.

[7] Despite our seeing that philosophy is a thing of considerable antiquity, we admit that its name is of recent date.* No one is able to deny that wisdom itself is not only ancient in fact but also in name. It was through its discovery of truths both sacred and human, as well as of each thing's origins and causes, that it acquired its glorious name among the men of old. Accordingly the Seven* were considered and named as *sophoi* by the Greeks and as 'wise' by our own countrymen, while, many generations earlier, Lycurgus, in whose times tradition has it that Homer also lived,* before this city's foundation, and, back in the age of heroes, Ulysses and Nestor were, as we have heard, men of wisdom* and accounted as such.

[8] And indeed tradition would not tell of Atlas holding up the heavens, or of Prometheus, nailed to the Caucasus, or of Cepheus, set among
the stars with his wife and son-in-law and daughter, had it not been that
their wondrous discovery of things caused their names to be transferred
to the fictions of myth.* This was the starting-point for the succession
of all those who directed their studies towards the contemplation of
nature being both considered and called wise, and that title they enjoyed
penetrated to the time of Pythagoras. According to the version of Plato's
pupil, Heraclides of Pontus, a man pre-eminent in learning,* the story
goes that Pythagoras* came to Phlius and in the company of Leon, that
town's leading citizen, discussed certain topics learnedly and at length.
Leon was struck by his intellect and eloquence, and asked him what art
he relied on especially. The reply Pythagoras gave was that he knew
no 'art' but was a philosopher.* Surprised at the novelty of the term,
Leon asked who philosophers were and what was the difference between
them and the rest of men.

[9] Pythagoras replied, so the story continued, that he thought human
life resembled the fair which was held with most splendid games, attended
by crowds from the whole of Greece. There were some there who sought
the glory and renown of the garland with their trained physiques, others
who were attracted by the gain and profit of buying and selling, but
there was a certain class of those, and that the most independent of
spirit, who sought neither applause nor profit but came to watch, and to
observe with close attention what was done, and in what manner. In the
same way we had come from another life and world to enter this life, as
if leaving some city for a crowded fair, and some were in thrall to glory,
some to money, whereas there were a few who devotedly studied nature,
thinking all else of no importance. These men, he said, he called devotees
of wisdom, that is, philosophers. At the games it showed true independence of spirit* to watch without seeking any personal gain, and
similarly in life far superior to all other pursuits was the contemplation
and examination of nature.

[10] Nor was Pythagoras simply the inventor of the name: in addition he developed the topics themselves. On his arrival in Italy following this discussion at Phlius, he enriched what was formerly called Magna
Graecia both privately and publicly with the most excellent doctrines
and arts; his teaching is perhaps something we may speak of at another
time. But from ancient philosophy down to Socrates,* who had been
instructed by Archelaus, the pupil of Anaxagoras, it was numbers and
motions that occupied philosophers, and from what sources all things
arose and to what they returned. The dimensions of the stars, the

distances between them, their courses and all celestial phenomena were investigated by them with passion. But Socrates was the first to call down philosophy from the heavens and to settle it in cities, and even to bring it into homes, compelling it to ask questions about life and morals and things good and evil.

[11] His techniques of discussion in their many forms, the wide compass of his topics, and the greatness of his intellect, immortalized in Plato's literary account,* produced several categories of philosophers who maintain opposing views. From those I have followed in particular the one I thought Socrates used, namely to keep my own opinion unknown, to remove from others' shoulders the burden of error, and in every discussion to seek what was most probable. As this was the custom Carneades* observed with great acumen and eloquence, I have made it my business on many other occasions as well as recently in my Tusculan villa to make my discussions conform to this practice. The conversation of the four days I have written up in the earlier books and despatched to you. On the fifth we took our seats in the same place, and this is how the subject of our discussion was put forward:

[12] A. Virtue, I think, is not sufficient for attaining the life of happiness. M. Well, my friend Brutus certainly thinks it is,* whose judgement, if you don't mind my saying so, I put far above your own. A. I don't doubt it, but what we are discussing here and now is not the extent of your affection for that man, but the merit of what I have stated as my view. That is what I wish to be discussed by you. M. Surely you don't deny that virtue is sufficient for attaining the life of happiness? A. I do, absolutely. M. Tell me, for living rightly, honourably, commendably—in a word, well—is there sufficient security in virtue? A. Certainly there is. M. Then can you possibly avoid calling one who lives badly unhappy, or deny that one you admit lives well is living happily? A. Why shouldn't I? Even under torture it is possible to live rightly, honourably, commendably, and on that account well, provided that you understand the sense in which I am using 'well'. I mean living with consistency, responsibility, wisdom and bravery.

[13] These qualities also are thrown upon the rack, and the life of happiness has no ambitions for that. M. Well, then, I ask, is the life of happiness left alone outside the door and threshold of the gaol, while consistency, responsibility, bravery, wisdom and the remaining virtues are hurried off to the torturer, and shrink from no punishment or pain? A. If you intend to make any headway, you must seek out some fresh arguments. Those you have used do not impress me in the slightest, not only because they are hackneyed but far more because, just as certain

light wines lose their potency in water, so those Stoic notions give more
pleasure when tasted rather than drunk.* For instance that band of
virtues you describe as set upon the rack brings before the eyes images
of the greatest nobility, making it appear that the life of happiness is
bound to make its way to them speedily and not allow them to be deserted by itself.

[14] But when one takes the mind away from those pictorial images
of the virtues to the true facts, there is left this naked question, whether
anyone can be happy for the time that he is being tortured. Accordingly
let us now examine this point. As for the virtues, have no fear that they
will protest and complain of being deserted by the life of happiness. If
no virtue exists without good sense,* good sense sees for itself that not
all good men are also happy, and it remembers many facts about Marcus
Atilius, Quintus Caepio and Manius Aquilius;* and, if you are resolved
on using images rather than actual facts, when the life of happiness tries
to go on to the rack, good sense itself restrains it, saying that it has
nothing to do with pain and torture.

[15] M. I am quite happy for you to proceed in such a fashion, although
you are being unfair in dictating to *me* how you want me to conduct our
discussion. But I put the question to you whether we should suppose
that something has been achieved in the last few days or nothing.
A. Something has indeed been achieved, and it is not inconsiderable.
M. And yet, if this is true, we have already worked our way through this
problem and virtually brought it to its conclusion. A. And what makes
you think that? M. Because unruly movements and agitations of souls,
roused and carried away by thoughtless impulse, show contempt for all
reason and leave behind no part of the happy life. What person who
fears death or pain, of which the one is often present, the other a constant threat, can avoid wretchedness? Again, if the same person, as frequently happens, is afraid of poverty, disgrace, dishonour, of physical
weakness and blindness, and finally of what has befallen not individuals
but powerful communities—slavery, can anyone who has those fears be
happy?*

[16] And what of the man who not only fears their coming in days to
come but actually suffers and endures them in the present? Add to the
same list exiles, sorrows, the loss of loved ones. Is it possible, I ask, for
a man who has been broken by these afflictions and crushed by misery not
to be wholly wretched? Next there is the case of the man we see to be
on fire with lusts that drive him mad, in a frenzy pursuing all things
with a desire that cannot be satisfied, whose thirst grows more insistent
and more fiery, the more liberally he gulps down pleasures from every

cup—would you not be right to call him most wretched? Again, when a man is carried away by the trivial and a rapture that has no basis, when he experiences joy without justification, is he not every bit as wretched as he supposes himself happy? So the wretchedness of these people is on a par with the happiness of those whom no fears frighten, no distresses consume, no lusts arouse, no aimless pleasure dissolves in listless pleasure. Just as we understand the sea to be calm when the waves are stirred by not even the slightest breeze, so we can reckon the mind calm and in a peaceful condition when there is no disturbance to cause it agitation.

[17] If, then, there is someone who thinks the power of fortune can be endured, together with all the tribulations that can afflict each mortal man, so that he is proof against fear or anxiety, if he feels no lust for anything, is carried away by no groundless pleasure of the mind, what reason is there why he should not be happy? And if it is virtue that brings this about, what reason is there why virtue of its own power alone should not make men happy? A. But you cannot maintain one point— that those who have no fear, no anxiety, no desires of the heart, who are not carried away by any uncontrollable feeling of joy, are not happy. And so I give you this point, and the other point we have already made some inroads into. It was established in our earlier discussions that the wise man is free from all mental disturbance.*

[18] M. Then, surely the inquiry is at an end. It seems the problem has reached a conclusion. A. That is pretty well the case. M. But that is the way mathematicians operate, not philosophers. When geometers wish to prove something, if there is anything they have previously proved that bears on a particular point, they take it as granted and approved. Only if something has not attracted any writing in the past, do they set about unravelling the problem. Philosophers, however, when they take up any topic that occupies them, heap on top of it all points of relevance, even if they have been discussed elsewhere. If this were not the case, why would a Stoic speak at length, once it had been established that virtue is sufficient for living the life of happiness? He would be satisfied with answering that he had shown already that nothing which was not morally good was good, and with this proved, it followed that the happy life was satisfied with virtue alone. Furthermore, he would say, just as the latter was a consequence of the former, so the former was of the latter,* that is, if the life of happiness is satisfied with only virtue, so goodness cannot exist in anything other than what is morally good.

[19] But this is not the way they behave. Separate books exist on 'what is morally good' and 'what is the ultimate good'. And though the latter

give rise to the fact that there is a power in virtue great enough for living the happy life, they nonetheless treat the theme separately. Every
subject, especially one as important as this, should be treated with its
own appropriate proofs and recommendations.* Do not imagine that
there is any utterance more glorious voiced by philosophy, or that there
is any promise it has made more fruitful or significant. What is the
promise it makes? Why, nothing less than this: it will ensure that whoever has obeyed its laws will be for ever armed against fortune, will have
in himself every security for a life lived well and in happiness, in short
for unending happiness.

[20] But with what it achieves* I will concern myself later. For the
present I value greatly the promise it makes. Xerxes was replete with all
the prizes and gifts of fortune but, not satisfied with his cavalry, infan-
try, huge fleet and weight of gold beyond measure, he offered a reward
to whoever could discover a pleasure that was new.* Even with that he
was dissatisfied. For lust will never find its limit. I could wish we were
able to lure someone by means of a reward to bring us some means of
believing this with greater conviction.

[21] A. That would be my wish, too, but I have a small point to ask
about. I do agree that, of the statements you have made, the one follows
the other: just as, if what is morally right is alone what is good, it follows
that the life of happiness is gained by virtue, so, if the life of happiness
consists in virtue, nothing is good apart from virtue. But this is not the
view of your friend Brutus on the authority of Aristus and Antiochus:* he
thinks virtue determines the life of happiness, even if something good
exists apart from virtue. M. What then? Do you suppose I will contradict
Brutus? A. You must do as you see fit. It is not for me to lay down the law.

[22] M. Then let us settle elsewhere the question of logical consistency. The disagreement you speak of I had frequently with Antiochus and
recently with Aristus, when I stayed at his house in Athens as 'Imperator'.*
It was my position that no one could be happy when beset by evils but
the wise man could be beset by evils, if such things as any evils of body
or fortune existed. The points being made had been put in writing
as well by Antiochus in several parts of his works, namely that virtue
without any assistance was capable of producing a happy life but not
a supremely happy one. He further held that most things received their
names from what formed the greater part of them, even though some
part was missing, citing such things as strength, health, wealth, honour,
glory, which their character, not their quantity, defined. Likewise the
life of happiness, even if it was imperfect in some part, maintained its
name on the basis of what formed by far the greater part of it.

[23] There is no need at present to go into detail on this, although it seems to me that the statements lack complete consistency. I fail to comprehend what the man who is happy needs in order to be happier—if something is lacking, he is not even happy—and, when it comes to their statement that every single thing gets its name and valuation from what forms the greater part of it, there are occasions when it is valid in the way proposed. But when they assert there are three categories of evils,* what are we to make of the man who is oppressed by all the evils of two of the categories, so that everything in his fortunes is against him, and his body is plagued and exhausted by every manner of pain, shall we say he just falls short of the life of happiness, not to mention that of supreme happiness?

[24] This is the position Theophrastus* was unable to defend. He maintained that whippings, torments, torture, overthrow of one's country, exile, loss of loved ones* contribute powerfully to living an ill and miserable life, but he did not venture to use a style that was exalted and dignified, as his thoughts were unassuming and low. The question is not how right he was—he certainly observed consistency. And so it is not my way to find fault with conclusions once you have granted premises. Now this most refined and learned of all philosophers is not greatly criticized when he speaks of three categories of good things;* he does, however, receive rough treatment from everyone, firstly for that book* in which he wrote of the life of happiness, and there advances many arguments to show why the man who is being subjected to torment and torture cannot be happy. It is even thought that in it he says the life of happiness does not mount the wheel (that is a kind of torture the Greeks use). He does not make that precise statement anywhere, it is true, but what he does say has the same force.

[25] And so, when the man to whom I have granted that bodily pains, and likewise the shipwrecks of fortune, are counted as evils, maintains that not all good men are happy, can I take issue with him, as good men can fall a prey to all the things which he reckons as evils? A rough handling comes to that same Theophrastus in the books and lectures of all the philosophers because in his *Callisthenes*￼ he showed approval for the maxim: 'Not wisdom, but fortune, rules our lives'. They say that nothing as craven has ever been stated by any philosopher. And they are right to say this, but I acknowledge that nothing could have been said with more consistency. If there are in the body so many things that are good, and outside the body so many things subject to chance and fortune, is it not a logical consequence that fortune, which is the mistress both of things foreign to and related to the body, is more powerful than wisdom?

[26] Or do we prefer to follow the teaching of Epicurus? There are
many fine things he often says. How logical and consistent they are do
not concern him. He has praise for a modest lifestyle. This fits a philosopher certainly, but only one who spoke like Socrates or Antisthenes,*
not one who claimed that the supreme good was pleasure. He says that
no man can live pleasantly unless his life also exhibits virtue, wisdom
and justice. Nothing could carry more weight or be more worthy of
philosophy, if it were not the case that the same man made pleasure his
point of reference for this selfsame virtue, wisdom and justice. What
better saying is there than this: 'Fortune has little effect upon the man
of wisdom'? But is the author of this statement the one who, after declaring that pain is not only the greatest evil but actually the only evil, can
succumb to the most acute pains throughout his whole body at the very
moment when he is boasting that fortune is not his equal?

[27] The same thought is expressed even better by Metrodorus:*
'I have outsmarted you, fortune,' he says, 'and seized and blocked your
lines of approach, so that you cannot get near me.' A fine remark, if it
came from Aristo of Chios* or the Stoic Zeno, who thought nothing evil
unless it was morally bad. But you, Metrodorus, who have stored away
'the good' in the depths and marrow of your body, and laid it down that
the highest good consists in a healthy physical condition with an assured
hope of this continuing, have you cut off fortune's lines of approach?
How? As we speak, you could be robbed of this 'the good' of yours.

[28] And yet this takes in the ignorant, and because of views of this
kind there are a great many people who think like this. But a man who
debates with a clear mind should have regard, not for what each person
says, but for what he ought to say. Take for instance the very view I have
adopted in this discussion we are having, my claim that all good men
are always happy. It is perfectly clear whom I call 'good'. Those who are
furnished and equipped with all the virtues whom we call at times 'wise',
at times 'good' men. Let us see who should be called happy. They are,
in my view, those who enjoy good things without any evil being in attendance, and, when we say 'happy', there is no other sense implicit in
the word than an unimpaired combination of good things with a total
detachment of all evils.

[29] Virtue is unable to achieve this if there is anything good besides
itself. A throng of evils, if we do regard them as evils, will present itself—
poverty, obscurity, isolation, loss of loved ones, severe physical pain,
failure of health, weakness, blindness, destruction of one's native land,
and finally, slavery. In these, so many and so distressing—and even more
can happen—the wise man can be involved. For it is chance which brings

these things, and chance can assail the wise man. But if they are evils, who can demonstrate that the wise man will always be happy, seeing that he can be involved at one time even in all of them?

[30] I cannot, then, easily allow my friend Brutus, or the teachers we shared,* or those philosophers of old, Aristotle, Speusippus, Xenocrates, and Polemo,* to say that the wise man is always happy in the same breath as they count the things I have just listed as evils. If any are attracted by that distinguished and impressive title, so deservedly applied to Pythagoras, Socrates and Plato, let them persuade themselves to despise those things whose glamour dazzles them—strength, health, beauty, wealth, offices of state, resources—and to think their opposites of no importance. Then in ringing tones they will be able to declare that neither fortune's assaults, nor the opinion of the masses, nor pain, nor poverty holds any terrors for them, that all that concerns them rests in their own control, and that there is nothing outside their power that they consider as good.

[31] As matters stand, it is quite impossible to allow them to combine giving voice to sentiments worthy of a man truly great and noble with counting among good and evil the same things as the masses. Inspired by this vision of glory Epicurus arises. He too, would you believe it, thinks the wise man is always happy. He is captivated by the grandeur of the thought, but never, if he listened to his own teaching, would he say so. What could be less consistent than for the same person to say pain is the greatest or the only evil and also to hold that the wise man will say, 'How agreeable this is!' at the very moment he is being tortured by pain? It is not, then, just their isolated statements we should judge philosophers by but unbroken consistency.

[32] A. You are prompting me to agree with you. But take care that your own consistency isn't also found wanting. M. In what way? A. Because I recently read book four of your *De finibus*. My impression was that there, when you were arguing against Cato, your purpose was to demonstrate, what I approve of, that there is no difference between Zeno and the Peripatetics apart from novel terminology.* But if this is the case, what reason is there why, if it is consistent with Zeno's belief that virtue possesses sufficient power for living happily, the Peripatetics should not be allowed to say the same thing? Substance is what we should examine, I think, not terminology.

[33] M. You proceed against me with documents that have been sealed, and submit as evidence what I said or wrote sometime in the past. You can deal in this way with others whose arguments are constrained by rules. I live from one day to another. I give voice to whatever strikes

my mind as probable, and so I alone am free.* Just the same, since we spoke not long ago about consistency, my own view is that this is not the point at which to ask whether Zeno's contention is true, and that of his pupil Aristo, that only what is morally right is good, but that, assuming it to be true, whether it followed that he should base the whole possibility of living happily on virtue alone.

[34] Let us, therefore, allow Brutus this at any rate, that the wise man is always happy: it is for him to consider how far he is self-consistent. Who is more deserving of the glory of this opinion than that considerable man? As for us, let us hold fast to our own view, that the wise man is as happy as possible. And if it appears that Zeno of Citium, an immigrant and unknown wordsmith, has inveigled himself into the Old Philosophy,* let the full weight of this opinion be traced back to its beginning in the authority of Plato, in whose work we often find this expression used—that nothing is to be called good except virtue. An instance occurs in his *Gorgias*,* where Socrates was asked if he didn't regard as happy Perdiccas' son Archelaus,* who at that time was held to be the most fortunate of men.

[35] 'I don't know', was his reply, 'I have never talked to him.' 'Really? Is there no other way for you to find out?' 'Not one.' 'So not even in the case of the great king of the Persians can you say if he is happy?' 'How could I do this, when I don't know how educated he is, how far a good man?' 'What? Do you think *that* is the foundation of a happy life?' 'It is certainly my belief that good men are happy and wicked men wretched.' 'So Archelaus is wretched?' 'Certainly, if he is unjust.' Don't you agree that Socrates makes the life of happiness depend completely on virtue?

[36] Moreover, what does the same man say in the funeral oration? 'The man in whom all things that contribute to living a happy life rest on himself alone, not depending upon other men's good fortune, or its opposite, and forced to waver at the mercy of what happens to another, this is the man who has secured the best way of living. It is he who possesses self-control, courage and wisdom, he who, when other blessings, and children in particular, are born and pass away, will obey and submit to that old proverb.* He will never indulge in excessive joy or sorrow, since he will always base every hope he has on himself alone.' Accordingly from that precept of Plato—from that holy and venerable spring, I am tempted to call it—will flow all our discourses.

[37] What starting-point, then, can we have which is more correct than our universal mother, nature? It was her wish that all she brought forth—not in the animal kingdom alone, but also whatever had so arisen from earth that it was supported by its own stems—should each

be perfect in its own kind. And so in the case of trees and vines and plants that are lower and cannot raise themselves high from the ground, some are evergreen, others are stripped bare by the winter and put on leaves when the season of spring supplies warmth; and because of the energy caused by a kind of internal thrust and the power of the seeds each has enclosed in it, there is nothing that fails to flourish, with the result that it produces flowers or food-crops or berries, and to the limit of their natures* all are perfect in everything, if no outside force prevents.

[38] But it is possible to see the power of Nature itself even more easily in animals, since they have been given sensation by Nature. She has decreed that some creatures should inhabit the waters as swimmers, others should enjoy the liberty of the sky in flight, some should creep along, some walk; of those very ones some should wander alone, some be part of herds, some savage, certain others tame, some hidden and buried in the earth. Each of these, maintaining its own function, since it cannot pass into the life of a living creature different from itself, abides within Nature's law. And as Nature has assigned to different animals individual characteristics, which each of them preserves as its own and does not depart from, so the human being has been given something considerably superior—although 'superior' is a term that should be applied to things which admit of some comparison. The soul of man has been culled from the divine mind,* and can be compared with nothing else except with God himself, if that is not a blasphemous statement.

[39] Accordingly, if this soul has been fully cultivated, if its acuteness of vision so cared for as to be blinded by no errors, the result is mind made perfect, that is absolute reason, which is also virtue. And if everything is happy that lacks nothing and is in its own kind full and complete, and that is what particularly defines virtue, then without doubt all who possess virtue are happy. And with regard to this I am in agreement with Brutus,* that is, with Aristotle, Xenocrates, Speusippus and Polemo.

[40] But in my view these men of virtue are also supremely happy. When a man is able to have confidence in the good things he has, what more does he need for living a life of happiness, or how can one who lacks such confidence be happy? But the man who divides good things into three* must lack this confidence. Who can have confidence in the strength of his body or in the permanence of fortune? Yet if the good is not secure, fixed and lasting, no man can be happy. What good of that kind, then, is possessed by your friends? I incline to the view that the famous saying of the Spartan is applicable to them. When a merchant was boasting that he had sent out many ships to every coast, he said, 'That fortune of yours is certainly not one to be desired, hanging as it does on

a ship's rigging.' Or is there any doubt that nothing which can be lost is to be reckoned as belonging to the category that makes up the happy life? For of all the constituent parts of a happy life none should wither away, none be snuffed out, or fail. The man who is afraid of losing any of these things will not be able to be happy.

[41] It is our claim that the man who is happy is safe, unassailable, fenced in and fortified, so that he feels not just a little fear but none at all. Just as the term 'innocent' describes, not the man who does little harm, but the man who does none, so we should regard as free from fear, not the man who has petty fears but who has none whatsoever. What is bravery other than a state of mind that shows endurance in facing danger, adversity and pain, and is far removed from all fear?

[42] This would certainly not be the case unless all good was found only in moral goodness. Again, if any man is or may be accompanied by a throng of evils, how can he possess that peacefulness so greatly longed for and pursued—and by peacefulness I mean the freedom from anxiety that is the basis of the happy life? How will he be able to stand tall and erect, despising all things that can befall a man, the kind of person we claim the wise man to be, unless he thinks that all things that may happen to him are within himself? When the Spartans were threatened by Philip* in a letter that he would prevent all their efforts, they asked if he would prevent them from dying. Will it not be much easier to find the man of our search with such spirit than an entire community? Moreover, if we add to this bravery of which I speak self-control, which controls all forms of agitation, what can a man lack for living happily who is rescued from anxiety and fear by his bravery, and is called away from lust and denied the chance to exult in excessive delight by self-control? I would show that these are produced by virtue, had they not been fully explained in the previous days' discussions.

[43] Wretchedness is caused by emotional disturbances, and the happy life by calmness, and disturbance takes two forms—anxiety and fear in expecting evils, ecstatic joy and lustful thoughts in misunderstanding good things,* all of which are at variance with wisdom and reason. Accordingly, if you see someone who is free, released and liberated from these impulses, so strong and yet so inconsistent and in conflict with one another, will you hesitate to call him happy? Yet this is the permanent condition of the wise man, and so the wise man is permanently happy. Furthermore every good gives rise to joy.* What gives rise to joy should be proclaimed and exhibited; such a thing is also glorious but, if glorious, certainly laudable; but what is laudable is surely morally good as well; so what is good is morally right.

[44] But what these people* count as good, they don't even them-selves describe as morally good. So the only good is what is good mor-ally, and from this it follows that only what is morally good is the basis of a happy life. We must not, then, describe or regard as good those things that a man may possess in abundance but still be completely wretched.

[45] Consider a person who excels in health, strength, beauty, acute and perfect senses—add also, if you wish, agility and swiftness, and grant him wealth, offices of state, military commands, resources and glory. If the man who possesses all these things is unjust, lacking in self-control, fearful, of limited or even no intelligence, will you hesitate to call him wretched? So what is the nature of these goods you speak of that enable a man in possession of them to be entirely wretched? Let us imagine that, as a heap consists of grains of one kind, so the life of happiness should be composed of identical parts. If this is the case, happiness must be the product only of goods which are good morally. If they consist of a mixture of parts that are not alike, nothing morally good can be produced from them. Take this away and what meaning will we be able to give happiness? For we should seek after anything that is good; but what should be sought after should certainly win approval; but what one approves should be considered pleasing and welcome; so it should also be held in distinction. If this is so, it must be worthy of praise; so every good thing is worthy of praise. It follows from this that only what is morally right is good.

[46] If we fail to maintain this, there will be many things we have to describe as good. I say nothing of wealth, which I do not count among goods, since anyone however unworthy can possess it. What is good is something not just anyone can possess. I say nothing of high birth or of public acclaim that is stirred up by the agreement of fools and men who lack morals. Even these insignificant things we have to call goods—nice white teeth, lovely eyes, an attractive complexion, and the things that win Anticlea's praise as she washes Ulysses' feet: 'gentle quality of speech, suppleness of body'.* If we think of these things as good, what will we find in the philosopher's authority to call more weighty or elevated when compared with the beliefs of the crowd or the rabble of fools?

[47] But wait a moment, what your friends* call 'goods' are called 'high-ranking' or 'preferred' by the Stoics!* Quite true, but the Stoics do not say that the happy life is unfulfilled without these things. The others, however, consider that without them it cannot exist, or if it is happy, they say it cannot be supremely happy. But our claim is that it can be supremely happy, and this view is confirmed by the following piece of Socratic logic. That chief of philosophers used to argue in this fashion: whatever the condition of a man's soul is, such is the man, and

whatever the nature of the man himself, such is the way he expresses himself in speech. Actions resemble a man's speech, and life his actions. But the condition of mind in the man who is good is worthy of praise, and of honour, too, as it is praiseworthy, from which it can be concluded that the life of good men is happy.

[48] For, in the name of gods and men, did we not establish sufficiently in our earlier discussions—or did we talk for our amusement and to pass the time—that the wise man is always free from every agitation of the soul to which I give the name of 'disturbance', that in his soul there always exists the most tranquil peace? Accordingly, if a man possesses self-control and consistency, and is without fear, distress, excitability or lust, is he not happy? But this is the nature of the wise man always, so he is happy always. Moreover, how is it possible for the wise man not to refer all his thoughts and actions to what is worthy of praise? Now he relates everything to living happily; the happy life, therefore, is praiseworthy, but nothing is praiseworthy without virtue; the happy life, therefore, is realized through virtue.

[49] We arrive at this conclusion in the following way as well: in the life of wretchedness there is nothing to proclaim or boast about, and the same is true of the life that is neither wretched nor happy. But in some lives there is something to proclaim, something worth boasting about and holding up to display, as in the case of Epaminondas:

> By my counsels the glory of the Spartans was shorn,*

or of Africanus:

> From where the sun rises over Maeotis' marshes
> No man is there who can match my deeds.*

[50] And if there is, the life of happiness is worthy of boasting, proclamation and display, for nothing else exists worthy of being proclaimed or displayed. Now that we have established this, you realize the conclusion that follows. Indeed, unless that same life which is morally good is happy, something else must exist which is better than the happy life. They will certainly admit that what is morally good is better. There will, then, be something better than the happy life. But is it possible to make a statement more illogical than this? Moreover, when they admit that vices possess sufficient power to make life miserable, are they not bound to admit that virtue possesses the same power to make life happy? Opposite consequences follow logically from opposites.

[51] At this point I wish to know what is the force of the celebrated balance of Critolaus.* In one scale he puts goods that belong to the soul,

in the other external goods and those belonging to the body, and he considers that the former are so much heavier that they outweigh earth and seas. What, then, prevents him or Xenocrates* also, that most influential of philosophers, who exalts virtue so greatly, disparaging and rejecting everything else, from making virtue the basis not only of the happy life but of the supremely happy life as well? Indeed, if this does not happen, the death of the virtues will ensue.

[52] The man who is susceptible to distress must also be susceptible to fear, for fear is the anxious expectation of distress that is to come. Again, if he is affected by fear, he is affected likewise by dread, alarm, panic and cowardice, and consequently there are times when he admits defeat, and does not think Atreus' well-known counsel applies to him: 'Then let them so prepare themselves in life that they know not how to be defeated.'* But the man above will be defeated, as I said, and not only will he know defeat but also servitude. Our claim, however, is that virtue is for ever free, for ever undefeated. If this is not so, virtue is destroyed.

[53] And if virtue provides sufficient guarantee for living well, it also provides sufficient for living happily. Virtue certainly provides sufficient for living bravely, and if bravely, also with great spirit, and indeed so that we are never frightened by anything, and are for ever undefeated. It follows that nothing causes regret, nothing is lacking, nothing stands in our way. Accordingly, everything is equable, complete, successful, and therefore happy. But virtue provides sufficient for us to live bravely, and so sufficient for us also to live happily.

[54] For just as folly never considers it has got sufficient, despite getting what it craves, so wisdom is always satisfied with what is to hand, and never feels sorry for itself. Do you think there was a similarity with the single consulship of Gaius Laelius—and that coming after a rejection—that is, if when a wise and good man such as he was is passed over at the election, it is not a case of the people being rejected by a good consul rather than one of him being rejected by a good people—but all the same, which would you prefer, if the choice were your own, to be consul once, like Laelius, or four times, like Cinna?*

[55] I have no doubt what *your* answer will be, and so I see someone I can trust. I would not put this same question to anyone at all. Another man would perhaps reply that he not only put four consulships before one but a single day of Cinna to entire lives of many illustrious men. If Laelius had laid a finger on any man, he would have answered for it. But Cinna ordered the beheading of his colleague in the consulship, Gnaeus Octavius,* of Publius Crassus,* of Lucius Caesar,* men of the foremost nobility, whose qualities had been observed in time of peace

and of war,* of Marcus Antonius,* the most eloquent of all men I myself have heard, and of Gaius Caesar,* who was in my view a model of finer feeling, wit, good humour and charm. Then is the man who caused these men's deaths happy? My view, on the other hand, is that he is wretched not only because of what he did but also because he behaved in such a way that it was permissible for him to do what he did—even if no man is 'permitted' to do wrong: we commit a solipsism through a misuse of language, for what anyone is allowed to do we describe as 'permissible'.

[56] Was Gaius Marius happier, I ask, on the day he shared the glory of his victory over the Cimbri with his colleague Catulus,* who was virtually a second Laelius, for I think of him as strongly resembling Laelius*—or in the hour of his victory in the Civil War when, furious with the friends of Catulus who were asking for mercy, he replied not once but several times, 'He must die.'* In this matter the man who obeyed these wicked words was happier than the man who gave so criminal an order. It is better not merely to suffer than to inflict a wrong but also to advance a little way to meet death, which is of itself already drawing near, as Catulus did, than to imitate Marius by murdering such a man and so invalidating his six consulships and besmirching the final stage of his life.*

[57] For thirty-eight years Dionysius* was tyrant of Syracuse, after he had seized power at the age of twenty-five. How beautiful was the city, how richly endowed with resources the community that he kept crushed in slavery! And yet concerning this man we have the written record of trustworthy authorities that, while he showed the utmost self-control in his way of life and unflagging application in the conduct of affairs, he was yet at the same time without principle or justness in his nature. It follows that all who view the truth correctly are bound to consider him most wretched. For even at the time when he thought his powers were unlimited, he failed to attain the very things on which he had set his heart.

[58] He came from good parents and respectable origins, although this point is recorded differently by different writers,* and enjoyed many friendships among contemporaries as well as good relations with his relatives. In addition he had a number of young men as lovers in the Greek fashion.* Despite all this, he trusted none of them but entrusted his physical protection to those he had selected when slaves from the households of wealthy men, having personally relieved them of the title of 'slave', and to certain refugees and uncivilized barbarians. In this way, owing to an immoral thirst for absolute control, he had in a sense shut himself up in gaol.* Furthermore, to avoid exposing his throat to

a barber, he instructed his own daughters in the use of a razor, with the result that the young princesses would trim their father's beard and hair, like hairdressers' assistants, employing a lowly and servile skill. Even so, once these girls grew up, he took from them the metal implement and trained them in the use of red-hot walnut-shells for singeing his beard and hair.

[59] He had two wives, Aristomache a fellow citizen and Doris a Locrian, and when he visited them at night, it was with the precaution of inspecting and examining everything thoroughly in advance. He surrounded the chamber in which he slept with a broad trench, constructing a small wooden bridge to serve as a gangway across the trench, and personally drawing in the bridge each time he closed the door of his chamber. And since he did not dare stand on platforms open to the public, it was his custom to deliver speeches from a high tower.

[60] Again, it is said that, when he wanted to play at ball—a pastime he engaged in frequently and enthusiastically—and was removing his tunic, he handed over his sword to a youth he loved. At this a certain acquaintance said by way of jest, 'Here's someone at any rate you're certainly entrusting your life to.' The young man smiled at this but Dionysius gave the order for both of them to be executed, the one for having pointed out a way to assassinate him, the other for having given his approval to the remark by smiling. The grief he felt after this act was such that nothing caused him greater distress throughout his life. He had killed someone he had loved with all his heart. The passions of those who lack self-control are in this way pulled in opposite directions. Acceding to one means resisting the other.

[61] Nonetheless, this tyrant himself made assessment of how happy he was. When one of his flatterers, Damocles,* detailed in conversation his resources, riches, the majesty of his rule, his profuse treasures, the magnificence of his palace, and said that no one had ever known such happiness, Dionysius replied, 'Then, Damocles, as this life delights you, would you like to taste it for yourself and put my good fortune to the test?' He said he was eager to do this, and so Dionysius ordered that the man be placed on a golden couch covered with gorgeous woven tapestries embroidered with superb works of art, and he set out several sideboards decorated with embossed silver and gold vessels. Next he gave the order for selected slave-boys of outstanding beauty to stand beside the table and to wait on him attentively, watching for his nods.

[62] Unguents and garlands were to hand. Perfumes were burned, the tables were loaded with the choicest dishes. Damocles thought himself fortunate indeed. In the midst of all this extravagance Dionysius

ordered that a gleaming sword fastened to a horse-hair be lowered from the ceiling, so that it was poised above the neck of that happy man. As a result he had no eyes either for those beautiful servants, or for the richly decorated silver-plate, and he failed to stretch his hand out to the table. Now the very garlands were slipping down to the ground. At last he begged the tyrant to let him leave as he no longer had any wish to be happy. Do you think Dionysius made it plain enough that there is no happiness for the man who is constantly threatened by some terror? And it was not even open for him to return to justice, and restore to his citizens their freedom and rights. In the thoughtlessness of his youth he had entangled himself in such errors and had committed such acts that he could not be safe if he regained his senses.

[63] But the extent to which he missed friendships, while living in dread of their proving false, was demonstrated by him in the case of the two followers of Pythagoras.* He had permitted one to act as a guarantor on a capital charge. When the other presented himself at the hour appointed for execution in order to discharge his guarantor, he said, 'If only I could be enrolled as a third friend with you both!' What a miserable thing it was for him to be without the company of friends, the enjoyment of social life, all intimate conversation, especially when he had received an excellent education from boyhood and was trained in the liberal arts! He was, we are told, a serious devotee of music, a tragic poet also—of what quality is of no relevance; in this art more than in others it is somehow the case that each person finds beauty in his own work. Never yet have I known a poet (and I have counted Aquinius among my friends) who did not consider himself excellent.* This is the way things are. 'You find delight in your work, I in mine.' But to return to Dionysius, he cut himself off from everything that lends civilization to human life. His life was shared with runaway slaves, criminals and barbarians, and he considered as his friend no man who was deserving of freedom or had any wish to be free.

[64] With this man's life, the most horrible, wretched and abominable I can imagine, I will not now compare the life of Plato or of Archytas,* men of learning and truly wise. I shall call up from his sand-table and measuring-rod a lowly little man who lived many years later in the same city, Archimedes.* In the time of my quaestorship* I searched out his tomb, which was unknown to the Syracusans, as they completely denied its existence, and enclosed all around, covered in brambles and thickets. I remembered some lines of verse I had been told were inscribed on his tomb, which stated that a sphere together with a cylinder had been set on the top of his tomb.*

[65] Now, as I was having a thorough look at everything around—there is a great crowd of tombs at the Agrigentine Gates—I noticed a small column rising a little way from the thickets on which there was a representation of a sphere and cylinder. At once I told the Syracusans—the leading men were with me—that I thought this was the very object of my search. Many men were sent in with sickles and cleared the site, opening it up.

[66] When access to the place had been created, we went up to the pedestal facing us. The epitaph was visible, with about half the lines missing where the line-endings had been worn away. So that celebrated Greek city, which had once been also a seat of great learning, would have remained in ignorance of the tomb of its most ingenious citizen, had it not learned of it from a man of Arpinum.* But let my discourse return to the point where its digression began. What man in the world who has any dealings with the Muses, that is, with refinement and learning, would not choose to be this mathematician rather than that tyrant? If we investigate their way of life and conduct, the mind of the one found nourishment in testing and exploring theories, together with the pleasure of exercising its ingenuity, which is the most delightful food of souls, that of the other in committing murder and wrongful acts, with fear as its companion, both by day and by night. Now compare Democritus, Pythagoras, Anaxagoras.* What kingdoms, what riches will you prefer to the studies in which those men found delight?

[67] That greatest good which is the object of your search must be located in the best part of a man. But what is better in a man than a mind which is intelligent and good? Accordingly, we must enjoy the good of such a mind, if we wish to be happy. Now, the good of the mind is virtue. Therefore the happy life must be defined by virtue. As a result all things beautiful, honourable, outstanding, as I have said above but it must, I think, be put a little more expansively, are full of joys. But since it is clear that the happy life consists of joys that are complete and uninterrupted, it follows that it proceeds from virtue.

[68] But it is not our intention to reach the truth of what we wish to reveal by words alone. We must set before our eyes what I may call certain incentives, to make us turn more readily to learning and understanding. Let us assume a man pre-eminent in the finest qualities, and let us for a moment dwell on this mental picture. In the first place he must be of outstanding intelligence: it is not easy for virtue to share the company of sluggish minds. Secondly, he must be passionately devoted to discovering the truth. From this will spring the well-known threefold progeny* of the soul, one based in knowledge of the universe and the

disentanglement of nature's secrets, the second in distinguishing things to be sought and things to be shunned and in forming a system of living, the third in judging what follows from each proposition and what is in conflict with it: in this reside all nicety of argument and all truth of judgement.

[69] How joyful, then, must the experience of the wise man's soul be when he makes his home and shares his nights with these interests! He has studied the movements and revolutions of the whole universe, and seen that innumerable stars fixed in the heavens are in unison with the motion of heaven itself as they keep their appointed locations, and seven others* maintain their several courses, being far distant from one another in height or depth, although their wandering motions define the approved and fixed paths of their courses. It is no surprise that the spectacle of all this was an inspiration to those men of old, encouraging them to further enquiry. From this was born the investigation into beginnings and, as it were, the seeds from which all things had their origin, generation and composition—what was the source of every kind of thing, be it inanimate, animate, voiceless or speaking, what its life and what its end, what change and alteration from one thing into another, what is the origin of the earth, what weights keep it in equilibrium,* what are the caverns that hold the seas in place,* what is the heaviness that causes all things to be carried downwards, constantly making for the centre of the universe, which is also the lowest in the sphere.

[70] The soul that is occupied with these matters and ponders them day and night is the recipient of that knowledge prescribed by the god at Delphi,* that the mind should gain self-awareness and realize that it is united with the divine mind, something which fills it with a joy that cannot be quenched. The very act of contemplating the essence and nature of the gods kindles the passion for imitating that mind's eternity,* not thinking of itself as limited to a short span of life, when it sees the causes of things linked in a chain to one another and by necessity bound together. Although they flow from eternity to eternity they are nevertheless governed by mind and reason.

[71] As our wise man observes this spectacle, looking upward, or rather around, at all parts and regions, what will be his calmness of soul when he turns again to contemplate matters human and more immediate! It is from this that his knowledge of virtue arises, that the kinds and divisions of the virtues blossom, that discovery is made of what is, in Nature's sight, the utmost in good things* and what is the ultimate in evils, to what end we should direct our duties,* and what rule we should choose for living our lives. Once we have investigated these and similar

questions, the most important outcome is what concerns us in this discussion, namely that, for the purpose of living a life of happiness, virtue is self-sufficient.

[72] The third follows, which flows and spreads through all parts of wisdom, which defines a thing, distinguishes kinds, forms sequences, comes to final conclusions, discerns between true and false—the art of rational discourse. This is the source not only of supreme usefulness in weighing judgements but in particular of a free-minded delight that is worthy of wisdom. But these are properties of leisure. Let that same wise man pass on to having regard for the welfare of the state. What could be more excellent than that, when his wisdom shows him what benefits his fellow citizens, his justice prevents him from channelling anything that is theirs into his own house,* and he makes use of the many different virtues that remain to him? Add the bounties that flow from friendships, in which the learned find not only counsel which shares their thoughts and almost their breath throughout all life but also supreme delight in daily cultivating one another's company. What, tell me, does this life lack to make it happier? It is packed with so many great joys that fortune itself must give place. But if taking delight in such goods of the soul, that is, in virtues, is happiness, and all wise men have the enjoyment of those delights, it must be admitted that all of them are happy.

[73] A. Even in torture and torments? M. Do you think I mean on a bed of violets or roses? Or will Epicurus,* who has merely put on the mask of a philosopher, bestowing this title on himself, be allowed to say what indeed, as matters stand, he does say, but nonetheless with my approval, that there is no time when the wise man, even if being burned, tortured or mutilated, cannot cry out, 'This counts for nothing with me!', especially since he defines evil as pain and a good as pleasure, mocking our 'morally good' and 'shameful' and saying that we busy ourselves with words and utter noises without meaning, and that we humans are affected only by the physical sensation of what is smooth or rough?* Now here is a man whose judgement, as I said, differs but little from that of beasts—shall we allow him to forget himself and to proceed to despise fortune at the time when all he considers good and bad lies in its power, shall we allow him to say that he is happy in extreme torture and torment at the time when he has decided that pain is not only the supreme evil but also the only one?

[74] And he has not provided himself with the remedies for enduring pain—mental strength, recoiling from disgrace, habitual practice of endurance, lessons in bravery, manly hardness,—but maintains he finds peace in the recollection of past pleasures alone, just as if a man

who was sweltering, struggling to endure the summer heat's intensity, wanted to remember that he had once immersed himself in the cool streams at my home in Arpinum. I fail to see how present ills can be assuaged by past pleasures.

[75] But since the wise man is permanently happy, as we are told by that philosopher who would not be entitled to make this assertion, if he intended to be self-consistent, what is to be done by those who think that nothing is desirable, nothing worth numbering among goods that has within it no moral goodness? My own advice is that Peripatetics also, together with the Old Academy,* should finally stop their stammering and dare to state openly and in clear tones that the happy life would descend into Phalaris' bull.*

[76] Assuming that there are three kinds of goods*—to get clear at last of the Stoics' complicated arguments,* of which I realize I have made more use than I normally do—assuming there are indeed those kinds of goods, provided that the bodily and external ones lie prostrate on the ground, and are called 'good' simply because they are 'to be chosen',* while those other divine ones extend their scope far and wide and touch the heavens—why should I not call the man who has gained them supremely happy rather than merely happy? But will the wise man regard pain with dread? For pain is the particular objection to this view. Against our own death and that of our loved ones, against distress and the remaining disorders of the soul, I think we have been adequately armed and prepared by the previous days' discussions.* It appears that pain is the most determined opponent of virtue. It takes aim with its burning firebrands and threatens to rob of their power bravery, greatness of soul and endurance.

[77] Will virtue then bow before this, will wisdom in its happiness, will the life of the steadfast man? How degrading, in heaven's name! When their flesh is torn by painful blows of the lash Spartan boys do not groan.* I have personally witnessed bands of youths in Sparta fighting with a competitiveness beyond belief as they use fists, heels, nails, even teeth to the point of losing life before admitting defeat. What barbarian country is wilder or more uncivilized than India? Yet in that nation those in the first place who are considered wise men pass their lives without clothing and endure the snows and winter harshness of the Caucasus without pain, and are burned without groaning after casting themselves into the flames.*

[78] Indeed the women in India, when the husband of any of them dies, take part in a contest and trial to discover which of them he loved best—it is the practice there that one man has several wives—and the

one who wins goes joyfully in the company of her relatives to be set on the pyre together with her husband, while the loser quits the contest in sorrow. Never could nature be defeated by custom,* for nature is always invincible. But we have sullied our souls with shady retreats, luxury, leisure, idleness, and sloth, we have made them soft and enervated with mere opinions and bad habits. Who does not know of the Egyptians' custom? Their minds are tainted with perverse superstitions, and would submit to any torment sooner than injure an ibis or asp or cat or dog or crocodile.* Even if they did anything of the kind without intending it, they would refuse no punishment.

[79] I speak of humans. What of beasts? Do they not endure cold and hunger, ranging over mountains and wandering through forests? Do they not fight so fiercely for their offspring that they receive wounds and shrink from no attacks, no blows? I make no mention of what is tolerated and suffered by men eager to win office, or who thirst for praise in order to win glory, or who burn with love in order to gratify their passion. Life is full of examples.

[80] But my discourse must observe a limit and return to the point where I digressed. The happy life will submit itself, I say, to tortures. It will escort justice, self-control, and in particular courage, greatness of soul and endurance, and it will not check its step on seeing the torturer's face. It will not stop, as I said, outside the door and threshold of the prison, once all the virtues have proceeded to torture with no mental terror. What could be more foul or more ugly than it when left alone, parted from its splendid companions? But this is by no means possible. The virtues are incapable of maintaining themselves without the happy life, nor that life without the virtues.

[81] And so they will not permit it to be evasive and will hurry it along with themselves to whatever pain and torture they will themselves be led. It is typical of the wise man to do nothing that could cause regret, nothing against his will, but everything nobly, consistently, weightily and honourably, not to expect anything as if it were bound to occur, not to marvel at anything once it happens, so that it appears to have occurred as something unexpected and strange, to apply everything to his own judgement, to stand by his own findings. I cannot conceive of anything being happier than that.

[82] For the Stoics indeed the conclusion is an easy one. Their contention was that the ultimate good was to agree with nature and live in harmony with it, and, as this is not only the wise man's fixed duty but also lies within his power, it must follow that the man who has in his power the highest good will also have the power of a happy life. Consequently

the life of the wise man is for ever a happy one. Now you have what I think can be stated most strongly about the happy life, and as things stand at present, unless you have some better suggestion to make, most truthfully as well. A. For my part I can make no better suggestion, but it would please me if I could prevail on you, if it is no trouble, since you are not constrained by the fetters of any definite school,* and you sip from all of them whatever most appeals to you by its semblance of truth—because a short time ago* you seemed to be encouraging the Peripatetics and Old Academy to have the courage to say freely and without reservation that the wise are always supremely happy, what I'd like to hear is how you think it is consistent for them to make that statement. You have raised a good number of objections to that view and proved them by Stoic reasoning.

[83] M. Then let me make use of the freedom which we alone* may assume in philosophy. Our discourse decides nothing on its own pronouncement but has regard for all sides of the question, so that it can be decided by others in its own right without appealing to anyone else's authority. Now it appears that what you want established is that, whatever the views of opposing philosophers about ultimate ends, virtue still possesses sufficient security for a happy life.* This, we hear, was argued habitually by Carneades* but it was as a way of opposing the Stoics, the constant target of his vehement refutations, and indeed his temper had grown hot against their teaching—my own approach will be to treat the question peacefully. If the Stoics have correctly established the ultimate good, the matter is settled: the wise man must be for ever happy.

[84] But let us examine the individual views of the remaining schools to see if it is possible that this splendid 'declaration' on the happy life is able to fit the views and teaching of them all.* Well, the views on ends that have been maintained and supported are, in my view, these. First, four simple ones: nothing good except moral goodness, the Stoic view; nothing good except pleasure, Epicurus' position; nothing good except freedom from pain, Hieronymus' view;* nothing good except enjoyment of the first goods of nature,* either all of them or the most important of them, as Carneades used to contend in opposition to the Stoics.

[85] These, then, are simple, the following compound: three kinds of goods, chief among them those of the soul, in second place those of the body, in third those that are external, as maintained by the Peripatetics and, not much different* from them, the Old Academy. Pleasure was linked with moral goodness by Dinomachus and Callipho. The Peripatetic Diodorus* combined freedom from pain with moral goodness. These are the views which have some permanence. Those of Aristo, Pyrrho,*

Herillus* and a number of others have simply disappeared. Let us see what these thinkers can do for us, leaving aside the Stoics, whose view I think I have upheld sufficiently. The case of the Peripatetics also has been made clear, with the exception of Theophrastus* and any followers of his who too weakly feel dread and abhorrence of pain. The rest at any rate are at liberty to do pretty well what they do, that is to elevate the dignity and worth of virtue. When they laud it to the skies in the exuberant manner typical of those eloquent people, it is easy to trample underfoot the rest and despise them by comparison. And it is not open to those who say renown must be sought with pain to deny that those who have gained it are happy. They may be involved in *some* evils but nonetheless this term 'happiness' has a scope that extends far and wide.

[86] They say that trade is profitable and farming productive, not if the one is always free from all loss and the other always free from all destruction by storms, but if each has, in the main, a healthy margin of success; so life, not only if it is loaded on all sides with goods, but if in the main and in the more important sense goods markedly preponderate, is correctly described as happy.

[87] According to the reasoning of these philosophers, then, the happy life will follow virtue even to execution, and accompany it as it goes down into the bull,* with the approval of Aristotle, Xenocrates, Speusippus and Polemo,* and no threats or cajoling will corrupt it into abandoning virtue. The same view will be held by Callipho and Diodorus, both of whom embrace moral goodness so warmly that anything lacking in it should, they hold, be ranked far behind it. The rest appear to be in something of a strait but still they succeed in swimming their way clear—Epicurus, Hieronymus, and any who concern themselves with defending Carneades' abandoned position. To a man they all think the soul is the judge of good things, and they join in training it to have the ability to despise things that merely *appear* to be good or bad.

[88] What you consider to be Epicurus' case will also be that of Hieronymus and Carneades, and indeed of all the remainder. For who is insufficiently equipped to face death or pain? Let us start, if we may, with the one we call weak and devoted to pleasure.* Does he fear death or pain, do you suppose, the man who calls the day on which he dies happy,* and when wracked by the greatest pains conquers them by the memory and recollection of the truths he has discovered? And he does not do this in a spirit that makes him seem to be babbling on the spur of the moment. Such is his view of death that he thinks that sensation is extinguished with the dissolution of the living creature, and what is without sensation, in his judgement, cannot in any way affect us. Also

he has fixed principles to adhere to when it comes to pain. For severity he finds consolation in short duration, for long duration in slightness.*

[89] Just how are those bombastic friends of yours better placed than Epicurus to combat those two things which cause the greatest distress? Or do Epicurus and the remaining philosophers not seem adequately prepared to face the other things which are considered evils? Who does not have a horror of poverty? Yet not a single philosopher does. How little contents Epicurus himself! No one has said more about a simple lifestyle.* Consider the things which make men desire money, so that they may have resources for love affairs, for furthering political careers, for daily expenditure. He is far removed from all these, so why would he nurse a great desire for money, or rather why should it trouble him in the slightest?

[90] Or if Anacharsis* the Scythian was able to think money valueless, will our own philosophers fail to do so? These are the words of a letter it is said he wrote: 'Greetings from Anacharsis to Hanno. My clothing is a Scythian blanket, my shoes the thick skin that covers the soles of my feet, my bed the earth, my relish hunger; I live on milk, cheese, flesh of animals. You may come to me, therefore, as to a man at peace. But those gifts that have brought you pleasure present to your fellow citizens or, if you like, to the immortal gods.' Virtually all philosophers of all schools apart from those twisted away from right reason by a corrupt nature have been able to share this same spirit.

[91] When a large quantity of gold and silver was being carried in a procession, Socrates remarked: 'How many things there are I don't want!' When envoys from Alexander brought Xenocrates* fifty talents, a huge sum of money in those times, especially at Athens, he took them to dinner in the Academy, serving only just enough, with no ostentation. They asked him the next day to whom he wanted the money paid. 'What,' he replied, 'did you not understand from yesterday's simple meal that I have no money?' When he saw that this had somewhat dampened their spirits, he accepted thirty minas* in case it appeared that he was being scornful of the king's generosity.

[92] But a more outspoken reply came from Diogenes, as a Cynic,* when Alexander asked him to say if he wanted anything. 'For the moment,' came the reply, 'just stand a little bit out of the sun'—Alexander, you see, had blocked him as he was enjoying the sun. Indeed this man was in the habit of discussing how much in his life and fortune he surpassed the king of Persia, pointing out that he lacked nothing, whereas the king would never possess enough. 'I don't miss the king's pleasures,' he would say: 'they can never satisfy him and he cannot possibly attain mine.'

[93] I assume you are aware how Epicurus distinguished the types of desires,* not perhaps with too much precision but still with benefit: some are natural and necessary, some natural and not necessary, some neither. It takes virtually nothing, he argued, to satisfy the necessary ones, for nature's riches are easily acquired. The second kind of desires, he held, were neither difficult to satisfy nor, indeed, to do without. He thought the third should be jettisoned entirely, as they were quite meaningless, and, so far from counting as necessary, had no relation to nature either.

[94] At this point Epicurus' followers enter into lengthy discussions. They belittle individually those pleasures whose general types they despise, but at the same time they wish to have a plentiful supply of them. Even indecent pleasures,* on which they discourse at length, they call easy, general and easily accessible, and they think that, if nature demands, they should be measured not by birth, position in life, or rank, but by beauty, age and form. It is by no means difficult, they held, to abstain from them if this is demanded by health, duty or reputation, and in general this kind of pleasures is to be desired if it is not harmful, but it is never beneficial.

[95] Epicurus' entire teaching on pleasure is such that he thinks pleasure of itself should always be desired and sought for because it *is* pleasure, and on the same principle pain is always to be avoided because of the very fact that it *is* pain. In consequence the wise man will always use a system of counter-balance such that he both avoids pleasure that will cause greater pain, and submits to pain that causes greater pleasure.* Although it is by physical sensation that all pleasurable things are judged, he carries these over nonetheless to the soul.

[96] And so he says that the body feels delight for as long as it feels present pleasure, and the soul feels the present pleasure jointly with the body but also foresees the coming of pleasure and does not let past pleasure slip by. The wise man, then, will always possess an unbroken web of pleasures, since the expectation of pleasures he hopes for is combined with the recollection of pleasures he has already enjoyed.

[97] Similar thinking is also applied to food. The grand display and costliness of banquets are belittled on the grounds that nature is satisfied with little refinement. Who fails to see that want is what seasons all those things? When Darius* was attempting to escape, he drank water that was muddy and fouled by corpses and pronounced it the most delightful drink he had ever tasted. He had never, of course, taken a drink when he was thirsty. And Ptolemy* had never been hungry when he ate. As he travelled once through Egypt ahead of his retinue, he was

given some coarse bread in a cottage and thought there was nothing more delightful than that bread. The story is told about Socrates that he was walking with some energy right up to evening and the question was put to him why he was doing this. He replied that by walking he was adding sauce to his hunger, so that he might take more pleasure in his dinner.

[98] Again, do we not see what food the Spartans ate in their messes? The tyrant Dionysius* once dined there and said that he had not enjoyed the black soup which was the dinner's main course. At this the man who had cooked it said, 'No surprise there—you didn't have what seasoned it.' 'And what was that?' asked the tyrant. 'Toil in hunting, sweat, running beside the Eurotas,* hunger, thirst—these are what give seasoning to the feasts of Spartans.' This is a lesson that can be learned not just from the practice of men but also from animals. Whenever anything is thrown to them, provided it is not foreign to their nature, they are content and look for nothing further.

[99] There are some whole states, trained in custom, that take pleasure in frugal living, as I described the Spartans just now. In describing the diet of the Persians Xenophon says* that they take nothing with bread except watercress. And yet, if nature should feel the need of some more savoury things as well, how many are produced from the earth and trees in ready abundance and of excellent sweetness! Add dryness* which is a consequence of this restraint in diet, add undiminished health.

[100] Contrast with this men who perspire, belch, and are stuffed with food like fatted cattle. Then you will understand that those who pursue pleasure the most vigorously are the least successful in attaining their quarry, and that delight in food lies in appetite, not in satiety. There is a story told of Timotheus,* a famous man in Athens and one of the foremost men of the state. He had dined with Plato and taken considerable pleasure in his entertainment. On seeing Plato the following day he said, '*Your* dinners are delightful, not just at the time but on the next day too.' There is the further fact that we cannot make proper use of our minds when we are full of quantities of food and drink. There is a famous letter that Plato wrote to the relatives of Dion. It contains a passage written in virtually these words: 'When I arrived there, I was not at all impressed by that so-called happy life, full of dishes from Italy and Syracuse—being full-up twice a day and never passing a night without company, and the other things that go along with this life, in which no man will ever be made wise, far less indeed possessed of self-control. What character can achieve so amazing a blend of elements?'*

[101] Accordingly, what charm can exist in the life that lacks good sense, that lacks the ability to control oneself? This throws light on the

mistake of Sardanapallus, the fabulously rich king of Syria, who ordered that this inscription be put on his tomb: 'All that I have eaten, all that my lusts have drained to satiety, are here in my possession; but many other things of note I have left lying there.' Aristotle observed on this: 'What else would one inscribe on the tomb of an ox, not of a king?'* He says he possesses in death things that even in life he could not have had beyond the moment of enjoying them.

[102] Why, then, should there exist a desire for wealth, or at what point does poverty not allow people to be happy? You take an interest in statues, I suppose, and in pictures. If there is anyone who takes pleasure in these, is it not true that men of slender means enjoy them more than those who possess them in abundance? There exists in our city a considerable supply of all these things for everyone's enjoyment. Those who own them privately do not see so many of them, and that less frequently, whenever they visit their country estates, and just the same they feel a pang of conscience when they remember how these things came into their possession.* I would run out of daylight, should I wish to plead the cause of poverty. The matter is plain to see, and each day we are admonished by nature itself on the subject of its needs, how few they are, how small, how inexpensive.

[103] Then surely the wise man will not be prevented from being happy by obscure or humble birth or even by failure to gain the people's support? Take care that the acclaim of the public and this coveted glory do not bring more trouble than pleasure. No doubt my admired Demosthenes* was being frivolous when he said he was delighted by the whispered remark of a poor woman carrying water, as is the custom in Greece,* who whispered to her companion, 'This is the famous Demosthenes!' What could be more frivolous? But what a great orator! But he had learned, you see, to address others, without communing a great deal with himself.*

[104] We should understand, then, that neither is glory in the people's eyes to be sought for its own sake nor is obscurity of origin to be dreaded. 'I came to Athens,' said Democritus,* 'and no one recognized me.' A steadfast and dignified man indeed, to glory in having no glory! Or is it possible that flute-players and those who can play the lyre use their own judgement when tuning their songs and melodies rather than that of the crowd, while the man of wisdom, who is endowed with a far more important art, will seek out, not what is most true, but what the mob wants? Or is anything more foolish than to regard those whom as individuals one despises, such as ordinary labourers with no manners, as amounting to something when taken as a group? The wise man indeed

will look down on our ambitions and frivolous pursuits, rejecting honours from the people even when bestowed without his asking, but we lack the knowledge to look down on them until we come to regret our error.

[105] There is a passage in Heraclitus,* the natural philosopher, about the leading citizen of Ephesus, Hermodorus.* He says that every member of the Ephesian community should be punished with death for making the following statement, when they expelled Hermodorus from the city: 'Let no single one of us be superior to his fellows; but if one does emerge, let him live elsewhere and among other men.' Is this not an attitude found in every people? Do they not hate every example of virtue that transcends the norm? Consider Aristides—I prefer to cite instances from the Greeks rather than ourselves—was he not expelled from his country precisely because men thought him excessively just? What a mountain of trouble, then, do men avoid who have no expelled at all with the people!* What gives more delight than leisure informed by scholarship? I refer to that scholarship through which we gain knowledge of the infinity of things and of nature and in this very world we know the heavens, lands and seas.

[106] Accordingly, once we have despised political advancement, despised also money, what is left to fill us with dread? Exile, I suppose, which is regarded as one of the greatest evils. If that is an evil because the people have become hostile and frustrated, how much should we regard this attitude with contempt was expressed a little earlier. But if absence from one's country is a wretched thing, then the provinces are full of wretched men, of whom only a few return to their country.

[107] 'But exiles have their property confiscated.' What of that? Is there not enough said about enduring poverty? Indeed if we examine the true facts about exile, not the disgrace of the name, how much, I ask, does it differ from living one's life constantly abroad? And in that condition the most distinguished of philosophers have passed their lives—Xenocrates, Crantor, Arcesilas, Lacydes, Aristotle, Theophrastus, Zeno, Cleanthes, Chrysippus, Antipater, Carneades, Clitomachus, Philo, Antiochus, Panaetius, Posidonius,* countless others, who once they had left their native cities never returned home. 'Yes, but they were not tarnished with disgrace as a result.' But is exile capable of bringing disgrace to the man who is wise? All of this discourse is concerned with the wise man, and such a fate cannot rightfully befall him. It is wrong to offer consolation to one who is rightfully exiled.

[108] Finally, the easiest argument in dealing with all misfortunes is the one applied by those who refer what they pursue in life to pleasure, so that they are able to live happily wherever this is available to them.

Consequently Teucer's remark can be fitted to every system: 'A man's homeland is wherever he prospers.'* Take the example of Socrates. When he was asked what country he regarded as his own, he replied, 'The world.'* He considered himself to be an inhabitant and citizen of the world. Then there is the example of Titus Albucius. Did he not show perfect equanimity when he studied philosophy in Athens as an exile? And yet that very punishment would not have befallen him, had he obeyed the teachings of Epicurus and shunned the life of politics.*

[109] In what way was Epicurus happier for living in his homeland than Metrodorus for living in Athens? Or did Plato surpass Xenocrates, or Polemo Arcesilas,* so as to be happier? What value should be accorded to a state that forces good and wise citizens into exile? Damaratus, the father of our own king Tarquin, was not able to endure the tyrant Cypselus, and so he fled from Corinth to Tarquinii, where he established his fortunes and fathered his children. Surely it was not folly in him to prefer freedom in exile to slavery at home?

[110] Then again, emotions, anxieties and distresses are relieved by forgetfulness when the mind is turned towards pleasure. So it was not without reason that Epicurus ventured to say that the wise man always has more good than bad, as he always has pleasures. From this, he thinks, the result of our enquiry can be deduced, that the wise man is always happy.

[111] 'Even if he lacks the sense of sight or of hearing?' Even then, for such things in themselves earn his contempt. In the first place, just what are the pleasures denied to the blindness you regard with such horror? After all, some people even argue that the other pleasures are to be found in the senses themselves, whereas what we perceive by sight is not to be found in any pleasurable sensation of the eyes in the same way as the perceptions of taste, smell, touch and hearing are to be found in the very part with which we have perception.* No such thing occurs in the case of the eyes. It is the mind that receives what we see. Now, the mind may experience delight in many different ways, even if sight is not employed. I am speaking of a learned and educated man, for whom living is thinking. When a wise man engages in thought he hardly ever enlists the assistance of his eyes to further his enquiries.

[112] If night does not do away with the happy life, why should day that resembles night do away with it? The saying of Antipater the Cyrenaic* is, it is true, somewhat coarse, but there is good sense in his point of view. When some females were lamenting his blindness, he said, 'What's the matter with you? Do you think there's no pleasure to be had at night?' The well-known Appius* of former days, who was blind for many years, was, as we understand both from the public positions he

held and his achievements, in no way barred by that personal misfortune from fulfilling his duties both public and private. We have been told that the house of Gaius Drusus* used to be filled with people who wished to consult him. Those who had the difficulty were not able to see for themselves their own concerns, and so had recourse to the guidance of a blind man. When I was a boy, Gnaeus Aufidius* the former praetor would state his opinion in the senate, assist friends in their deliberations, wrote a history in Greek and in literature had vision.

[113] Diodotus the Stoic, who was blind, lived for many years at my house.* Now—and this is something scarcely to be believed—this man not only engaged in philosophy much more tirelessly even than before, and played the lyre in the tradition of the Pythagoreans,* but he also had books read to him night and day, pursuits in which he did not need eyes. Furthermore, something which scarcely seems possible without eyes, he continued to teach geometry, giving verbal instructions to pupils on those points from which and to which they should draw each line. The story goes that Asclepiades, an Eretrian philosopher* not without distinction, was asked by a man what blindness had brought him. 'I have a larger escort,' was his reply, 'larger by a single slave.' Just as it would be possible to endure even the most grinding poverty, if we could bring ourselves to behave as certain Greeks do every day,* so blindness could be easily tolerated, if aids to our infirmities were put at our disposal.

[114] When Democritus lost his eyesight,* he was, of course, unable to distinguish between what was black and what white. But despite this he could distinguish between good and bad, just and unjust, morally good and immoral, expedient and inexpedient, great and small. He could live happily without appreciating changes of colour, he could not live happily without understanding the universe. Furthermore, this man thought that the mind's acuity was actually hampered by eyesight, and when other men frequently failed to see what lay at their feet, he travelled into all infinity,* so that no ultimate point checked his progress. The tradition also exists that Homer was blind. But what we see is not his poetry but his painting. What district, what coast, what place in Greece, what aspect or form of battle, what line of battle, what pulling at the oar, what movements of men or beasts has he not depicted in such a way that he has enabled us to see what he himself did not? Well then, do we think that neither Homer nor any man of learning ever experienced mental delight and pleasure?

[115] Or if this were not the case, would Anaxagoras* or Democritus himself, of whom we spoke, have forsaken their lands and inherited

property and devoted themselves wholeheartedly to this godlike delight of learning and enquiry? This is why the prophet Tiresias,* whom the poets portray as wise, is never brought on stage lamenting his own blindness. In Polyphemus' case, however, when Homer portrayed him as savage and wild, he makes him actually talk to the ram and congratulate it on its good fortune, because it can go where it likes and get what it likes.* And in this he was right, for the Cyclops himself had no more intelligence than the ram.

[116] As for deafness, what evil is there really in this? Marcus Crassus* was hard of hearing, but it was a different thing, and more annoying, that he heard hard things said about him, even if, as I thought, unfairly. Our followers of Epicurus as a rule are ignorant of Greek,* and his Greek followers of Latin. Consequently the former are deaf to the language of the latter, and vice-versa. In the same way we are all undoubtedly deaf when it comes to those languages we do not understand, and they cannot be counted. 'But they fail to hear the voice of the man who sings to his lyre.' No, nor the screech of a saw when it's being sharpened, nor the squealing of a pig when it's throat is being slit, nor the clamour of the roaring sea when they want to get some rest. And if music happens to give them pleasure, they should reflect firstly on the happy lives that many wise men lived before it was invented, and secondly on the far greater pleasure that can be derived from reading than from hearing it.

[117] Again, as shortly before we were guiding the blind to the pleasure of hearing, so we may guide the deaf to the pleasure of sight. A man who is able to hold conversation with himself will not need another with whom to converse. Let everything be piled together, so that the same man is afflicted by blindness and deafness, and let him be burdened furthermore with the most relentless physical pain. This in the first place generally finishes a man off by itself. But if it happens that the pain is long and drawn out, and nonetheless tortures him with an intensity that gives no reason for him to endure it, why on earth, in heaven's name, should we struggle? There is at hand a refuge from the storm, since death is right there, the everlasting place of shelter where no sensation exists. When Lysimachus was threatening him with death, Theodorus told him, 'That's no small achievement of yours, if you have got yourself the power of a Spanish fly.'*

[118] When Perses was begging not to be led in triumph, Paullus* made this remark to him: 'The matter lies in your own hands.' We had a great deal to say about death on the first day, when we were reflecting on death itself, and quite a lot on the day after, when our discussion was

about pain. Anyone who recalls this runs very little risk of thinking either that death should not be wished for or at any rate should make us afraid. For my part, the rule I think should be kept in life is the one observed at the Greeks' drinking parties: 'Let him either drink or go.' This is correct. Someone should either enjoy the pleasure of quaffing equally with others or else he should take his leave earlier, to avoid encountering the violence of the drunk, when he is still sober. And so by running away one can leave the wrongs fortune has done that you cannot endure. This advice given by Epicurus is repeated in as many words by Hieronymus.*

[119] But if those philosophers who think that virtue in itself has no importance and maintain that everything we call morally right and commendable is mere emptiness decked out in a resounding phrase without meaning—if just the same they hold that the wise man is always happy, what, I ask, ought those philosophers to do who derive their thought from Socrates and Plato? Some of these say that the superiority of the goods of the soul is so pronounced that the goods of the body or external goods are eclipsed by them, while others regard these not even as goods, finding the home of all goods in the soul.*

[120] It was Carneades* who, like a respected referee, used to decide this dispute between them. Since the Stoics regarded as 'advantages'* whatever the Peripatetics regarded as 'goods',* and yet the Peripatetics did not attach more value than the Stoics to wealth, good health, and the other things of the same kind, he said that, when facts, not words, were the criterion for assessing the question, there was no ground for disagreement. So it is for philosophers of the other schools to determine how they can maintain this position; to me it is gratifying that, in maintaining the permanent ability of the wise to live well, they affirm something worthy of the utterance of philosophers.

[121] But since we must take our leave in the morning, let us commit to memory these discussions of the last five days. Indeed it is my intention to write them up as well—in what way can I make better use of this leisure I have, whatever form it will take?* And these additional five books I will dedicate to my good friend Brutus, who not only encouraged me to write philosophy but actually gave me no rest until I did. How much benefit I will bring to everyone else in this enterprise I could not easily say, but for the cruel sorrows and various troubles that have encompassed me on all sides, no other relief could have been found.

ON OLD AGE

SYNOPSIS

CATO THE ELDER

ON OLD AGE

[1]   O Titus, should some aid of mine assuage
       The cares that in thy bosom rage
       And, there lodged fast, torment thy heart,
       What boon wouldst thou to me impart?

For I may speak to you, Atticus, using the very same verses in which
Flamininus is addressed by

       That man of meagre means but rich in loyalty.

And yet, I know full well it cannot be said of you, as of Flamininus,

       Thyself thou dost torment, my Titus, night and day,*

for I know your equanimity and self-control, and I appreciate that you
brought home from Athens* not a surname alone but refinement of
thought as well, together with practical judgement. Nonetheless I suspect that the same set of circumstances that causes me distress sometimes troubles you quite seriously; finding how to console ourselves
for this is too arduous a task, however, and one we should defer to
another time.

[2] At the present, however, I have decided to write in dedication to
you something on the subject of old age, for I wish to bring both you
and me relief from this common burden of old age, which may not yet
be following at our heels but is certainly advancing upon us;* and yet
I know for certain that you indeed bear this burden and will continue
to bear it, as you do all things, with the self-control of a philosopher.*
But when I formed the intention of writing something on this subject, you were the one who constantly suggested himself to me as
worthy of a tribute which the pair of us might benefit from alike. For
myself, I have found such delight in the writing of this book that it
has not only wiped away all the vexations of old age but has even turned
it into a condition of pleasurable ease. Never, then, can philosophy
receive the measure of praise that is its due, since the man who follows its precepts is enabled to spend every period of his life free from
annoyance.

[3] Now on other matters I have had much, and will frequently have much, to say; this book which I send to you takes as its theme old age. But I have ascribed the entire conversation, not to Tithonus, as the Cean Aristo did,* for a myth would lack sufficient authority, but to the elderly Marcus Cato,* in order to give the language greater weight. I have represented the scene as his house, and there I have Laelius and Scipio* expressing their amazement that he endures old age with such ease, while he replies to them. If it strikes you that his arguments contain more learning than he was accustomed to display in his own books, put this down to Greek literature, of which he was a keen student in his later years, as is well known.* But why need I say more? For from this point onwards the words of Cato himself will reveal to you all my thinking on old age.

[4] SCIPIO: Many times, together with Gaius Laelius here, I have been amazed, Marcus Cato, both by your outstanding, not to say matchless, wisdom in matters generally, and especially by the fact that you have never given me the impression of finding old age irksome; in the eyes of most old men it is so tedious that not Etna itself,* they declare, is a burden their shoulders would find more heavy.

CATO: I think, Scipio and Laelius, it is something of no great difficulty that causes you amazement; for men who lack within themselves the means to live a virtuous and happy life find every stage of life a burden; but men who wish to derive everything good from themselves cannot regard as evil whatever is inevitably imposed by nature's laws. To this class in particular belongs old age; all men desire to obtain it, yet find fault with it once obtained—so great is the inconsistency and perverseness that attend on stupidity. They say old age steals upon them faster than they would have supposed: in the first place, who forced them to make this mistaken judgement? For how much sooner does old age creep up on youth than youth on childhood? Again, how much less irksome would they find old age, if they were in their eight hundredth year rather than their eightieth? For however long it may be, time past, once it has ebbed away, cannot soothe or offer any consolation to a foolish old age.

[5] And so, if you are in the habit of marvelling at my wisdom (if only it were worthy of your estimate and my surname!)*, I am in this sense wise that I follow Nature, the best of guides, and obey her as a god.* Now since Nature has written out skilfully the other parts of life's drama, it is not likely that she has ignored the final act, like some lazy poet; but nonetheless there had to be something final, and, as with the fruit of orchards and produce of the earth, something shrivelled, as it were, and liable to fall, when the fullness of time brought it to ripeness; this the

wise man must bear with compliance. For what else is resisting Nature but fighting the gods as the Giants did?

[6] LAELIUS: Well, Cato, you will be doing us a great kindness (if I may speak also for Scipio), if, as we expect, or rather as we wish, to live to be old,* you give us instruction well in advance on what principles we can most easily endure the burden of increasing years.

CATO: Of course I shall do this, Laelius, especially if it is going to gratify the pair of you, as you say.

LAELIUS: Provided it is no trouble to you, Cato, since you have, as it were, travelled the long road we must also take, we really wish to hear what kind of a place it is that you have reached.*

[7] CATO: I will do what I can, Laelius; for I have often been present when contemporaries of mine complain—and in the old proverb 'like with like most happily flock together'. What things used to make them lament, those former consuls* Gaius Salinator and Spurius Albinus, men close in years to myself!—sometimes that they had lost their pleasures,* without which they thought life not worth living, sometimes that they were scorned by those who had been in the habit of showing them respect. In my view, they were not directing their criticism where it was due; for if it was the fault of old age that this happened, I should have had the same experience, together with all other men of advanced years; in many cases I know that old age drew no complaints from them, since they were not distressed at being set free from the chains of desire for pleasure and they were not despised by their relations. But in the case of all complaints of that kind the fault lies in a man's character, not in his age; for old men who are self-controlled and free from bad temper or boorishness find old age bearable, while an absence of tact or of finer feeling make every stage of life a nuisance.

[8] LAELIUS: You are quite right, Cato; but perhaps someone might say that you consider old age more tolerable because of your means, your resources and your standing in people's eyes, while such advantages cannot be the lot of many.

CATO: There is something in that point, Laelius, but it is far from the whole truth; there is the reply they say Themistocles gave in an altercation with a man from Seriphos who had told him he owed his brilliant reputation to his country's glory, not his own: 'It's true enough that I would never have been famous if my home was Seriphos, and neither would you, if your home was Athens.'* The same point can be made about old age: in extreme poverty old age cannot be easy to bear, even for a man of sense, and for a fool old age can only be a burden, even in the utmost wealth.

[9] Without doubt, Scipio and Laelius, the most suitable weapons for defending old age are the qualities and practice of virtues; if these are cultivated in every stage of life, they yield wonderful fruits, once a man has lived a lengthy and full life; this is not only because one never loses virtues, not even at the very end of life, although that is no small matter, but also because a man's awareness of a life well spent and his recollection of many actions well performed are a source of the greatest happiness.*

[10] I was as fond of Quintus Maximus,* the man who won back Tarentum, as if we had been of the same age, though he was old and I young. For there was in that man a dignity seasoned by affability, and old age had worked no change on his character; although he was not greatly advanced in years when I began to cultivate his acquaintance, he was still of considerable age. For I was born in the year after he had held his first consulship and when he was consul for the fourth time* I was just a young fellow when I set out for Capua with him as a private soldier, and, five years later, for Tarentum. Four years after that I became quaestor, holding this office in the consulships of Tuditanus and Cethegus, at the very time when he, though considerably old, spoke in support of the Cincian law on fees and gifts.* He was quite elderly but waged war like a young man and by his persistence he softened the youthful energy of Hannibal. My friend Ennius* writes admirably of him:

> One man by his delay restored our state,
> Preferring safety to the mutterings of the crowd:
> Hence now the longer does his glory last,
> The more its brilliance dims the past.

[11] And as for Tarentum, what watchfulness, what judgement he showed in capturing it back! Indeed, when Salinator (who had been in the citadel when the town was lost) was speaking to him in my hearing in these boastful tones, 'It was thanks to me, Quintus Fabius, that you took back Tarentum', he replied with a smile, 'Quite so, for I wouldn't have won it back, if you hadn't lost it.'* But he was no more distinguished in war than in civil life; while consul for the second time, though his colleague Spurius Carvilius preferred to take no action, he resisted to the best of his ability the people's tribune Gaius Flaminius in his attempt to defy the authority of the senate by distributing to individual citizens the Picene and Gallic land, and, despite holding the office of augur, he dared to say that whatever was done to safeguard the republic was done under the best auspices, and whatever endangered the welfare of the republic was against the auspices.*

[I2] I have come to know many outstanding qualities in that man but nothing invites more admiration than the way in which he endured the death of his son,* a distinguished man and one who had held the consulship; the funeral speech he delivered then is in my possession and, whenever I read it, what philosopher do I not find contemptible?* And it was not only in the light of day, in the sight of his fellow-citizens, that he was great; in the privacy of his own home his excellence was greater still: what conversation, what moral instruction, what great famil-iarity with past history, what great knowledge of augural law! He had read widely in literature, for a Roman;* he retained in his memory all affairs, not domestic only but foreign as well. I was as enthusiastic to benefit from his conversation then as if I already had a premonition of what indeed came about, that with his death I would have no one from whom to learn.

[I3] Why, then, have I said so much about Maximus? Because, of course, you see that it would be an offence to heaven to call such an old age as his unhappy. And yet not everyone can be a Scipio or a Maximus, recalling cities he stormed, battles he fought on land and on sea, wars he waged, triumphs he won; there is also the peaceful and gentle old age of a life spent quietly, with integrity and with discrimination, such as we hear was Plato's, who died in the act of writing, in his eighty-first year; such as was the life of Isocrates, who tells us he was in his ninety-fourth year when he wrote the book entitled *Panathenaicus*, and lived on for five years more; his teacher Gorgias of Leontini reached a total of one hundred and seven years without ever ceasing in his enthusi-asm for his work. When the question was put to him why he wished to remain alive so long, he said, 'I have no reason to find fault with old age.'

[I4] What an outstanding reply, how worthy of a man of letters! For what fools attribute to old age are their own failings and their own faults. This was not true of Ennius, of whom I spoke recently, who writes:

> Like the brave steed that in the final lap
> Many an Olympic trophy won,
> He takes his rest, by weariness now undone.

It is his own old age he is comparing to that of the brave and victorious horse. Both of you can remember him clearly; for it was only nineteen years after his death that the present consuls, Titus Flamininus and Manius Acilius, were elected; his death, moreover, was not until Caepio and Philippus were consuls, the latter for the second time, at the time when I, then sixty-five years old,* spoke in support of the Voconian law* with loud voice and strong lungs. But he at the age of seventy, for such was the length of Ennius' life, was enduring the two burdens that are considered the most taxing, frugality and old age, in such a way that he seemed almost to take pleasure in them.

[15] Indeed, when I reflect on this, I find four reasons why old age seems to be unhappy:* one, that it calls us away from active pursuits, a second, that it makes the body less strong, a third, that it takes away from us virtually all pleasures, and the fourth, that it is not far removed from death. Let us, if you will, examine each one of these reasons and determine what importance and validity they separately contain. Old age withdraws us from active pursuits. What are these? Those that are carried out by means of youthful vigour and strength? Are there, then, no tasks for old men which may be performed by their minds, though their bodies are without strength? Was there, then, no employment for Quintus Maximus,* none for Lucius Paulus your father and the father-in-law of my own son,* that best of men? And the other old men, like Fabricius, Curius and Coruncanius,* when they were protecting the state through their judgement and authority, did they lack employment for their gifts?

[16] In the case of Appius Claudius it was his misfortune that, in addition to his old age, he should be blind; yet when the verdict of the senate inclined towards making peace and a treaty with Pyrrhus,* he did not hesitate to say those well-known words that Ennius described in verse,

> Those minds of yours that ere now stood so firm and true,
> Where have they gone, so madly swerving from their course?

and so forth, in the most impressive style; for you both know the poem, and anyway the speech of Appius* himself has survived. And this was delivered by him in the seventeenth year after his second consulship,* although ten years had passed between the two consulships and he had been censor before he first held this office;* from this it is understood that he was quite advanced in years at the time of the war with Pyrrhus; and in any case this is the version passed down to us by tradition.

[17] Therefore those who say that old age has no part to play in use-ful activity have no proof to bring, and are like those who would say a helmsman takes no part in the sailing of a ship, since it is others who climb the masts, who run up and down the deck, who empty the bilge-water, while he sits peacefully at the stern, just holding the tiller. He does not do what young men do; but in fact what he does is much better and much more important. It is not by strength or physical speed or swift-ness that great things are achieved but by judgement, authority and

thought; these are qualities which, as a rule, so far from deserting old age, positively enrich it.

[18] It may be, of course, that you think I lack employment these days, when I do not wage wars, I, who have been engaged in various forms of warfare, as a private soldier, a tribune, a lieutenant, a commander-in-chief:* yet I direct the senate in which wars should be waged and how; Carthage has now long been plotting our ruin but far before this time have I declared war on her; I will not cease from fearing her until I learn that she has been completely destroyed.*

[19] And I pray that the immortal gods reserve for you, Scipio, the distinction of completing what your grandfather left undone! Thirty-three years have passed since his death, but each succeeding year will receive the memory of that hero and pass it on. He died in the year before I became censor, nine years after my own time as consul,* and when I was holding the consulship, he was elected for the second time to that office.* If, therefore, he had lived to his hundredth year, would his old age have made him dissatisfied? I think not. For he would not be spending his hours on running or jumping, on long-distance spear-throwing or close-quarter sword-play, but on judgement, on reason and on thought; if these qualities were denied to old men, our ancestors would not have called their chief council of state the senate.*

[20] Among the Spartans, indeed, the men who occupy the highest magistracy are named 'the elders' in accordance with their actual age.* But if you wish to read or to hear of foreign history, you will discover that the greatest states have been undermined by the young and put back on their feet and restored to stability by the old.

How lost you, pray, so great a state as yours so soon?—

That is the question they ask, as we read in the poet Naevius' *The Lydian:** they are given various answers but this one is most to the point,

We heard a crop of fresh young speakers, silly lads.

Evidently rashness belongs to the budding-time of life, wisdom to the harvest-time.

[21] Ah, but the memory declines. No doubt if one fails to give it exercise, or again if one is naturally rather dull-witted. Themistocles had learned the names of all his fellow-citizens by heart: you don't suppose, surely, that in his later years he was in the habit of greeting Aristides as Lysimachus?* For my part I know not only present citizens but their fathers and grandfathers as well; and in reading their epitaphs I do not

fear the superstition that it will make me lose my memory;* for it is the act of reading those very inscriptions that makes me recall to mind men who are now dead. Certainly I have never heard of any old man forgetting the place where he had buried his treasure: everything that concerns them they remember, agreed times for appearance in court, who their creditors are and who their debtors.

[22] What of old jurists, pontiffs, augurs and philosophers, how much do they remember? Old men retain their mental powers, provided that their interest and application last the course; and those powers exist not only in the case of famous men who have held high office but also in private life, outside the hurly-burly of politics. Sophocles composed tragedies into extreme old age;* when his attention to literature was thought to be making him neglect his business affairs, he was summoned to court by his sons, with the intention of removing him from control of his property on the grounds of senility, just as in our law it is customary for heads of families to be deprived of control of their property if they are guilty of mismanagement;* on that occasion it is said that the old man read out to the jurors that play which he had just written and was then revising, and asked them if they thought the poem was the work of a half-wit; after this recitation he was acquitted by the verdict of the court.

[23] Old age, then, no more compelled this man to give up his intellectual pursuits than it imposed silence on Homer or on Hesiod, on Simonides and Stesichorus, on the men I spoke of before, Isocrates and Gorgias, on those princes of philosophy, Pythagoras and Democritus, Plato and Xenocrates, on Zeno and Cleanthes of a later date, or the man you have both seen in Rome, the Stoic Diogenes.* In the case of all these was the length of their lives not matched by mental activity in their various pursuits?

[24] But come now, to pass over such godlike pursuits as these, I could name Roman farmers from Sabine territory,* friends and neighbours of mine, who are virtually never absent when the more important tasks are being performed, such as the sowing, harvesting and storing of crops; although in the case of annual crops this is less remarkable—for no one is so old as to think he cannot live for one more year—yet these same fellows labour in those tasks which they know have no relevance whatever to themselves: 'He plants the trees for the next generation to enjoy,' [25] as our Statius* says in his *Young Comrades*. And however old a farmer may be, if you ask him for whom he is planting, he replies without any hesitation, 'For the immortal gods, who have decreed that I should not only receive this from my forbears but also pass it on to

posterity.' And the same Caecilius wrote to better purpose about the old man who looked ahead to 'the next generation' than he did in these lines,

> In truth, Old Age, if you did bring no harm but this alone,
> When you arrive, it would alone suffice for me,
> That one, by living long, sees much he has no wish to—

and much, perhaps, he does wish to; and as regards the things one does not wish to see, even youth encounters these on many occasions. But there is more that is objectionable in these lines of the same Caecilius,

> But most wretched in old age I consider is this,
> Realizing at that age that one is oneself a bore to others.

[26] A delight rather than a bore: for just as wise old men are delighted by young men who possess good qualities of mind, and old age becomes easier to bear for those who are cultivated and appreciated by the young, so young men delight in the instructions of the old through which they are led into the study of virtue; and I certainly do not feel that both of you take any less delight in me than I do in you. But you see that old age, so far from being feeble and idle, is in fact busy and always doing and striving to effect something, that is, something of the same nature each time as their pursuits of earlier years were. What of those who even learn something new, as was true of Solon, whom we see boasting in his verses that he grows old learning something new every day, and as I have done, learning Greek in my old age?* Indeed I have seized upon it as greedily as if I desired to satisfy a long-standing thirst, so that I might familiarize myself with the very things which you see me now making use of as examples* in my discourse. When I heard that Socrates had done this in the case of the lyre,* I would have liked to have done that too (for the ancients learned the lyre);* but at reading their literature I have certainly worked hard.

[27] Nor indeed do I now yearn for the strength of being young (for that was the second heading* under which the faults of old age were detailed), any more than as a young man I yearned for a bull's strength, or an elephant's. A man should use the strength that he has, and in all that he does he should act in accordance with that strength. For what remark can be more contemptible than that made by Milo of Croton?* When he was now an old man and was watching the athletes training on the racecourse, they say that he looked at his arms and said, with tears in his eyes, 'Well, these are certainly dead now'—they're not as dead as you yourself are, you buffoon; for it was never your real self that earned you renown but your lungs and your arms. Far removed from this were

Sextus Aelius and, many years earlier, Tiberius Coruncanius, and, more recently, Publius Crassus, men who gave their fellow-citizens instruction in the law;* their skill in jurisprudence continued right up to their dying breath.

[28] I fear that an orator's effectiveness may decline in old age, for physical strength and the power of his lungs are necessary to his function, not intellect alone. But in old age somehow or other brilliance in the voice's quality of resonance actually improves; for myself, it has so far not deserted me, and you see my advanced age. Nonetheless, what suits an old man best is a quiet and gentle style of speech; and when an old man is eloquent, the elegance and mellifluous quality of his voice compel the listeners' attention in their own right. And if one is unable to practise oratory oneself, one can still give instruction to a Scipio or a Laelius: for what is more delightful than an old age surrounded by the pursuits of youth?

[29] Do we not even leave to old age such strength as to teach and instruct young men and equip them for every task befitting their function in life? Can there be anything more splendid than this service? It was certainly my belief, Scipio, that Gnaeus and Publius Scipio,* and your two grandfathers, Lucius Aemilius and Publius Africanus,* were fortunate in being attended by numbers of young men of good family; and no teachers of liberal arts should be regarded as unhappy, even if their strength may have succumbed to old age and failed them; and yet more often it is the follies of youth, not of old age, that are responsible for that very eclipse of one's strength: for youth spent in gratifying desires without restraint hands on to old age a body that is exhausted.

[30] Indeed Cyrus, in the pages of Xenophon, in those words he spoke on his deathbed when he was now a very old man, says that he was never aware of his old age becoming feebler than his youth had been.* For myself, I remember when I was a lad Lucius Metellus, who was elected chief pontiff four years after his second consulship and proceeded to hold that priesthood for twenty-two years,* possessing such great vigour in the final stage of his life that he did not miss his youth. I have absolutely no need to speak of my own case—although that is certainly the right of an old man and permitted to one of my age.

[31] Do you see how in Homer Nestor very often proclaims his own virtues?* For he was by that time observing the third generation of men; and he did not have to fear that in proclaiming the truth about himself he would appear to any great extent either eccentric or loquacious. For indeed, as Homer says, 'From his tongue flowed speech sweeter than honey';* and this melodious style had no need of physical strength; and yet the famous commander of Greece nowhere prays for

ten men like Ajax but for ten like Nestor; if he has this fortune, he has no doubt that Troy will perish soon.*

[32] But I return to my own case: I am in my eighty-fourth year.* Now, I would wish to be able to make the same boast as Cyrus; but nevertheless this I can say: I certainly do not possess the strength I had, either as a private soldier in the Punic war or as quaestor in the same war or four years later when I did battle at Thermopylae under the command of the consul Manius Acilius Glabrio;* but nonetheless, as you both see, old age has not quite robbed me of vigour or cast me down; the senate-house does not find my powers absent, any more than the speakers' platform, friends, clients or guests of mine. For I have never given my approval to that old and popular proverb that advises one to become old early if one wants to be old for long; in fact I would prefer to be old for less long rather than to be old before my time. And so no one who has wished to have an audience with me has so far found me engaged in advance.

[33] But, the objection comes, I have less strength than either of you.—Well, *you two* don't have the strength of the centurion Titus Pontius;* this doesn't make him more excellent than you, does it? If only one keeps control of one's strength, and each man strives as hard as he can, then he will certainly not feel great regret at the loss of his strength. They say that Milo walked the length of the racetrack at Olympia while carrying an ox on his shoulders: would you prefer to be given this strength of body or the strength of intellect of Pythagoras?* In short, enjoy the advantage of physical strength while it is yours and do not lament its passing when it is not—unless, perhaps, you think youths should be sorry to have lost their boyhood and young men of more years their adolescence. The racetrack of life is fixed, and nature has only one path, which is run once only; and each part of life has been given its own appropriate quality, so that the weakness of childhood, the high spirits of youth, the seriousness of middle age and the maturity of old age each bears some of nature's fruit which should be reaped in its own season.

[34] I think, Scipio, that you hear regularly of the doings of your grandfather's friend and host, Masinissa,* who is today ninety years old: that when he begins a march on foot, he never mounts a horse, and when on horseback he never dismounts; that no rainfall or frost induces him to cover his head; that his body is extremely dry,* and consequently he carries out all the duties and functions of royalty. Accordingly even in old age exercise and self-control can maintain something of one's former robustness. So old age has no strength?—but strength is not even demanded of old age: consequently both by law and by custom men of my age are exempt from those public services* which can only be

performed through the use of strength, and so there is no requirement for us to do even as much as we can perform, far less what we cannot.

[35] Yes, but, we are told that many old men are so weak that they cannot perform any function that duty or even life itself lays upon them.— But this is a failing which is not peculiar to old age but a general result of ill-health: how weak, Scipio, was your adoptive father, Publius,* the son of Africanus, how frail, or rather non-existent, his health! Had this not been the case, he would have come into prominence as another luminary of the state; for to his father's nobility of character he had added a greater richness of learning. Small wonder, then, that old men are sometimes weak, when even the young cannot escape this! We must stand up to old age, Laelius and Scipio, and make up for its failings with due care; we must fight against old age as we would against a [36] disease; we must have a regimen of health;* we must take part in moderate exercises, taking just enough food and drink to restore our strength, not to overwhelm it. And it is not in fact just the body that we must support with our help; the mind and soul are much more in need. For these, too, grow dim with old age, unless, like a lamp, one supplies them with regular drops of oil; and the body, of course, becomes heavy with fatigue from exercise, but the mind is lightened by exercising itself. For when Caecilius* talks of 'the old fools of comedy', he is thinking of characters who are too trusting, forgetful and slack; these are not the faults of old age but of old age that is inactive, lazy and given to falling asleep. As insolence and sexual appetite are more to be found in young men than in old, yet not in all young men but only those of bad character, so that foolishness of the old which is usually called 'senility' belongs to shallow old men, not to old men in general.

[37] Appius was both blind and old, yet he kept control of four sturdy sons,* five daughters, a great household, and many clients; for he kept his mind taut, like a bow, and he did not become apathetic or give in to old age. He maintained not only authority but total command over his family; his slaves feared him, his children revered him, everyone loved him; in that house there flourished ancestral custom and discipline. [38] For old age wins honour, only if it defends itself by its actions, preserves its rights, surrenders to no one else's power, and to its last breath holds sway over its family. For I approve of the old man in whom there is something of the young man no less than the young man who has something of the old man in him; the man who follows this principle will be able to be old in body but never in mind. The seventh book of my *Antiquities** is now in preparation; I am collecting all the records of our ancient history; for all the famous cases I have pleaded, now

more than ever I am putting the finishing touches to my speeches;*
I am working on augural, pontifical and civil law; I am also devoting much
time to the study of Greek literature, and, following the Pythagoreans'
practice, in order to train the memory I call to mind in the evening what
I have said or heard or done each day.* These are my exercises for the
intellect, these, my mental gymnastics; as I perspire and toil away at
these, I do not greatly miss my physical strength. I am present as an
advocate for friends, I often attend the senate;* to both places I bring
subjects for debate I have pondered deeply and for many an hour, and
these I maintain through strength of mind, not of body. Even if I was
unable to carry out these activities, I would still derive pleasure from
the couch I use for study, as I reflected on those very things I could no
longer do. But what enables me to do these is the life I have led: for
when one lives in the constant and energetic pursuit of these studies,
it goes unnoticed when old age creeps up on one; in this way gradually
and imperceptibly age enters its final stage, not abruptly terminating by
force but over a long period of time losing its light.

[39] There follows the third ground for abusing old age, the charge
that it lacks pleasures.* What an outstanding gift it is that age bestows,
if indeed it takes from us the most harmful fault that bedevils our youth!*
Now, my excellent young men, hear what that especially impressive and
distinguished man Archytas of Tarentum* had to say in an ancient
speech passed on to me when I was a young man at Tarentum serving
with Quintus Maximus.* No more deadly plague than carnal pleasure,
he said, had been given by nature to mankind, and in their desire for
this pleasure the passions surged on recklessly and without control to
make it their own; [40] from this is born the betrayal of one's country,
from this the overthrow of states, from this secret negotiation with the
enemy; in short, there was no crime, he maintained, no wicked deed that
the desire to gratify pleasure did not drive men to undertake; indeed
rape, adultery and all vicious crime of this sort were prompted by no
other enticements than those of pleasure;* and since nature, or, it may
be, some god has given man nothing more excellent than his intellect,
there is nothing more hostile to this divine gift and boon than pleasure;
[41] for, he urged, where lust holds sway, there is no place for restraint,
and it is impossible for virtue to establish itself anywhere in the kingdom of pleasure. In order to make this more easily understood, he told
his listeners to imagine a person aroused by the most intense physical
pleasure that can be experienced: he thought that no one would doubt
that such a man, for as long as he was in the throes of this delight, was
incapable of any mental activity or of achieving any goal by means of

reason or reflection. Nothing, then, he concluded, was as hateful, nothing as deadly as pleasure, seeing that, when it was indulged too much and for too long a time, it snuffed out the light of the mind, consigning it to darkness. My Tarentine host Nearchus, who had continued to be a staunch friend of the Roman people,* said that he had heard from older acquaintances that Archytas had spoken these words in conversation with Gaius Pontius the Samnite, father of the man who had inflicted defeat on the consuls Spurius Postumius and Titus Veturius at the battle of Caudium;* and also present to hear that declaration, he said, had been Plato of Athens, who, according to my investigations, did indeed come to Tarentum in the consular year of Lucius Camillus and Appius Claudius.*

[42] Now, what was my reason for quoting Archytas? In order that you might understand that, if we are unable to reject pleasure by means of reason and wisdom, we should be extremely grateful to old age for depriving us of the desire to do what we ought not to do. For pleasure is an obstruction to the exercise of judgement, it is an enemy to reason, it blindfolds, so to speak, the mind's eyes, and has no traffic with virtue. It gave me no pleasure to expel from the senate Lucius Flamininus, the brother of that gallant gentleman Titus Flamininus, after he had held the consulship seven years previously but I took the view that it was necessary to censure his lustful behaviour: for when that man was consul in Gaul, he was begged by a courtesan at a dinner party to behead one of the men who were being held in chains for some capital offence. As his brother Titus (my immediate predecessor) was censor at the time, he escaped punishment, but in the eyes of Flaccus and myself* self-indulgent conduct of this sort, so vicious and abandoned, could not in any way win approval, since to his crime against one person he added dishonour to the state.

[43] Many times I have heard from my elders, who in their turn said they had heard it as children from old men, that Gaius Fabricius* used to be amazed by the story told him when he was an ambassador at the court of king Pyrrhus by Cineas the Thessalian, that there was at Athens a man who advertised himself as wise and used to say that everything we did should be measured in accordance with pleasure; now when Manius Curius* and Tiberius Coruncanius* heard this from Fabricius, they used to wish that the Samnites and Pyrrhus himself might be won over to this belief, as they could be overcome more easily once they had given themselves to pleasure. Manius Curius had lived in the close company of Publius Decius, who five years before the former gained the consulship had offered up his own life to safeguard his country in the year

when he was consul for the fourth time; this same man was known to both Fabricius and to Coruncanius; based on their own experience and on the heroic act of the Decius I have spoken of,* they were firmly of the view that there exists beyond doubt a goal that is naturally noble and honourable, which is sought for its own sake and pursued by all men of finer spirit, who have only contempt and loathing for pleasure.

[44] Why, therefore, do I speak at such length about pleasure? Because not only is it no ground for criticism of old age but actually to its highest credit that it feels no great longing for pleasures. It lacks the banquet with its high-piled tables and wine-cups regularly refilled: it lacks, then, as well drunkenness, indigestion and sleeplessness. But if some concession is to be made to pleasure (since we do not easily resist its allurements—for, as Plato puts it brilliantly, pleasure is the bait of wickedness, obviously because men are caught by it like fish),* although old age lacks the banquet where excess prevails, it can still enjoy a moderate gathering for dinner. I often used to see when he was returning from dinner as an old man Gaius Duilius, son of Marcus, and the first Roman to win a naval victory over the Carthaginians;* it gave him pleasure to be preceded by a rope-torch soused in wax and a flute-player, honours he had assumed as a private citizen without any precedent—so great was the privilege his glory gave him.*

[45] But why do I speak of others. Let me now return to myself. Firstly I have always had club companions—in fact it was at the time of my quaestorship* that clubs were organized, with the adoption here of the rites of the Great Mother*—and consequently I used to dine with these companions, in moderation indeed, but our spirits showed a certain effervescence in accordance with our time of life, which, as the years pass, brings each day a greater sense of calm to everything; for I used to measure my delight in these same social gatherings less by the physical pleasures they brought than by the opportunity to meet and have conversations with friends. For it was a happy choice of our ancestors to give the name of *convivium* to the practice of friends reclining together at feasts, as it connotes a communion of life, improving here on the Greeks, who call this same thing sometimes 'a drinking together' and sometimes 'an eating together', so that they appear to praise most what matters least in that association.*

[46] Now, for my own part, my delight in conversation brings me delight even in 'afternoon feasts',* and these not only with men of my age, very few of whom now remain, but also with your generation and yourselves; and I am most grateful to old age, which has increased my appetite

for conversation and has removed that for food and drink. But if there is anyone who takes delight even in such things (so that I may by no means appear to have declared war on pleasure, when perhaps nature allows a certain measure of it)* it is not my understanding that old age lacks an appreciation even of these very pleasures. Certainly I find delight in the custom instituted by our forefathers of appointing masters of ceremony at feasts, and also in that of conversation over the wine starting at the top couch, as was our ancestors' practice;* I also enjoy cups that are small in size and filled with a sprinkling of wine, like those we read of in Xenophon's *Symposium*,* cooled in summer and, again, in winter heated by the warmth of the sun or a fire. These gatherings indeed I am in the habit of frequenting even when I am in the Sabine country,* and each day I make up a party of neighbours which we make last late into the night, talking on as wide a variety of topics as possible.

[47] But, I hear it said, in old men the tingling that pleasure affords, if I may use the phrase, is not so great.—This may be true, but equally diminished is their longing for these pleasures: and nothing that one does not long for can cause distress. It was a good reply Sophocles gave when, now in old age, he was asked by a man if he still indulged in sex. 'Heaven forbid!' he said. 'Indeed I am delighted to have escaped from this as if from a savage and cruel master.'* For those who desire such things perhaps it is annoying and irksome to lack them; but for those who have indulged in them to the point of satiety it is more pleasant to lack them than to have them—though of course a man who does not miss them cannot be said to lack them, and therefore what I mean to describe as more pleasant is this state of 'not missing'.

[48] But while youth enjoys these very pleasures more keenly, in the first place they are petty things, as I have said, that they enjoy, and, secondly, old age may not possess such pleasures in abundance but it is not entirely lacking in them: as Ambivius Turpio* gives greater pleasure to the spectator in the front row of the theatre, yet also pleases the one in the back row, so youth gazing upon pleasures nearby gains more delight perhaps from them, but old age also derives enjoyment enough from a more distant view.

[49] But what a blessing it is for old age that the soul, after, so to speak, ending its campaigns against lust, ambition, strife, enmity and all the passions, has itself for company and lives with itself!* Indeed if it has any sustenance, so to speak, in study and learning, nothing is more delightful than a leisured old age. I used to see your father's friend, Scipio, Gaius Galus, working himself to death in his enthusiasm for measuring, as it were, the heavens and the earth—how often daylight

surprised him when he had started working on some chart by night, how often night found him engaged on a task begun at break of day! What delight he took in predicting for us, long in advance, eclipses of sun and moon!*

[50] And, in the case of studies which are less demanding and yet subtle, what about the enjoyment Naevius* had from his *Punic War*, or Plautus from his *The Grim Fellow* or *The Cheat*? I myself saw Livius as an old man who, despite producing a play in the consulships of Cento and Tuditanus six years before I was born, lived right on to the time when I was a young man.* Why need I speak of the zeal for both pontifical and civil law shown by Publius Licinius Crassus,* or of that we find in our own Publius Scipio,* elected Chief Pontiff only a few days ago? And all those men I have mentioned I have seen burning with enthusiasm for their pursuits in their old age; take Marcus Cethegus, justly called by Ennius 'the marrow of Persuasion',* what enthusiasm I saw him display when he spoke in public, even as an old man! What, then, are the pleasures to be had from feasting, games or harlots compared with these pleasures? And in fact these things in the case of wise and well trained men increase in proportion to the passing of the years, so that there is merit in the saying of Solon which is in one of his pieces of verse, as I have said,* that he learned many new things each day as he grew old: there can surely be no greater pleasure than this one of the mind.

[51] I come now to the pleasures that farmers know,* in which I take incredible delight; they are in no way restrained by old age and seem to me to bear the closest resemblance to the life of the wise man.* For farmers have an account in earth's bank,* and it never refuses to accept an investment or ever gives back what it has taken without interest, but pays sometimes at a low rate, usually at a high one. And yet what gives me pleasure is not the produce alone but the soil itself, its power and nature; whenever it receives the scattered seed in its softened and subdued bosom, it at first hides it from view (this gives rise to the term 'harrowing', derived from a word meaning 'to hide'), then it causes it to grow outwards, having warmed it by the steam it generates in its embrace, and draws out the green shoot that grows into stalks; this, supported by the root fibres, gradually matures and, raised on a knotted stalk, is enfolded in a sheath, once it has, so to speak, reached man's estate, and when it has emerged from this sheath, the ear comes into sight with its grain piled up in the ordered formation of the ear, and is protected against the sharp attacks of smaller birds by the rampart of spikes.

[52] Why should I speak of the early growth, cultivation, and later growth of the vine? I cannot get my fill of enjoyment of this process—so

that you may realize what brings relaxation and delight to my old age—for I say nothing of the natural force of all plants, a force that, from the tiny fig-seed or the grape-pip or the smallest seeds of all other fruits and plants, produces such mighty trunks and branches; are they not enough to cause wonder and delight in any man, mallet-shoots, cuttings from trunk and branch, rooted cuttings and runners? As for the vine, which naturally is prone to droop and falls to the ground unless it has support, it raises itself by its tendrils which, like hands, it uses to embrace whatever it has caught hold of; and as it turns and twists with many a course, now in this direction, now in that, the skilful farmer keeps it in check by means of his knife that prunes, to stop it running to wood with its cuttings and spreading too far in all directions.

[53] And so, with the start of spring, there emerges from, so to speak, the joints of the cuttings what is termed a bud; arising from this, the grape shows itself, which both the soil's moisture and the sun's heat cause to grow; at first it is very bitter in taste, then with ripening it becomes sweet and with its garment of foliage it has no lack of moderate warmth and keeps off the more ardent rays of the admiring sun; what can be more delightful to the taste or, at the same time, more beautiful to the eye? What I find a source of delight is not only its usefulness but also, as I said before, its cultivation and very nature—the evenly spaced rows of frames with cross-piece set at the top, the tying up and propagating of the vines, the pruning of some branches, as I have described, and the leaving of others to grow freely. What need have I to refer to irrigation or to the ditching and digging over of fields, which make the soil grow much more fertile?

[54] Why need I speak of the usefulness of manuring?* I have dealt with this already in the book I wrote on agriculture; on this topic the learned Hesiod, although he wrote on agriculture, said not one word; but Homer, who lived, in my view, many generations before,* represents Laertes as seeking to assuage his longing for his son in cultivating the soil and manuring it. Indeed it is not only fields of corn, meadows, vineyards and woodlands that bring fertility to the farmer's domain, but gardens as well, and orchards; then there is the pasturing of his beasts, his swarms of bees, and the endless variety of flowers; and not only does he delight in the planting out of his vines but also in their grafting, which requires more dexterity than any other of agriculture's tasks.

[55] I could enlarge upon all the several delights that belong to the farmer's life, but I feel what I have already described has taken too much space; but you will forgive me, for my enthusiasm for the life of farming has carried me away and old age is naturally given to wordiness*—and

it is not my wish to acquit it of every fault. So then it was in this sort of life that Manius Curius* spent his final years, after he had triumphed over the Samnites, the Sabines and Pyrrhus; indeed when I gaze at his country house—for it is no great distance from mine—I cannot show enough admiration either for the abstemiousness of the man or for the way life was lived in those days.

[56] When the Samnites brought a great mass of gold to Curius* as he sat by his hearth, they were turned away scornfully; for he said it was not possessing gold that seemed glorious to him but exercising command over those who possessed it. Could such a noble character make old age anything but happy? But I return to farmers, to avoid losing my thread: on the land in those days there were senators, that is *senes* or old men,* if the story is true that Lucius Quinctius Cincinnatus was at the plough when he received the news that he had been made dictator; it was on his order as dictator that the Master of Horse Gaius Servilius Ahala killed Spurius Maelius when he was attempting to establish a tyranny.* It was from the farmhouse that both Curius and the other old men were summoned to the senate, and this is why those who summoned them were given the name of *viatores* or wayfarers.* Surely the old age of these men was not one to invite pity, when they found delight in cultivating their land? Indeed in my own estimate I am inclined to think that no life could be more blessed; not only in view of the duty performed, since cultivation of the land promotes the welfare of the entire human race, but because of the charm I have spoken of, and the sufficiency and abundance of all the things which contribute to the nurture of mankind, as also to the worship of the gods—so that I may now make my peace with pleasure, in view of the delight that certain people take in these things; for when the owner of a farm is conscientious and industrious, his storeroom and cellars are always well filled with oil and wine and provisions, his whole farmhouse suggests wealth, it has an abundant supply of pork, goat's meat, lamb, poultry, milk, cheese and honey. And then there is his garden, which farmers themselves call 'their second flitch';* among spare-time activities hawking and hunting further supply the seasoning for these dishes.

[57] Why need I speak at greater length of meadows in their greenness, or of trees planted in rows, or of the beauty of vineyards and olive groves? I shall be concise: nothing can be more abundant in usefulness or more attractive in appearance than farmland that is well cultivated; and old age not only presents no obstacle to one's enjoyment of this but actually invites and entices one to this end. For when can an old man more pleasantly grow warm from sun or fire, or, conversely, when can

he cool himself with greater benefit to his health by means of shade and running streams?

[58] Let men keep, therefore, their weapons, their horses, their spears, their wooden clubs and exercise balls, their hunting and running competitions; let them leave us old chaps, out of many sports, our knuckle-bones and dice—or let them take or leave whichever of these they like, since old age has no need of them to be happy.

[59] Most useful for many projects are the books of Xenophon, and I beg you to carry on reading* these attentively. How comprehensively he praises agriculture in that book devoted to the management of estates, the one entitled 'The House-holder'! And so that you both may understand that he regarded nothing so worthy of a king as a keen interest in the cultivation of land, in a conversation which he has in that book* with Critobulus, Socrates talks of how Cyrus the Younger, the Persian prince remarkable for his natural ability and the glory of his rule, on receiving a visit at Sardis from Lysander of Sparta,* a man of supreme bravery, who brought him gifts from the allies, displayed courtesy and kindness towards Lysander in all his hospitality but in particular showed him a certain park that had been planted with care;* Lysander admired the stateliness of the trees planted in rows in dice-formation, the clean and well-tilled soil, and the sweetness of the odours emanating from the flowers, and then expressed his admiration not only for the attention to detail but also for the skill of the man responsible for the planning and arrangement of this work; the reply of Cyrus, as Socrates tells us, was this: 'But it was I who laid them all out, I who set them in rows, I who saw to their arrangement; and many of those trees were planted by my own hand'; then, Socrates ends, Lysander, looking at Cyrus' purple robe and physical splendour, and his Persian costume adorned with much gold and many jewels, said, 'Men are quite right to call you happy, Cyrus, since you are not only virtuous but fortunate as well.'*

[60] This fortune, therefore, is one that we old men may enjoy, and it is not our time of life that hinders us in the pursuit of other activities and, in particular, the cultivation of the soil, even to the final stage of old age. Indeed there is the tradition that Marcus Valerius Corvinus continued his pursuit of agriculture to his hundredth year, living and working on the land after passing the ordinary span of life; between the time of his first and sixth consulships there was an interval of forty-six years*—so the span of life decreed by our ancestors as indicating the beginning of old age* was the length of the public career he enjoyed. And the final period of his life was happier than the middle one in the sense that he had greater authority and less labour.

[61] But the crown of old age is authority: how great was this in Lucius Caecilius Metellus,* in Aulus Atilius Calatinus!* He received the following epitaph:

> 'All nations agree that he alone who lies here
> foremost was among his country's men.'

For the entire poem carved on the tomb is well known; his authority, then, was weighty for good reason, as all men agreed in praising his achievements. What greatness did I see not long ago in the Chief Pontiff, Publius Crassus,* and in his successor in that priesthood, Marcus Lepidus!* Why need I speak of Paulus or of Africanus, or of Maximus, whom I have already mentioned?* The authority of these men resided not in their judgement alone but in the very nod of their heads. In particular when old age has been honoured with public office it possesses an authority of greater value than all the pleasures of youth; [62] but remember that throughout this entire discussion the old age which I am praising is the one established on the foundations of youth. The result of this is, as I once stated* with the approval of all who heard it, that the old age that defends itself with speeches is a wretched one; grey hairs and wrinkles cannot suddenly seize the prize of authority, but earlier years spent honourably gather authority's fruits at the last.

[63] For these very things that seem inconsequential and everyday win a man esteem—receiving clients, being sought after, having others give way to us or rise at our approach, being escorted to and from the forum, being asked for advice; these are marks of respect that are scrupulously observed both among us and in other states according to the excellence of their morals. The story is that Lysander of Sparta (whom I have lately mentioned) was accustomed to say that Sparta was where old age had its most honourable dwelling place; for nowhere is greater deference paid to a man's advanced years, nowhere is greater honour bestowed on old age. Why, there is even a story we hear that when an old man entered the theatre at Athens during the dramatic festivals, no place was offered to him anywhere in all that seated throng; but when he went to the special area where Spartans sat in seats reserved for them as ambassadors, it is said that they all stood up and invited the old man to take a seat;* [64] when applause from all quarters of that great audience had greeted their action, one of the Spartans said that the Athenians knew correct behaviour but were unwilling to practise it. There are many admirable customs in your college of augurs,* gentlemen, but particularly relevant to our subject is the one whereby a man is given precedence in stating his opinion according to the seniority of his years; and the older

augurs are preferred not only to those whose official rank is higher but to those who hold the highest offices of all.* What, then, are the pleasures the body gives us that should be compared with the rewards we have from authority? Those who have put these gifts to glorious use seem to me to have played their parts well in the drama of life, and not, like untrained players, to have collapsed in the last act.

[65] But, we are told, old men are peevish, fretful, bad-tempered, difficult: if we inquire, some are also misers. But these are faults of character, not of old age; and yet peevishness and those faults I mentioned have some excuse, which, though not wholly legitimate, is capable of being understood: they think that they are the objects of disrespect, condescension and mockery; besides when the body is weak, every blow causes vexation. But all these trials are made more pleasant by good habits and qualities of character; and this can be understood both in life and on the stage in the case of those brothers in the *Adelphi**—what harshness we find in the one, what geniality in the other! That is how things are: for not every human character grows sour with old age, any more than this happens with every wine. Strictness in old age wins my approval, but here, as in other things, I would have it in moderation: moroseness I have no time for at all.

[66] As for miserliness* in the old, I do not see the point of it: for can anything be more absurd than a traveller increasing his luggage the nearer he gets to his journey's end?* There remains the fourth reason, which appears to cause my time of life particular distress and anxiety: the approach of death, which, of course, cannot be far distant from old age. Oh, what a wretch he is, the old man who has not seen in all the course of his long life that he should not be cowed by death! Plainly it should not be taken seriously, if it completely destroys the soul, or it should actually be desired, if it conducts the soul to some place where it will exist for ever;* but certainly no third possibility can be found.

[67] Why, then, should I fear, if after death I am going to be either not unhappy or happy? Although who is so foolish, even if he is young, as to be convinced that he will be alive when evening comes? Indeed, youth has far more incidents of death than my time of life: young men fall victim to disease more easily,* their illness produces more suffering, and curing them is a more arduous process. And so few reach old age: if this were not what happens, life would be lived better and more wisely; for it is in old men that understanding, reason and judgement are to be found, and had it not been for old men, no states would have existed at all. But I return to the imminence of death: what is this charge you level at old age, when you see it is one that can be made equally against youth?

[68] That death is common to every age came home to me when I lost my excellent son,* and to you, Scipio, when you lost your brothers,* men expected to rise to the highest positions in the state. But, you say, the young man hopes to live for a long time, a hope the same man cannot have when he is old.—But this hope lacks wisdom: for what is more fool-ish than to take as certain what is uncertain, what is false as true?—But, you reply, the old man does not even have anything to hope for.—Well, he is in so much the better situation in that he has attained what the young man hopes for: the young man wishes to have a long life, the old man has had one.

[69] Although, heavens above, what is there in man's nature that lasts for long? For grant the longest span of years, let us hope to rival the age of Tartessus' king (for, as I have seen it recorded,* there was at Gades a certain Arganthonius* who ruled as king for eighty years and lived for one hundred and twenty), but in my view nothing is 'long-lasting' if it has a definite end; for when that time arrives, then what has preceded it vanishes at once; all that remains is what you have won by virtue and honourable actions. Hours and days, months and years, go by; past time never returns and no one can know what is to follow; each man should be content with the time he is given for living.

[70] For the actor does not need to appear in every scene of a play in order to please his audience but only has to win favour in whatever parts he plays, and the wise man need not stay on stage right up to the final curtain; for a short span of years is long enough for a man to live a good and honourable life. But if more years fall to him, he should no more grieve than farmers do, when the pleasant springtime has passed and summer and autumn have come. For spring, as it were, is the token of youth, and gives promise of the fruits to come; the rest of the seasons are suited to gathering in these fruits and storing them away; [71] but the fruit of old age is, as I have said many times, the recollection of abun-dant blessings earlier won. Now everything that comes about in accord-ance with nature should be counted as good;* but what is more in accordance with nature than for the old to die? Yet the same end befalls young men, though nature opposes and fights against it. And so when young men die it seems to me akin to a strong flame being extinguished by a torrent but when old men die it is like a fire going out of its own accord without any force being applied, once the fuel has been used up; and just as apples when green require an effort to be plucked from trees but fall of themselves if they are ripe and matured, so it is force that takes life from young men, ripeness from old; this thought of 'ripeness' in fact causes me so much delight that, the nearer I draw to death, the

more I feel like someone who sees the land and is about to come into harbour after a long voyage.

[72] But old age does not have any fixed end, and a man lives his last years in the proper way if he can still fulfil the tasks his duties prescribe and at the same time have no regard for death; this leads to old age actually having more spirit in it than youth, and more courage. This explains the reply that was given to the tyrant Pisistratus by Solon, when in answer to the former's question, 'Just what do you rely on that you oppose me with such boldness?' we are told Solon said, 'Old age'.* But the best end of living is when a man's mind is unimpaired and his faculties in order and nature itself dismantles the same work that it has itself assembled. As a ship or a building is most easily destroyed by the very man who constructed it, so is man best unmade by nature, his maker; now, every structure that has been assembled recently is dismantled with difficulty but the old and weather-beaten one comes down with ease. So it follows that old men should neither greedily seek to hold on to what little is left of their lives nor give it up without good cause.*

[73] And Pythagoras forbids us to abandon our guard-duty in the garrison of life unless we are under orders from our commander, that is, from a god.* The wise Solon has a couplet in which he says he does not want his death to be without the grief and lamentations of his friends; his wish, I suppose, is to be in his friends' hearts; but I am inclined to think that Ennius improves on this with his lines:

> Let no man honour me with tears
> Or weep to see me on the bier . . .*

He does not think death, which is attended by immortality, should occasion grief.

[74] Now in the process of death there can be some sensation, and this for an old man lasts a fleeting moment; after death, to be sure, the sensation is either desirable or non-existent. But this is a thought that should be practised from youth, so that we may look death in the eye; without this practice no man can be in a calm frame of mind. For certainly death must come, and we do not know if it will be on this very day: what man, then, can be steadfast of mind, who every hour fears the threatening approach of death?

[75] On this matter I do not think there is need of very lengthy discussion, when I recall, not Lucius Brutus, who was killed in bringing liberty to his country,* not the two Decii, who rode at full tilt to a death they had chosen,* not Marcus Atilius, who set out to his execution in order to honour the agreement he had made with the enemy,* not the

two Scipios, who saw fit to obstruct the Carthaginian march with their own bodies,* not your own grandfather, Scipio, Lucius Paulus, who gave his life in the shameful defeat at Cannae to pay for the rashness of his colleague,* not Marcus Marcellus, whose death not even the most pitiless enemy allowed to go unrecognized by the honours of a funeral,* but rather when I recall our own legions, as I have written in my *Antiquities*,* many a time marching out with eager and resolute hearts to a place from which they thought they would never return. Shall wise old men, then, tremble at a thing which holds no fear for young men, and not only untutored ones but simpletons at that?

[76] Undoubtedly, if one has had his fill of all pursuits, he has had his fill of life. Boyhood has certain pursuits: surely it does not follow that these are missed by young men? Early youth has its pursuits: surely these are not needed by the mature or, as it is called, middle stage of life? That period, too, has its pursuits: not even these are sought in old age; there are, in the end, certain pursuits that belong to old age: accordingly, as the pursuits that belong to earlier times of life wane, so do those also of old age; when this happens, a man has had his fill of life and the time is ripe for him to meet his death.

[77] For I do not see why I should not dare to tell you what I myself feel about death, for it seems to me I have a clearer understanding of it, the nearer I get to it.* It is my belief that your fathers, Publius Scipio, and you, Gaius Laelius, men of the greatest distinction and most dear to me, are living yet, yes, and living the life that alone deserves the name of life; for while we are enclosed in this bodily structure, we perform a sort of task that necessity has imposed, and heavy labour it is. For the soul is heavenly in origin, brought down to us from its dwelling on high and, as it were, plunged in the earth,* a place incongruent with its divine and eternal nature. But I believe that the immortal gods implanted souls in human bodies, so that there would be beings to protect the earth and who, as they contemplated the heavenly order, would imitate it in the regularity and constancy of their lives. And I have not been driven to hold this belief simply by the forces of reason and philosophical debate but also by the reputation and authority of the greatest philosophers.*

[78] I used to be told that Pythagoras and the Pythagoreans, virtually fellow countrymen of ours,* who once had been called 'Italian philosophers', had never doubted that we possessed souls emanating from the universal divine mind; moreover I had revealed to me the arguments concerning the immortality of souls that Socrates set out on the last day of his life, that man whom the oracle of Apollo had judged to be

the wisest of all.* Need I say more? This is my conviction, this, what I believe: since the soul possesses such great rapidity of movement, such a powerful memory of things past and ability to foretell things to come, so many arts, sciences and inventions, it cannot be that such a nature embracing such knowledge is mortal; and since the soul is constantly in motion and has no source of motion because it is self-moving, it will have no limit to its motion either, because it will never leave itself; and since, we learn, the nature of the soul is of one substance and it contains no admixture which is unlike or dissimilar to it, it cannot be divided: if this cannot take place, it cannot perish; an important proof for the idea that men know several things before they are born is the fact that already children, when learning difficult subjects, grasp countless facts so quickly that it seems they are not learning them then for the first time but are recalling and remembering them.

[79] This is, effectively, the teaching of Plato;* in Xenophon's work,* however, the elder Cyrus, as he is dying, says this: 'Do not think, my dearest sons, that, when I leave you, I will cease to have any existence. For while I was with you, you did not see my soul, but understood it to be in this body from the deeds I performed: therefore continue to believe it exists still, even if you do not see it at all.

[80] And indeed the honours paid to famous men after their deaths would not survive, if the souls of these very men did not cause us to preserve the memory of them longer. For myself, I could never be per-suaded that our souls had life while they occupied our mortal bodies but perished when they left those bodies; or, indeed, that the soul became unthinking when it had escaped from the unthinking body but rather that it only gained wisdom when it was freed from every admix-ture of the body and had begun its pure and uncontaminated existence. And even when a man's nature is dissolved by death, it is clear where each of the other bodily constituents goes, for they all depart to the place of their origin: but the soul alone is unseen, both when it is in the body and when it has departed. Now indeed you see that nothing so much resembles death as sleep; [81] and yet it is when we are asleep that our souls especially reveal their divine nature; for they foresee many things in the future when they are unfettered and at liberty:* from this it is understood what their nature will be when they have wholly set themselves free from the shackles of the body. And so, if the truth is as I have said,' he ended, 'henceforth pay me the respect you would a god: but if my soul is going to perish together with my body, still you, in showing reverence to the gods who preserve and rule over this beautiful universe, will keep me in dutiful and sacred memory.'

[82] These were the sentiments of the dying Cyrus; now let me, if you please, give my own. No one will ever persuade me, Scipio, that either your father Paulus or your two grandfathers Paulus and Africanus, or Africanus' father or his uncle,* or many eminent men whom I need not now name, would have attempted such great exploits for posterity to remember unless they were aware that posterity belonged to them. Or (to boast somewhat about myself, as old men will do) do you think that I would have undertaken such great labours, by day and night, at home and abroad, if I was going to limit my glory by the same boundaries as my life? Would it not have been far better to spend a peaceful life of leisure, free from all effort and struggle? But somehow my soul was constantly alert, looking ahead towards posterity, as if it would only live at last when it had departed from life. And indeed, were it not the case that souls are immortal, it would not be true that the souls of all the best men especially strive after immortality and glory.

[83] And what of the fact that all the wisest men die with the greatest tranquillity of mind, but all the most foolish with the least? Does it not seem to you that the one soul, because it has deeper and wider vision, sees that it is setting out for a better destination, while the other, because its sight is less sharp, does not? Indeed, gentlemen, I am swept away by my eagerness to see your fathers, whom I honoured and loved, and I long to meet not only those men I have come to know personally but also those of whom I have heard and read and written myself.* Yes, and when I set out to join them, no man, I assure you, will easily draw me back, or boil me up to youth again, as if I were Pelias; and should any god bestow on me the gift of returning from this old age to infancy and howling in my cradle, I would stoutly refuse and have no wish whatever to be called back from the finishing line to the start, so to speak, when I have run the course.

[84] For what advantage does life possess? Or rather what trouble does it not? But let us grant it does possess advantage, yet it is one we can certainly have too much of or find limited. For I am not inclined to complain of life, as many men have done, and learned men at that, and I am not dissatisfied that I have lived, since I have lived in such a way that I think I was not born in vain; and I take my leave from life as if it were an inn, not my home: for nature has given it to us as a hostelry in which to break our journey, not a permanent residence. O glorious day, when I shall set out to join that divine gathering of assembled souls, and leave behind this swirling mass of impurity! For I shall go to meet not only those men of whom I spoke but also my own Cato,* the finest man, the most renowned for dutifulness, this world has ever seen;

his body was burned on the pyre by me, whereas on the contrary it was fitting that mine be burned by him;* but his soul, not abandoning but gazing back on me, has truly gone to that place where he knew I myself must come. Men have thought I bore this loss of mine with bravery—it was not that I bore it with a heart untroubled, but I kept consoling myself with the thought that our separation and leave-taking would not be long.

[85] It is for these reasons, Scipio, for you said this was a source of amazement for both you and Laelius, that old age is no burden to me; not only is it not irksome, but even a source of pleasure. But if am wrong in my belief that the souls of men are immortal, I am glad to be wrong, and, while I live, I have no wish for this error to be wrested from me; but if, as certain insignificant philosophers hold, I will have no sensation when dead,* I do not fear that these philosophers when dead will poke fun at this error of mine. But if we are not going to be immortal, still it is a desirable thing for a man to meet his end at his proper time: for nature has imposed a limit on living in the same way it has on all other things; again, old age is, so to speak, the final scene in life's drama, from which we ought to escape when weariness overcomes it, especially if we have had our fill. These are the words I had to say on the subject of old age: my wish is that both of you reach this stage, so that you may be able to prove by the test of experience what you have heard from me.

ON FRIENDSHIP

SYNOPSIS

LAELIUS, ON FRIENDSHIP

[1] The augur Quintus Mucius Scaevola* was in the habit of recounting many anecdotes about his father-in-law, Gaius Laelius,* which were always told with attention to accuracy and in a pleasant fashion, and each time he discussed that man, he had no hesitation in calling him 'the wise'.* Now, when I had assumed the toga of manhood,* I was taken by my father to Scaevola on the understanding that, so far as I could and it met with his wishes, I would never leave the old man's side. And so I would memorize many shrewd arguments he made, together with many of his concise and pointed remarks, and I made it my task to improve my own education through his learning. When he died, I transferred my allegiance to the pontiff Scaevola, a man who, I venture to assert, was the most eminent in Rome both in mental acuity and a sense of what was fair.*

[2] But I will speak of him at another time; for the moment I will return to the augur. There is one occasion among many that I recall, when he was sitting at home on his semi-circular bench, as was his custom, with myself present and only a few friends, and his conversation turned to a subject that was common talk at the time. Now you remember, Atticus, as you were a close friend of Publius Sulpicius, how astonished, or indeed shocked, everyone was, when, as a tribune of the people, he set himself up in deadly hatred as an opponent of Quintus Pompeius, the consul of the day, a man with whom he had lived on the closest and friendliest terms.*

[3] And so it came about that Scaevola, having mentioned this very matter, went on to describe to us a discussion on friendship that Laelius had held with him and with his other son-in-law, Gaius Fannius, the son of Marcus, a few days after the death of Africanus.* I committed to memory the main points of that discussion and these I have set out in this book in my own fashion; I have, so to speak, brought the characters themselves on stage to avoid inserting too often 'I said' and 'he said', and to give the impression that they are present and personally engaged in conversation.

[4] When you pleaded with me frequently that I should write something on the subject of friendship, it struck me that here was a topic worthy of universal interest as well as our own close association; I was, therefore, not unwilling to oblige you and to bring benefit to many. But as in my *Cato the Elder*, which was written to you on the subject of old

age, I represented Cato in his old age as the leading speaker, since no character seemed more suited to talking about that stage of life than he, as one who had not only been elderly for a very long time but also had flourished in old age itself to a greater extent than other men; so, on learning from our forbears that Gaius Laelius and Publius Scipio had enjoyed an especially memorable friendship, I drew the conclusion that Laelius was a suitable character to expound the very views on friendship that Scaevola remembered from his own conversations with him. And dialogue of this kind, founded on the authority of men of earlier times, particularly men of distinction, seems in some way to carry more weight;* and so, as I read my own work, I am sometimes so struck that I imagine that it is Cato, not I,* who speaks.

[5] But as on that occasion I wrote on old age as one old man to another, so in this book I have written on friendship as a most affectionate friend to another.* In the former case it was Cato who spoke, whom in his day virtually no one exceeded in years and no one in wisdom; in the present work Laelius, a wise man (for such was his reputation) and one distinguished for his own glorious friendship, will speak on friendship. Be so good as to put me out of your mind for a short while and to imagine that it is Laelius himself who speaks. Gaius Fannius and Quintus Mucius have paid their father-in-law a visit following the death of Africanus; the conversation starts with them, Laelius replies, and to him belongs the entire discourse on friendship in which, as you read it, you may recognize a portrait of yourself.*

[6] FANNIUS: That is so, Laelius; a better or more illustrious man than Africanus never existed. But you should consider that the eyes of all men are fixed on you; you alone are the one they both call and regard as wise. In recent times that honour used to be accorded to Marcus Cato, and we know that Lucius Acilius was hailed as wise in our fathers' time, but each man for a different reason, Acilius because he was considered learned in civil law,* Cato because he was experienced in many fields. Both in the senate and the forum many instances were recorded of his displaying shrewd foresight or resolute action or acuteness in debate, and for that reason by the time of his old age he enjoyed, as a virtual surname, the title 'the wise'.*

[7] You, however, present a different case again, being wise not just because of your character and endowments but also because of your learning and intellectual pursuits; and this term is applied to you, not in the sense that the ordinary people use it, but rather as learned men are accustomed to do. And such a man, tradition tells us, was not to be found anywhere in the rest of Greece—for the so-called Seven Wise

Men* are not allowed into the category of the wise by those who are more scrupulous in judging these things—except in the case of one man at Athens; and he, indeed, was judged by Apollo's oracle the wisest of men.* You are credited by them with the wisdom that makes you consider everything that concerns you as lying within your own responsibility, and all life's vicissitudes capable of being overcome by virtue. This is the cause of the question being put to me, and, I am sure, it is also put to Scaevola, how you are managing to bear the death of Africanus, and this is particularly the case, since you were not present when we met on the Nones of this month for our customary practice in the gardens of Decimus Brutus* the augur, although you had always been most punctilious in attending that function on that day.*

[8] SCAEVOLA: It is indeed, Gaius Laelius, a question frequently put, as Fannius has said, but the reply I give is what I have observed, namely that you endure in a controlled way the pain caused you by the death of a man who was not only most eminent but very dear to you; that you could not have failed to be moved by this and that such a reaction would not have been consistent with your humane character. As for the fact that you were not present at our college on the Nones, my response is that this was caused by ill health, not grief.

LAELIUS: An excellent reply, Scaevola, and one that was correct; for no personal inconvenience should have kept me from fulfilling the duty you speak of, one that I have always observed when in health, and I do not think any such circumstance could occasion the neglect of any duty on the part of a man of reliable character.

[9] Now Fannius, as to your saying that such great merit is attributed to me, merit such as I neither recognize nor lay claim to, it is kind of you, but I feel your estimate of Cato does not do him sufficient justice. For either no man has ever been wise, which is the view I really think preferable, or if any man has been, that man was Cato. Without citing other instances, how well he bore the death of his son!* I remembered the case of Paulus* and I had witnessed the behaviour of Galus*; but their sons died in boyhood, while Cato's was a full-grown man whose merits the world had noted.

[10] And so beware of rating more highly than Cato even that very man whom you mentioned as the wisest of all* in Apollo's judgement; for Cato is praised for his actions, the other for his words. But as far as I am concerned, let me now address you both at once and I will give you my own views. If I were to say that I have been unaffected by grief at the loss of Scipio, it would be for men of wisdom to estimate how far I am right, but I would certainly not be telling the truth. For I am indeed

affected by grief at being deprived of such a man as, I believe, there will never be again, and, as I can state without qualification, a friend such as there has never been before. But I do not lack remedies: I bring myself particular consolation* from the comforting thought that I am not a prey to the delusion that causes most men torment when their friends pass away. It is my belief that nothing bad has happened to Scipio; if it has happened to anyone, it has happened to me; but to let your own inconveniences* cause you grave distress is to show love, not for a friend, but for yourself.

[11] But who would say that fortune has not treated that man wonderfully well? For unless he wished to live for ever, a wish he did not remotely entertain, what wish that the gods would allow a man to have did he fail to attain, this man who by means of amazing merit at the moment he became a youth surpassed the highest expectations his countrymen invested in him when he was a boy? He never sought the consulship but was made consul twice, on the first occasion, before he was of legal age, the second time at the time that was proper for him but for his country almost too late;* the two cities that were the implacable foes of our empire he overthrew, so terminating not only existing wars but future wars as well. What need have I to mention his most genial character, his affection for his mother and generosity* towards his sisters, his kindness to his relatives and the fairness he showed to all men? You know these qualities well. And the love he inspired in the citizen body was shown by the display of grief at his funeral. How, then, could he have derived any benefit from a few more years? For old age may well be no burden, as I remember Cato arguing in a discussion he had with Scipio and myself* the year before he died, but it nonetheless takes away that freshness which Scipio enjoyed even to the end.

[12] His life, therefore, really was of such a kind that nothing could be added to it either by good fortune or by fame; and the sense of dying was taken away by the swiftness of his end. It is difficult to speak of the nature of his death; you are both aware of people's suspicions:* yet this I may state with truth, that of the many joyous days he enjoyed in his life, days filled with admiring crowds, the finest of all was the day before he passed away, when the senate had been adjourned and he was escorted home towards evening by the senators, the people of Rome, the allies and the Latins,* so that it seemed that from so eminent a station of worth he had passed to the company of the gods rather than to the shades below.

[13] For I do not agree with those who have lately begun to argue* that the soul perishes together with the body, and that all things are destroyed by death. The authority of the ancients carries more weight with me,

either our ancestors, who paid such reverential rites to the dead, which they would undoubtedly not have done if they thought that nothing could affect them; or those who lived in this land and by their principles and precepts educated Great Greece,* which now is no more but flourished then, or the man whom the oracle of Apollo* judged wisest, who did not, as he frequently did, say sometimes one thing and sometimes another,* but consistently held the same opinion, that human souls are divine and a return to heaven lies open to them when they have quit the body, a journey that is the swifter and easier, the better and more just the man.

[14] The same opinion was held by Scipio: indeed, as though he had a premonition of it, only a few days before his death, when both Philus and Manilius* were present, together with several others, and you also, Scaevola, had come with me, he discussed our commonwealth for three days,* devoting almost all of the last part of this discourse to the immortality of the soul, things which he said he had heard from Africanus in the course of a dream. If it is indeed true that the souls of all good men at death make the easiest of escapes from what we may call the imprisoning fetters of the body, what man can we suppose had an easier journey to the gods than Scipio? For this reason I fear it may be more in keeping with an envious spirit than a friendly one to feel grief at such a fate as his. But if, on the contrary, the truth is rather that the soul and the body suffer the same death and no sensation survives, then it follows that, as there is nothing good in death, so there is certainly nothing bad in it.* For once a man's sensation has been lost, the result is the same as if he had not been born at all, and yet the fact that Scipio was born is both a source of joy to us and will bring delight to this nation, as long as it exists.

[15] Accordingly, as I have said already, in his case matters have turned out as well as they could have, but in mine to less advantage, as it would have been fairer for me, who entered this life before he did, to be the first also to take my leave of it. However, I derive such enjoyment from recollecting our friendship that I feel my life has been one of happiness because it was spent in the company of Scipio. I used to share with him my concerns on matters both public and private, I associated with him at home and abroad on military service, and we had what constitutes the very essence of friendship, namely complete community of wishes, interests and opinions.* And so I am not so pleased by my reputation for wisdom,* mentioned recently by Fannius and certainly undeserved, as I am by my hope that the memory of our friendship will last for ever; and I take all the more delight in this thought since in all the course of history scarcely three or four pairs of friends have reached our

ears;* I believe there is hope that the friendship of Scipio and Laelius
will be known in this group to posterity.

[16] FANNIUS: There can be no doubt, Laelius, that this will happen.
But since you have mentioned friendship and we are at leisure, I would
be most grateful, and so too, I expect, would Scaevola, if in accordance
with your usual practice when asked questions on other subjects you
would discuss your feelings on friendship, what kind of thing you judge
it to be and what advice you offer in regard to it.

SCAEVOLA: I will indeed enjoy this, and it was the very request I was
trying to make when Fannius anticipated me. And so you may be confident you will be doing each of us a considerable favour.

[17] LAELIUS: Well, for myself I should have no objection, if only
I had confidence in myself, for the subject is an excellent one and, as
Fannius has remarked, we are at leisure. But who am I, or what aptitude
do I possess? It is men of learning and men of Greek race who have the
habit of requesting that a subject be proposed for debate* at short notice.
This is no easy task and one that requires considerable practice. So in
the matter of a philosophical discussion of friendship, my advice is that
you ask those who profess this art; all that I can do is to exhort you to
give friendship precedence over all other things in the life of man;* for
there is nothing that conforms so well to nature, nothing that brings so
much benefit whether we are experiencing good fortune or bad.

[18] But let me say, as my first point, that in my view friendship can
exist only among men who are good. Now I have no wish to prune that
definition right back to its roots, as those men do who show more subtlety
in discussing these matters—perhaps correctly but not very beneficially
for ordinary purposes. They say that no one is a good man if he does
not possess wisdom. This may well be true, but their understanding of
wisdom is such that no one on earth has to this day attained it.* But
what we should concentrate on are those things which are available in
ordinary life, in our own experience, not those things which are only
imagined or wished for. Never would it be asserted by me that Gaius
Fabricius, Manius Curius and Tiberius Coruncanius,* whom our ancestors judged to be wise, were wise by the standard the philosophers apply.
And so let them keep to themselves their name of wisdom, which attracts
both envy and misunderstanding, as long as they grant that those men
were good. Yet not even this will they do; they will say that only a wise
man is entitled to be called good.

[19] Let us therefore proceed using our own homespun wisdom, as
the saying goes. Men who behave and live in such a way that praise is
bestowed on their honesty, integrity, fairness and generosity, and who

are entirely free from greed, sensual desire and presumption, and possess great strength of character, like those men I recently named—such men let us regard as good, in accordance with their reputation hitherto, and also worthy of receiving this name, since, as far as is humanly possible, they follow Nature, the best guide for living well.* It seems clear to me that we were born into this world with a certain natural tie of association between us all,* but one that gains in strength the nearer we are placed to one another. And so there is a greater closeness with our fellow countrymen than with foreigners, and relatives are closer than strangers; with these, Nature itself has created a tie of friendship, but it is one that lacks stability;* for friendship surpasses family connections in this respect, that goodwill can be eliminated from family connections but not from friendship; once goodwill is removed the name of family connections remains but that of friendship vanishes.

[20] The clearest way, however, to appreciate the power of friendship is this, that out of the infinite number of ties that bind the human race together and have been fashioned by nature itself, friendship is something so compressed and so narrowed that every example of true affection is found either between two persons, or among just a few.* For friendship is nothing other than a shared set of views on all matters human and divine,* together with goodwill and affection, and I am inclined to think that, with the exception of wisdom, it is the greatest gift bestowed on man by the immortal gods. Some give preference to wealth, some to good health, some to political power, some to public honours; many even prefer pleasure. This last is suited merely to animals,* while the earlier ones are unpredictable and unstable things, dependent not so much on our own intentions as the capriciousness of fortune. There are, of course, those who place the highest good in virtue,* and this is indeed a noble sentiment, but this very virtue is the creator and protector of friendship, and without virtue there are no means by which friendship is able to exist.*

[21] Let us proceed to understand the word virtue in the light of our familiar experience of life and of linguistic usage, not taking our measure of it, as some philosophers do, from the grand language we employ in defining it, and let us number as good men those who are so regarded, men like Paulus, Cato, Galus, Scipio or Philus.* They satisfy the ordinary standard of life, but as for those who are nowhere to be found at all, let us give them no thought.

[22] Among men such as these, then, friendship possesses such great advantages that I can scarcely number them all. In the first place how can life be, in Ennius' phrase,* 'a life worth living', if it does not

rest on the mutual goodwill of a friend? What is more agreeable than to have someone with whom you can feel free to discuss all matters as if you were communing with yourself?* In times of good fortune how could your enjoyment be so great if you did not have someone whose delight in it equalled your own? As for bad fortune, truly it would be hard to bear without the one person who would find it a heavier burden even than yourself. And, in any case, the other things that are desired generally bring advantage, each one for a particular end: wealth for the uses it brings, influence for the honour it confers, public office for the praise it bestows, pleasures for the delight they afford, good health for the freedom from pain and the ability to take part in physical activities. But friendship embraces numerous ends: wherever you turn it is at your side, it is nowhere excluded, is never untimely, never troublesome. And so we do not use fire and water, as they say, on more occasions than we use friendship (I am speaking now not of ordinary and common-place friendship, delightful and helpful though this is in itself, but of true and perfect friendship* of the kind that belonged to those few men who are remembered for it. For friendship makes good fortune shine with greater brilliance and, by sharing and dividing bad fortune, eases its weight on one's shoulders.

[23] Moreover, while it is the case that friendship contains a host of considerable advantages, it surely surpasses all other things in this respect, that it casts a bright light of hope into the future and does not allow a man's spirit to grow weak or to stumble. For the man who looks at a true friend is looking, as it were, at a reflection of himself.* For this reason friends who are absent become present, those in need become rich, those who are weak become strong, and, a more difficult thing to say, those who are dead become alive: so great is the esteem that follows after them among their friends, so deep-felt the longing, so potent the memory, that it seems through this that the departed ones are happy in death, the living who grieve worthy of men's praise. But only remove from the world the tie of goodwill and not one house or city will be able to stand, and not even the tilling of the land will continue. If this point is not properly grasped, then one can understand the power of friendship and amity by considering that of dissension and strife. For what house stands so firm, what state is so strong that it cannot be completely torn to pieces by hatred and discord? From this one may judge how great is the good inherent in friendship.

[24] The story goes that a certain learned man of Agrigentum was inspired to tell in Greek verses how in nature and in the whole universe all things that stand fixed and all things that move are united by friendship

and scattered by strife.* And indeed this declaration is one that all men on earth both understand and approve in fact. Accordingly if ever it is required of a friend to perform a service either in facing or in sharing dangers, where is the man who would not celebrate such action with the highest praise? What loud applause echoed recently through the whole theatre when the new play of my friend and guest Marcus Pacuvius* was performed! It was the scene where the king was unaware which of the two men was Orestes, and Pylades said that *he* was Orestes so that he might be killed in his friend's place but Orestes continued to assert, as was true, that *he* was Orestes.* The audience got to their feet to applaud this imaginary incident; what do we suppose they would have done had it been true? Nature on this occasion asserted its power easily, seeing that people judged the action of another to be correct, though they could not have carried it out themselves. Well, I think this is as far as I am able to express my opinions on friendship; if there remains more to be said— and I believe there is much more—be good enough to put your questions to those whose business it is to discuss such topics.*

[25] FANNIUS: But we prefer to ask you. I may well have put questions often to such men and indeed taken pleasure in hearing them respond, but your argument is of a somewhat different texture.

SCAEVOLA: You would say that all the more, Fannius, had you been present in Scipio's gardens recently when politics came under discussion.* What an advocate of justice we had on that occasion against the studied speech of Philus!

FANNIUS: Ah, but that was an easy enough task, for the most just of men to defend justice.

SCAEVOLA: But consider friendship. Isn't it also easy for a man who has won the greatest renown for preserving that with the utmost loyalty, steadfastness and sense of justice?

[26] LAELIUS: Oh, here we have the application of force! I see that both of you are bent on compelling me by whatever means you can. For it is not only difficult but not even fair to stand in the way of the enthusiasm of my sons-in-law*, especially in a worthy cause. So be it. On the frequent occasions I have given thought to friendship, it has always struck me that a point which deserves the deepest thought is this: is it because of our weakness and insufficiency that we desire to have friendship, so that through the giving and receiving of favours each of us may get from another and repay in turn what he cannot attain for himself, or whether, though this reciprocity might indeed be an inherent quality within friendship, there is not a different cause, more ancient and finer and deriving more from nature itself. For the first thing that promotes

the establishing of goodwill is love (*amor*), from which is derived the word 'friendship' (*amicitia*). For it is true that many times practical advantages are obtained even by those who are cultivated under a pretence of friendship and honoured to gain a temporary benefit; but in friendship there is nothing false, nothing pretended, and whatever there is within it, is genuine and proceeds willingly.

[27] It is therefore my view that friendship has its origin in nature rather than in need,* and that it derives more from an attachment of the mind together with a sense of affection than from a calculation of how much advantage the relationship will bring. The nature of this feeling can be observed even in certain animals, which love and are loved by their offspring for a certain period of time, in such a way that it is easy to see their feelings.* This is much more noticeable in mankind; first in the affection that exists between children and their parents and which only some abominable crime is capable of destroying; secondly, if we find someone whose character and personality are in harmony with our own, and a kindred feeling of love arises, because in that person we fancy we see, as it were, a gleam of integrity and virtue.

[28] For there is nothing that inspires affection more than virtue, nothing that attracts us more powerfully to love the one who possesses it, since it is their virtue and integrity that makes us in a certain way feel love even for those whom we have never seen. Who is there who does not dwell with a certain affection and goodwill on the memory of Gaius Fabricius and Manius Curius,* despite never having set eyes on them? But who is there who does not hate Tarquin the Proud, Spurius Cassius, or Spurius Maelius?* There were two generals with whom we fought for supremacy in Italy, Pyrrhus and Hannibal;* against the former because of his good character our feelings of hostility are tempered, the latter because of his cruelty will always be hated by our people.

[29] Now, if the force of good character is so great that we love it, whether in men we have never seen, and, more impressively, even in an enemy of our country, what wonder if the minds of men are stirred when they think they are observing virtue and integrity in persons with whom they can form an association? Yet the strengthening of love is caused by the receiving of kind acts, by the observation of the other's warm feelings and by the increase of familiarity. When these are added to that initial stirring of the mind and of amorous feeling, goodwill surges up like a flame, truly amazing in its intensity. If any men suppose that this stems from weakness and from the desire of each of us to secure someone who will enable us to gain what we lack, then the origin they leave friendship is a mean one indeed, very far from aristocratic, if I may so express it,

as they would have us see it as born of Poverty and Insufficiency.* If this were the case, the man who had least self-confidence would be the one most fit for friendship; but reality is far different from this.

[30] For a man excels in seeking out and maintaining friendships in direct proportion to his capacity for self-reliance and his being so fortified by virtue and wisdom that he has need of no one else, considering all things that concern him as within his own control. I ask you: was Africanus in need of me? Of course he wasn't and I wasn't in need of him either; but I loved him through my admiration for his excellent nature, and he in turn loved me through, it may be, the reasonable opinion he had formed of my character. His goodwill was increased by familiarity; but although many considerable advantages did result, it was not from the hope of those that the causes of our affection at first sprang.

[31] For as men such as we are kind and generous in our behaviour, not so that we may exact remuneration—for we do not loan out our kindnesses at interest but are naturally disposed to generosity—so we regard friendship as worthy of pursuit not because we are influenced by hope of gain but because the affection has all its fruits within itself.*

[32] Utterly different from this is the view held by those who, like beasts of the field, refer all things to pleasure.* And this is not surprising, for they have thrown away all their thoughts on a thing so low and contemptible and are incapable of raising their eyes to anything that is lofty and noble and divine. Let us, therefore, dismiss these persons from our discussion, and let us ourselves understand that the sense of experiencing love, and that affection consisting in goodwill, are born from nature, once indication has been given of moral worth; and when a man has been attracted to this, he attaches himself to it and draws closer, so as to enjoy the company and personality of the one he has begun to love; and it is his aim to equal him in affection, matching his love, and to become readier to do favours than to ask for them in return, the one partner competing with the other in a rivalry that brings them honour. In this way the greatest advantages will be gained from friendship, and at the same time it is the case that its origin is not in weakness but in nature, a beginning at once truer and nobler. For if friendships were cemented by expediency, they would dissolve as soon as that expediency was removed; but since nature is incapable of change, it follows that real friendships last for ever.* There you have my thoughts on the origin of friendship, unless you may have something to add to this.

FANNIUS: No, please continue, Laelius; I take it I may answer on behalf of my friend here, as he is younger than I.*

[33] SCAEVOLA: Quite right, Fannius: and so let us carry on listening.

LAELIUS: Then listen, my fine friends, to some ideas that were very often aired by Scipio and myself when we were discussing friendship. Yet, it's true enough, he used to say that nothing was harder than for friendship to last to the very end of one's life;* for often it turned out either that the friendship was no longer in the interest of both parties, or they ceased to have the same political views, and many times he said that a change occurred in men's characters when good fortune deserted them or the years grew more irksome. And this principle he would illustrate from the start of one's career, when the most enthusiastic friendships among boys are often put aside along with the toga praetexta;* [34] but if they continue them into early manhood, they are nonetheless dissolved as a result of rivalry, sometimes over a marriage arrangement, sometimes because of some advantageous situation from which they cannot both benefit. But if any journey further in friendship, they often find its foundations are shaken when they become competitors for public office; for there is no greater plague afflicting friendships than, in the case of most people, the desire for money, but among the higher echelons of society it is the rivalry to secure public office and glory,* which has caused the deadliest enmities to arise between men who were the closest friends.

[35] He also said that disagreements which were serious and usually justified arose when men were asked by friends to do something which was not right, to abet them in gratifying some illicit passion, or to assist them in doing wrong to another, and on their refusal to comply, however honourably they were acting in this, they were nevertheless accused of disregarding the laws of friendship by the people with whose wishes they were unwilling to comply. As for those who had no compunctions about asking anything whatever from a friend, he said that by that very act of asking they were declaring a willingness to do anything whatever to oblige a friend. The recriminations of these people, he maintained, produced two results: old friendships were usually destroyed and, into the bargain, everlasting enmities were engendered. So many trials, he would say, hovered like evil fates over friendships that it took not just wisdom but also good luck to escape them all.

[36] Accordingly, if we may, let us examine first of all the extent to which love should go in friendship. Is it our view that, if Coriolanus had any friends, they were duty bound to take up arms with him against their own country? Or when Vecellinus or Maelius was attempting to make himself king, should they have been helped by their friends?*

[37] As for Tiberius Gracchus when he was bringing turmoil on the body politic,* we saw him left without any support by Quintus Tubero

and his friends of the same age. But when Gaius Blossius of Cumae,* a guest of your family, Scaevola, came to me to plead for pardon, as I was helping the consuls Laenas and Rupilius* in an advisory role, he put forward this as a reason why I should pardon him, the fact that he had valued Tiberius Gracchus so highly that he thought he should carry out anything that man wished him to do. At this I asked him, 'Even if he wanted you to set the Capitol on fire?' 'He would never have wanted that,' he replied, 'but had it been his wish, I would have obeyed.' You see what a monstrous thing to say that was; and in fact he carried out just that, or even more than he said; he did not simply follow Tiberius Gracchus' rash plans but actually instigated them, and showed himself to be not only an accomplice in Gracchus' madness but the one who led the way. And so in this infatuated state, frightened by the new court of inquiry that was set up, he fled to Asia, offered his services to his country's enemies and in time met with the severe and merited punishment that the Republic demanded.* It is, therefore, no excuse for wrongdoing that you have committed wrong for the sake of a friend; for since it was a belief in each other's virtue that brought you together as friends, it is difficult for the friendship to continue, if one forsakes the path of virtue.

[38] But there would be nothing wrong in laying down a law, that it is right, either to grant a friend his every wish, or to obtain our every wish from them, given that we are endowed with perfect wisdom; but the friends I am speaking of are those before our eyes, the ones we are able to see or have heard of in history, those known to everyday life; from men who belong to this category should we draw our examples, but especially, I accept, from those who approximate most to wisdom.

[39] We see that Aemilius Papus was a friend of Fabricius Luscinus* (this we have had passed down by our forefathers), and that they were consuls together on two occasions and were colleagues in the censorship; there is also the tradition that Manius Curius and Tiberius Coruncanius* were at that time on the closest terms of friendship with them and with one another. It is, therefore, impossible to suspect that any of these asked to do anything that contravened their sense of honour, their oath of office or the interests of their fellow countrymen. Where men of this calibre are concerned, what is the relevance of pointing out that if such a request had been made, it would have failed, seeing that those men had the highest moral standards, and it would be equally wicked either to carry out such a deed when asked or to ask that it be carried out. And yet Tiberius Gracchus did attract followers in Gaius Carbo,* in Gaius Cato,* and in his own brother Gaius, whose support, though somewhat lukewarm in the early stages, is now most enthusiastic.*

[40] Accordingly, let us enact this law concerning friendship, that we should not request shameful things, nor carry them out, if asked. For it is a shameful excuse and one that must in no circumstances be accepted for a man to plead, in the case of wrongdoings in general and especially of those against the Roman state, that he acted in the interests of a friend. Indeed, my friends Fannius and Scaevola, our position is such that it is our duty to look far into the future towards the accidents that may befall the Republic in days to come.* Already the established way of doing things, instituted by our ancestors, has to some extent veered from the straight course.

[41] Tiberius Gracchus attempted to make himself a tyrant, or rather he succeeded in this aim for a few months. Had the people of Rome ever heard of or witnessed such a thing before? As for what his friends and relatives did to Publius Nasica,* following him even after his death, I cannot describe it without tears. In the case of Carbo, we kept him in check as best we could,* for the end of Tiberius Gracchus was still fresh in people's minds. But as to what I expect from the tribunate of Gaius Gracchus, I am not inclined to prophesy. This malaise creeps onward from day to day, and once a thing like this has begun, it slides downhill without a break to disaster. You see in the case of the ballot how much harm has been done even before now, first by the Gabinian law, and then two years later by the Cassian law.* Already, it seems, I see the people estranged from the senate, and the most important decisions being reached to suit the will of the mob; for more men will learn how such action can be set in motion than how it may be resisted.

[42] Why do I say this? Because nothing of this sort is attempted by anyone unless he has accomplices. To good men, then, we must issue this instruction, that, if through some chance they fall into friendships of that kind, they should not regard themselves as so bound by this that they fail to sever themselves from friends when the latter do wrong in some important matter; but for bad men we should establish a penalty, and one that is certainly not less for those who follow another than for those who themselves have led the way in treasonous activity.* Who was more distinguished in Greece, or more influential, than Themistocles? But that man, after he had liberated Greece from the prospect of slavery by his exercise of supreme command in the Persian war, and after envy had caused him to be driven into exile, did not put up with the unjust treatment of his ungrateful countrymen, as he was duty bound to do: he acted as Coriolanus did twenty years earlier towards his countrymen. Yet neither of these men found a single supporter to assist him in fighting against his country; and so both men committed suicide.*

[43] Accordingly, not only should such a conspiracy of wicked men not be protected by the excuse of friendship but rather it should be punished with the utmost severity in order to stop any man from thinking it permissible to follow even a friend who is waging war on his own country; and yet, in view of the course things have begun to take, I am inclined to think this very thing will come about one of these days;* but I feel more concern for the state of the Republic after my death than I feel for its state today.

[44] So let this be enacted as the first law of friendship:* that we should ask of friends only what is honourable and that we should act honourably on behalf of friends; we should not even wait to be asked, but should constantly show enthusiasm, never hesitation; as to counsel,* we should not be afraid to offer it freely; in friendship the influence of those friends who give good advice should be of first importance, and it should be applied when there is need for advice, not only openly but sharply as well, if occasion demands, and, once applied, it should be obeyed.

[45] Now some men, who are regarded in Greece as wise, I am told, have held some views on this that I find very strange (but there is no topic those fellows will not pursue with their subtleties): some of them hold that excessively close friendships are to be shunned, in case it proves necessary for one person to worry about the welfare of several; each man, they argue, has enough and to spare of his own concerns, and it is irksome to be excessively involved in those of others; the easiest way is to keep as slack a hold as possible on friendship's reins, so that you can draw them in or give them out as you please; for the key to securing a happy life, they conclude, is freedom from care, which one man cannot enjoy if, so to speak, his mind is in labour on behalf of several.*

[46] Again, there are others, I am told, who say, with even less regard for human nature (I touched briefly on this topic a little earlier) that it is for the sake of defence and assistance that friendships should be sought,* not out of kindness and affection; accordingly, the less strength and stability a man possesses, the greater should be his desire to form friendships. The consequence of this argument would be that the protection extended by friendship should be looked for more by the weaker sex* than by men, by the poor more than the rich, by the victims of disastrous fortune more than by those accounted happy.

[47] What remarkable wisdom is this! It is as if they were to deprive the universe of the sun, these people who deprive life of friendship, which is the best and most delightful of all the gifts we have received from the immortal gods. For what is this freedom from care they speak

of? In appearance, indeed, it is attractive; but the truth is that in many situations it should be rejected. It is hardly proper not to undertake any honourable task or action, or to abandon it once undertaken, in order to spare oneself trouble. But if we keep running away from anxiety, we must run away from virtue, which inevitably experiences some anxiety when it is exposed to things contrary to it, finding them repulsive and hateful; as kindness is repelled by malice, self-control by excess, bravery by cowardice; in the same way one may see that just men are most pained by examples of injustice, courageous men by cowardliness, decent men by indecency. Accordingly, it is characteristic of a well-ordered mind to take joy in good things, and to feel distress at their opposite.

[48] And so, if distress of mind is predicable at all of a wise man* (which it surely is, unless we consider that human feeling has been wholly uprooted from his mind), what reason is there why we should remove friendship entirely from life just to avoid having to involve ourselves in some unpleasantness because of it? If you remove the mind's ability to feel emotion, what difference is there, I do not say between a beast of the field and a man, but between a man and the trunk of a tree or a rock or anything else of the same kind? We should not listen to those who would have virtue a thing of hardness, clad in iron, so to speak; indeed, in many situations, and particularly in friendship, it is tender and pliable, so as to expand, as it were, with a friend's good fortune and contract with his bad. And so the worry I spoke of, that we often have to undergo on a friend's behalf, has no more power to take friendship away from life than it has to make us give up virtuous actions because they entail certain anxieties and annoyances. Now, since, as I said before,* it is virtue that draws friendship together, if there should be the appearance of some sign of virtue shining out, as it were, and inviting another person of like mind to join with and attach himself to someone, then, when that happens, it is inevitable that love should arise.

[49] For what can be so ridiculous as to take delight in many empty things, such as honour and fame, buildings or dress or personal adornment, but not to take the keenest delight in a mind furnished with virtue, the one thing which has the capacity for loving or, to coin a phrase, loving back?* For nothing creates more pleasure than receiving a return for one's kindness, or exchanging warm-hearted assistance with another.

[50] Again, suppose we further grant what can quite properly be granted, that nothing has such a capacity for attracting and drawing things to itself, as likeness has in drawing persons together in friendship: then undoubtedly it will be granted as a fact that good men love good men and are attracted to one another, since they are joined as if by a family

relationship or a bond of nature; for there is nothing that seeks to attain things like itself more eagerly or greedily than nature. Accordingly, Fannius and Scaevola, let us agree on this point at least: that, where good men are concerned, between them and other good men goodwill is virtually inevitable, and that this has been determined by nature as the source of friendship. But this same goodness belongs also to men in general; for virtue is not inhuman or brutish or arrogant, in that it is its way to watch over entire nations and to consult their best interests, which it certainly would not do if it had a complete distaste for the affection of ordinary folk.

[51] Again, it is my view that those who imagine that friendships are based on advantage are removing the most delightful bond of friendship. For it is not so much the material gain won through a friend that gives pleasure, as the love of the friend itself; and the very time when what comes from a friend brings delight is when it comes with genuine feeling. And so untrue is it that friendships are cultivated out of need, that it is those who have the least need of another's wealth and resources, and particularly of his virtue (which affords the greatest protection), who are the most generous and kindest of men. And yet I suspect it may not be a good thing either for friends never to lack anything at all; for when would our goodwill have had the chance to show its strength, if Scipio had never been in need of my advice or my assistance either at home or abroad? The friendship did not follow from the quest for advantage, but advantage did follow from friendship.

[52] It will be our duty, then, not to listen to men who are saturated in self-indulgence, whenever they argue about friendship, of which neither in practice nor in theory have they any true understanding.* For what person, in the name of all gods and men, would want to be surrounded by boundless wealth and to live in an abundance of all he might desire, if it meant he should not love anyone or be himself loved by anyone? This is, indeed, the life lived by tyrants,* one in which, of course, there can be no trust, no affection, no confidence in the permanence of goodwill, where every action creates suspicion and anxiety, and friendship has no place.

[53] For who would love either the man he fears, or the man by whom he believes he is feared? It is true that tyrants are cultivated by men who affect friendship for a time, to gain their own advantage. But if, as often happens, they should chance to fall from power, then one understands how poor they were in friends. The story goes that Tarquin,* when he was in exile, remarked that the only time he realized which of his friends were faithful and which unfaithful was when he was no longer able to reward either according to their merits.

[54] And yet, given his arrogance and imperviousness to other men's feelings, it amazes me that he could have any friends at all. Now, just as this man's character, as I said, prevented him from winning true friends, so the riches and influence enjoyed by men of power often stand in the way of true friendships. For not only is fortune itself blind but also it generally makes blind the men it has embraced, with the result that, as a rule, they are swept away by pride and inflexibility. Nothing in the world can be more intolerable than a fool who is blessed by fortune. And we may observe that men who previously were affable in character are changed by power and influence and prosperity; they spurn old friendships and favour new ones.

[55] But what is more foolish, when men have the resources, the influence and the opportunity to gain whatever they wish, than to acquire the other things which money can buy—horses, servants, splendid clothes, costly tableware—but not to acquire friends, who are, if I may so put it, the best and finest kind of furniture for life? Indeed, when they are procuring the other things, they do not know for whom they make these purchases or for whose sake they go to all this trouble; for each of those things belongs to the one who can gain them by his strength. But when it comes to the friendships he has, each man enjoys a permanent and fixed ownership of them, so that, even if those acquisitions, which are, effectively, gifts of fortune, should continue as his property, it remains true that a life devoid of friends and abandoned by them cannot be a happy one.

[56] But enough on this topic. We now must establish in the matter of friendship what are its limits and what are, so to speak, the boundary-markers we are to choose for it. On this subject I see that three views are held, none of which gains my approval: first, that the attitude we have towards a friend should be the same as the attitude we have towards ourselves; second, that our goodwill towards friends should correspond fairly and equally to their goodwill towards us; third, that the value put on a man by his friends should be exactly the same as that he puts on himself.*

[57] I do not agree in the slightest with any of these three opinions. There is certainly no truth in the first one, that a man's attitude to a friend should match his attitude towards himself: consider the number of actions we undertake for friends that we would never undertake for ourselves, such as begging and entreating a favour from an unworthy fellow, or attacking and abusing someone in more forceful terms than we would normally use.* Behaviour of this kind would be quite disgraceful in arguing our own case, but where a friend's interests are

concerned, it brings no disgrace whatever. And there are many occasions when good men substantially curtail their own advantage, or acquiesce in its curtailment, so that, rather than themselves, their friends may reap its benefit.

[58] The second view is the one that defines friendship by an equal exchange of favours and goodwill. Now this surely calls friendship to account in a manner too niggardly and petty, in ensuring that the accounts of favours received and bestowed tally in the register. True friendship, it seems to me, is something richer and more abundant than this; it does not keep a close eye on the account, in case it has paid out more than it has received; for there is no need to fear that something may be lost, or may spill on to the ground, or that one may tie up in a friendship an inequitable amount of one's assets.

[59] But undoubtedly the worst of the three definitions is the third, which requires that the value put on a man by his friends be exactly the same as that he puts on himself. For not infrequently the self-confidence of certain people is low, or their hopes of bettering their lot have been broken. It is not, then, the part of a friend to have the same estimate of such a person as he has of himself, but rather to strive with all his energy to rouse his friend's low spirits, and to awaken in him the spirit of hope and a more positive frame of mind. Accordingly, we must establish a different definition of true friendship, once I have told you something that used to raise the strongest objections from Scipio. He used to remark that no saying more hostile to friendship could have been thought up, than that of whoever said that one should love as if one day he were going to hate. And, he said, he could not be induced to accept the commonly held belief that the author of this statement was Bias, who was regarded as a man of wisdom and one of the Seven:* it had to be the view of some vile person, or an ambitious politician, or someone who regarded everything in relation to furthering his own power. How can anyone be a friend to a man if he thinks he can some day be that man's enemy? Why, in that case he will be bound to desire and pray that his friend may do wrong as often as possible, so as to give him all the more handles, as it were, for finding fault; and, conversely, he will be obliged to feel anxiety, hurt and envy when his friends act well or enjoy good luck.

[60] So this advice, whoever is its author, really has the effect of doing away with friendship. What should rather have been laid down as a rule is that we exercise such care in forming friendships that we should never begin to love someone whom we could one day hate. Indeed, it was Scipio's belief that, even if we had been less than fortunate in making

our choice, we should tolerate this, rather than turn our minds to finding an opportunity for a quarrel.

[61] These, then, are the limits I think we ought to employ. Whenever
the characters of friends are without blemish, there should be between
them a complete community of thoughts and inclinations in all things
without any exception. And even if by some chance it happens that the
wishes of friends are not wholly honourable and yet are in need of our
support in matters which affect their life or reputation, we should turn
aside from the straight path as long as utter disgrace does not ensue.*
There is a definite extent to which friendship permits us to forgive misdemeanours. But we must certainly not ignore the claims of reputation,
nor should we regard the goodwill of our countrymen as a feeble weapon
for achieving life's goals; and, whereas it is a shameful thing to solicit
this by means of flattery and fawning, it is quite wrong to disdain true
virtue, which brings with it popularity.

[62] But it was a regular complaint of Scipio—for I keep returning
to Scipio, who constantly spoke about friendship—that men paid less
attention to it than to all other things; every man could tell you how
many goats and sheep he owned, but he could not say how many friends
he had; and he said that men take care when it comes to getting the
former but are careless in the matter of choosing friends, having, so to
speak, no sure signs and marks* to help them judge those who are suitable for friendship. The men to choose, therefore, are strong and steadfast and dependable, a class of which there is a considerable dearth.
And it is no easy matter to judge except by putting them to the test,
a test which must, however, be made in the course of the friendship
itself. In this way friendship runs ahead of judgement, and eliminates
the opportunity for putting to the test.

[63] It is, then, incumbent on the wise man to restrain the initial
surge of goodwill, as he would pull on a chariot's reins, so that one may
pursue friendship only after submitting our friends' characters to the
test, as we would test the strength of horses. Some men often demonstrate their unreliable nature when an insubstantial sum of money is
concerned; others, however, whom a small sum cannot corrupt, are
found out when the sum is considerable. But if in fact some individuals
are found who think it shameful to put money before friendship, where
shall we find those who do not prefer public honours, offices of state,
military commands, power and wealth to friendship, so that, when these
are set on one side and the demands of friendship on the other, they do
not greatly prefer the former? Human nature is weak when it comes to
rejecting power, and even when men have won this by disregarding

friendship, they think the fact will go unnoticed because their reason for disregarding friendship was not trivial.

[64] And so true friendships are very hard to discover among those who occupy positions of power and engage in public life. For where would you find a man who would be happy for a friend to gain political office in place of himself?* Again, leaving this out of consideration, consider how irksome and difficult most people find association with those who have suffered misfortune: it is no easy thing to find men who would stoop to this level. Although Ennius was in the right when he said 'A faithful friend is found when fortune is fickle',* the majority of men are still convicted of inconstancy and unreliability by one or other of these two traits, when they overlook their friends in prosperous times or abandon them in misfortune. Any man, then, who in either situation has shown himself to be steadfast, consistent and immovable in friendship, should be judged to belong to a breed of men that is especially rare and almost divine.

[65] Now the basis of that stability and steadfastness that we seek in friendship is trustworthiness; nothing is stable which is without trustworthiness.* Besides, it is reasonable to select someone who is frank in nature, sociable and sympathetic, that is, one who is affected by the same things as oneself; and all these things tend towards trustworthiness. A personality that is multi-faceted and devious cannot be trustworthy, and, indeed, a person who remains untouched by the same influences as you are, and who is unsympathetic by nature cannot be either trustworthy or reliable. We should add to this that a friend ought never to be eager to bring forward accusations or to believe them once they are brought; all this has relevance to that steadfastness which I have been discussing for some time now. Accordingly, it comes about that the truth of my remarks at the outset is established: friendship cannot exist except in good men. For it is incumbent on a good man, whom we are at liberty to call also a wise man,* to keep these two rules in friendship: first, that there should be no dissembling or pretence (for even an open display of hatred is more worthy of a free man than concealing one's opinion behind a misleading face) and second, that he should not only rebuff accusations brought by any person but neither should he himself entertain any suspicions and constantly think that some offence has been committed by a friend.

[66] To this we must add the ingredient of a certain pleasantness of conversation and manner, which is a by no means trivial seasoning for friendship. Sternness and strictness in all matters may well possess a certain quality of impressiveness, but friendship ought to be more relaxed and genial and agreeable, and tend more towards courteousness and tolerance.

[67] But here there arises a question of some difficulty: whether there are times when we should prefer new friends who deserve our friendship to old ones, as we are accustomed to prefer young horses to old ones. This sort of doubt is beneath the dignity of a civilized person. We should not become weary of friendships as we do of other things. The oldest should bring us the greatest pleasure, as do those wines which improve with age, and there is truth in the saying that a man must eat many bags of salt together, if he is to fulfil friendship's requirements.*

[68] Now, while we should not reject novelty, if like a green cornfield it offers hope of a healthy harvest in time, we should still maintain old friendship in its proper place, for the force of lengthy acquaintance and habit is not inconsiderable. Why, even in the case of horses, to return to my earlier comparison, unless some particular reason prevented it, there is no one who would not use one he has grown used to rather than a new and unbroken one. Indeed habit exerts its force not only in the case of horses, which are living creatures, but also where inanimate things are concerned, since we take pleasure in places where we have stayed a long time, even when they are mountainous and wild.

[69] But it is of the greatest importance in friendship that inferiors should be treated as equals. Not infrequently an individual will stand out above the rest, as Scipio did in what I may call our crowd. At no time did he put himself before Philus or Rupilius* or Mummius,* or friends of lower rank; and in the case of his brother Quintus Maximus,* who was no doubt a distinguished man, though not at all on his level, he had regard for his greater age and so treated him as his superior. His wish was that through him all his friends could enhance their standing in the eyes of other men.

[70] This is a practice that all men should follow and seek to imitate. If a man possesses some outstanding quality, be it moral or intellectual or based on wealth, he should share it with his friends and impart it to those around him, so that if he was born of lowly parents or has relatives who are weaker in intelligence or fortune, he should increase their wealth and be a source of honour and prestige for them. It should be as we find in legends, where those who have lived the life of slaves through ignorance of their lineage and family, when they are recognized and found to be the sons of gods or kings, still keep their affection for the shepherds whom they regarded for many years as their fathers. And this must, of course, happen all the more where true and undoubted parents are concerned. It is when it is shared with our nearest and dearest that the greatest benefit of intelligence or virtue or any outstanding quality is felt.

[71] Accordingly, just as the superior partners in a friendship or association should make themselves equal to the inferior, so the inferior should not feel resentment at being surpassed by their friends in talent, fortune or standing in the world. Many of these people either complain constantly about some particular matter or actually make it a cause of reproach, all the more so if they think they have done anything which they can speak of as an act of service or friendship or as having cost them a certain amount of effort. A disagreeable class of people it certainly is who reduce their services to a reproach, when duty prescribes that these are acts to be remembered warmly by the receiver and not repeatedly mentioned by the doer.*

[72] And so, just as those who are superior should not stand on their dignity in a friendship, so those who are inferior should, so to speak, lift themselves up. There are people who make friendship a chore by supposing that they are being passed over; but this practically only happens to those who consider that they actually deserve to be passed over. These should be relieved of such a view not only by reasoned discussion but also by practical assistance. [73] But when it comes to the amount of consideration one should show, each friend should be given, firstly, as much as you are able to manage yourself, and, secondly, as much as the person whom you like and seek to help is able to take.* For no matter how much you excel, you cannot raise all your friends to the highest honours, as Scipio was able to do when he made Publius Rupilius consul but failed in the case of that man's brother Lucius. But even if you were able to confer on another man any honour you pleased, you would still have to consider that man's ability to support it.

[74] As a rule friendships should be judged only after the intellect and age of both parties have reached full maturity and strength. If one was enthusiastic about hunting or ball-games in boyhood, that is no reason for keeping as friends those one liked at that time because they had the same passion. On that principle the greatest claim on our goodwill will be that of our nurses and tutors, simply because they have known us for such a long time. They are not of course to be neglected but [should be valued] in some other way. Otherwise lasting friendships cannot endure. Different ways of life are accompanied by different interests, and different interests drive a wedge between friendships. Indeed there is no other reason why good men cannot be the friends of bad men, or bad men of good, except that there exists between them the greatest possible difference of way of life and interests.

[75] The following rule can also be laid down, that there should not be, as often happens, an excess of goodwill towards one's friends, which

gets in the way of their real interests. Indeed, to return to legends, Neoptolemus would not have been able to capture Troy, had he been willing to listen to Lycomedes, in whose home he had been raised, when he tried amid floods of tears to stop him making that journey.* There are often strong reasons why it is necessary for us to part from friends; and anyone who seeks to block these, saying that he will find it hard to bear his friend's absence, is not only unmanly and soft in nature but for that very reason not sufficiently capable of behaving as a friend should.

[76] And in every case one should consider both what it is that you are asking of a friend and what you are prepared to do in order to oblige him. There are times, moreover, when an unavoidable loss must be borne in terminating friendships (our discussion slips now from comradeships enjoyed by the wise to friendships of the ordinary kind).* Frequently the faults of friends burst out, sometimes affecting their friends themselves, sometimes strangers, but the loss of reputation they cause still washes back over the friends. Friendships like this, then, should be dissolved through gradually reducing the habit of spending time together, and, as I have heard Cato say,* they should be unravelled rather than torn apart, unless some flagrant act of wrong has been perpetrated which is hardly to be tolerated, so that it is not right or honourable or even within the bounds of possibility that there should not be an immediate estrangement and separation.

[77] But if, as often happens, some change of character or interests comes about, or if there arises a difference of views in political matters (for I speak now, as I said a short while ago, not about friendships of the wise but those of ordinary men), we will have to guard against creating the impression that not only has a friendship been ended but also a quarrel begun. There is nothing that so detracts from honour than waging war against someone with whom you have lived on terms of friendship. As you are both aware, Scipio brought his friendship with Quintus Pompeius to an end on my account, and due to a disagreement in politics he ceased to be friends with our colleague Metellus.* In each instance he behaved with dignity and self-control, and, though offended, he stopped short of rancour.

[78] One should take pains, therefore, first of all to prevent separations of friends; but if something of this sort does come about, we should strive to give the impression that the friendship has burned out naturally, and has not been suddenly snuffed out. But we must also guard against the transformation of friendships into serious quarrels, leading to confrontations in public, abuse and insults. Yet even such exchanges should be tolerated if they can be, and the previous friendship should be

respected to the extent that the perpetrator of the wrong should be held to blame, not the victim. In short, there is only one precaution and provision against all these faults and misfortunes, namely that one should not begin a friendship too quickly and one should not form attachments with those who do not deserve it.

[79] Now, by 'those who deserve friendship' I mean those who contain within themselves the reason why they should be loved—a rare breed; and indeed rarity belongs to all fine things, and there is no task more difficult than to discover a thing that is in all respects perfect of its kind. But most men do not recognize anything in human life as good unless it brings some profit, and, as with the beasts on their farms, they give the most affection to those friends who they think will bring them the greatest profit.

[80] The result is that they deny themselves the fairest and most natural form of friendship, which men desire in itself and for its own sake; and they do not grasp from their own experience the power of this friendship, its quality and greatness. For each man loves himself, not with the aim of acquiring from himself the reward of affection, but because we all naturally value ourselves; and, without the application of this same principle to friendship, a true friend will never be found, for such a man is, as it were, another self.*

[81] But if this is plain to see in animals,* birds, fish and beasts, both tame and wild, first that they love themselves (for this feeling is born in every living creature alike), then that they desire and eagerly seek out animals of the same kind with which to form attachments, and do this with a sense of longing and with something akin to human love, how much more naturally does this occur in man, who both loves himself and searches for another whose mind he may so mingle with his own as virtually to produce one out of two.*

[82] But many people out of perversity, not to say shamelessness, want a friend to be the kind of man they cannot be themselves, and require friends to provide what they themselves fail to give in return. The equitable thing, however, is first of all to be a good man yourself and then to look for another who resembles you. It is among such men that we can ensure that stability of friendship we have been discussing all this while, when people united by ties of goodwill will first of all master those desires that enslave other men, then will delight in fairness and justice, each man undertaking any task for the other's sake, and never asking the other for anything unless it is honourable and right; and they will not only give each other support and affection but also respect; for the man who removes from friendship the feeling of respect* removes its greatest ornament.

[83] Accordingly a fatal error is made by those who suppose that friendship creates the licence to indulge every kind of self-indulgence and to commit every kind of crime. Friendship has been given to us by nature as a helper in virtue, not a companion in criminality, so that, as the highest goals cannot be attained by virtue in isolation,* it should reach them when joined with another as its ally. If any men there are between whom there exists, has existed or will exist an alliance like this, we must regard theirs as the finest and happiest comradeship on the road to nature's highest good.

[84] This, I say, is the alliance in which dwell all the things men consider worthy of pursuit—honour, glory, peace of mind and delight: those things whose presence makes life happy and whose absence unhappy. And inasmuch as this is the finest and greatest thing, if it is our aim to obtain it, we must give our attention to virtue, without which we cannot attain either friendship or anything else we desire. But those who think they have friends while ignoring virtue, come to realize their mistake in the end, when some considerable misfortune forces them to learn from experience.

[85] Accordingly (for not once but several times it must be said) one should judge before making friends, not make friends before forming a judgement.* But our remissness in many matters makes us suffer, and this is particularly the case in the way we select and treat our friends; we make plans the wrong way round and revisit cases that are closed, contravening the old proverb;* for once we have become involved in reciprocal ties, either through long-standing association or even the exchange of services, suddenly, at the outbreak of some cause of offence, we sever friendships when they have run only half their course.

[86] We should, then, deplore all the more such carelessness in regard to a matter which is the most essential. For the one thing in human affairs on whose value all men unanimously agree is friendship. Even virtue itself is despised by many men, who describe it as imposture and ostentation; many look down on wealth, finding contentment in a little and pleasure in a modest way of life; as regards honours, which fill some men with a burning desire, how many regard these with such contempt that they think nothing more trivial or less important! The same is true of other things that some people think wonderful: in every case there are many who regard them as worth nothing; but when it comes to friendship, all to a man think the same thing: those who are engaged in politics, those whose delight is science and learning, those who mind their own business, taking no further interest in public affairs, and, last of all, those who devote themselves completely to the pursuit of

pleasure. They all believe that without friendship life is nothing, if, that is, they wish to live to any degree at all the life of civilized men.*

[87] For friendship steals into everyone's life in some way or other, and does not allow any mode of life to be untouched by its presence. Indeed, even if anyone exists whose nature is so harsh and wild that he shuns and hates the company of men, as we are told a certain Timon of Athens* was, yet even he would not be able to endure not finding someone to whom he could spew out the venom of his bitterness. And this could be recognized most easily if something like the following situation were possible: that some god might remove us from this human throng and set us in some desolate place, providing us there in abundant supply with all the things desired by nature but depriving us of the power to set eyes on any human being at all. Who would have such an iron soul that he could endure a life such as this? Would solitude not rob him of the enjoyment of all his pleasures?

[88] So it is a true saying that I have heard our elders say was regularly expressed by Archytas of Tarentum,* I think, and which they themselves had heard from the generation before them: if anyone were to ascend into the heavens and there see clearly the beauty of the stars and the true nature of the universe, that wondrous sight would afford him no delight, though it would be most delightful if he had someone to whom he could describe the experience. So it is that human nature loves nothing solitary* and constantly, as it were, leans towards some support, and the dearer the friend, the greater the pleasure derived from this. But although this same nature of ours demonstrates by so many signs what it wants, and what it seeks and longs to have, yet somehow or other we become deaf and fail to hear the warnings it gives. The experience we have of friendship is varied and diverse, and often there spring up causes of suspicion and offence, which the wise man will sometimes ignore, sometimes make light of, and sometimes tolerate. There is one instance where it is necessary not to take offence seriously in order that the advantages inherent in friendship might be preserved, as well as the requirements of honesty. Often it is necessary to give not just advice but also criticism to friends, and these, when done with good will, should be taken in good part.*

[89] But in some way or other it is true what my good friend says in his *Woman of Andros*: 'Complaisance gets us friends, the truth, hatred'.* The truth can create trouble, if indeed it gives rise to dislike, which poisons friendship; but complaisance is much more troublesome, as it is tolerant of a friend's misdeeds and allows him to rush away out of control. The greatest fault, however, is in the one who rejects the truth and

is driven to a position of self-deception by his complaisance. Accordingly, in this matter it is necessary to employ all reason and care, firstly that advice is offered without acrimony, and secondly that criticism is free from insult. And in the case of complaisance (since we are happy to adopt Terence's word), let courtesy be present, and let flattery, that encourages faults, be banished afar, since it is not even worthy of a free man, let alone a friend; we do not live on the same terms with a tyrant as we do with a friend.*

[90] But if a man's ears are so closed to the truth that he is unable to hear what is true from a friend, one should lose all hope for the health of his morals. In this regard, as so often, Cato had something witty to say:* some people, he said, owe a greater debt to bitter enemies than to friends who wear smiles of approval, as the former often speak the truth, the latter never. It is ridiculous that when men are criticized, they do not feel annoyed by what should annoy them, but they are annoyed by what should not; they are not pained by having done wrong, but take it amiss that they are receiving a rebuke, whereas on the contrary they ought to be upset at their offence and pleased to be corrected.

[91] And so, since it is characteristic of true friendship to give as well as to receive advice, in the former case freely but not unkindly, in the latter patiently and not reluctantly, so we should think that there is no greater plague for friendships than fawning, flattery, obsequiousness—however many names you may give it, it deserves to be branded as a fault peculiar to dishonest and insincere men who say everything with a view to pleasure and nothing with a view to the truth.

[92] Now, pretence in any form is immoral, for it pollutes the truth and removes one's ability to see it, but most of all it is opposed to friendship, as it destroys that truthfulness without which the name of friendship cannot have any significance. Inasmuch as the effect of friendship is, as it were, to make many minds become one,* how can this come about if not even in one individual man will there be a mind that is always one and the same, but rather one that is changeable and fluctuating and many-sided?

[93] What can be as fickle and crooked as the mind of someone who changes to suit not only the wishes and views of another but even the expression of his face or his every gesture?—'Someone says no, no say I; he says yes, yes, say I; in short I've given myself orders to agree with everything', as Terence also says, this time in the character of Gnatho.* It would be entirely silly to use this man as an example of a friend, [94] but there is no shortage of people like Gnatho who are superior to him in position, fortune and reputation, and they are the ones whose flattery

grates on the ear, when their empty remarks are supported by their powerful status.

[95] But it is possible to separate a flatterer from a true friend and to distinguish between them by applying a watchful eye, just as all things false and feigned may be distinguished from what is genuine and real. A public assembly may be composed of the most ignorant men but it generally manages to tell the difference between a demagogue,* that is, a dishonest politician who flatters his audience, and a dependable man who has both honesty and authority.

[96] What words of flattery did Gaius Papirius recently pour into the ears of the assembly to ingratiate himself, when he was proposing a law that tribunes of the people might be re-elected!* We put the arguments against this, but I shall say nothing of myself, as I much prefer to speak of Scipio's part. Immortal gods! What dignity, what majesty there was in his speech! One could tell easily that he was not merely one of the Roman people but their leader. But you were both there, and the speech is available. Accordingly a law of the people was rejected by the votes of the people.* Again, to return to myself, you remember when Quintus Maximus, brother of Scipio, and Lucius Mancinus were consuls, how popular apparently was the law on priesthoods proposed by Gaius Licinius Crassus:* election to the priestly colleges was to be handed over to the people. He was the first politician to face towards the forum when addressing the people.* Nevertheless, piety towards the immortal gods (together with our counter-arguments) easily defeated his tena-penny oratory. And this was done when I was praetor, five years before my election to the consulship.* Thus the issue was decided more on its own merits than through the influence of one holding the highest office.

[97] But if on the public stage, that is to say the assembly of the people, where there lies the greatest scope for falsehood and confusion, the truth still prevails, if only it is exposed and brought into the light of day, what should be the case with friendship, which depends for its existence wholly on truthfulness? There, unless you can, as the saying goes, both see an open heart and reveal one of your own, you cannot be assured of anything or know anything for certain, not even the satisfaction of loving or being loved, as you do not know how genuine these emotions are. And yet this flattery we spoke of, however destructive it may be, cannot harm anyone except the man who is taken in by it and finds delight in it. And so it happens that the man who opens his ears particularly to flatterers is the one who flatters himself and takes more delight in himself than in anything else.

[98] I grant that virtue loves itself; it knows itself better than any other does, and understands how much it is deserving of love; however, it is not virtue I am now talking about, but the opinion people have of their virtue. Not as many people are endowed with virtue as wish to appear to be so endowed. These are the people who take pleasure in being flattered, and when they are exposed to talk that is fashioned to suit their fancy they regard this meaningless verbiage as proof of their own merits. There is, then, no friendship when one party is unwilling to hear the truth and the other is ready for the telling of lies. And we would not find any humour in the flattery of parasites in comedies, if there were no boastful soldiers. 'You tell me that Thais is really very grateful to me?' It would have been sufficient to make the reply 'Yes, very'. 'No, hugely,' he says.* The flatterer always exaggerates whatever his eager listener thinks important.

[99] Accordingly, although that kind of empty flattery carries weight only with those who attract and invite it themselves, yet even men of a more serious and steadfast nature should be warned to guard against being taken in by flattery in its more subtle form. The man who employs flattery in an open way does not go undetected by anyone, unless he is a complete fool; but we need to exercise persistent care against the clever and sly type in case he worms his way into our confidence. It is far from easy to recognize this sort of fellow, since his eagerness to please often appears as opposition to one's views, and his flattery masquerades as contrary argument, until in the end he concedes the battle and admits himself beaten, so that the victim of his cruel deception appears to have been right from the start. Nothing brings more shame on a man than being made a fool, and all the more care must be taken to avoid this happening to us.

> Of all the old fools you see in every play
> Not one is half as duped as you've made me today!*

[100] Even on stage this is the silliest character portrayed, that of the gullible old men who take no thought for the future. But in some way or other our discussion has meandered from the friendships of men without fault, that is, from men who are wise (the wisdom I speak of is that which a human being is thought to be capable of attaining)* and descended to friendships of little worth. Accordingly, let us return to that original topic, and finally bring to an end our thinking on that. It is virtue, virtue, I say, Gaius Fannius, and you, Quintus Mucius, that both creates the bond of friendship and makes it last. Here lies all harmony, all permanence, all trust. Whenever it rises up and displays its light,

and discerns and recognizes the same thing in another, it moves towards it and in turn receives the light it provides, which causes love or friendship to leap into flame, for both derive their power from loving; and loving is quite simply showing affection for the one you love for his own sake, without considering any need one has or advantage one might gain. But advantage does blossom forth from friendship, even if it was not the goal you were particularly aiming at.

[101] It was this feeling of goodwill that prompted me as a young man to feel affection for those men of older years, Lucius Paulus, Marcus Cato, Gaius Galus,* Publius Nasica,* and Tiberius Gracchus, father-in-law of my dear Scipio.* This feeling shines out even more among contemporaries, as between Scipio, Lucius Furius, Publius Rupilius, Spurius Mummius,* and myself. But in turn, now that old age has come to us, we find pleasure in the affection of young men such as yourselves and Quintus Tubero,* and, for my own part, I take delight also in the company of Publius Rutilius* and Aulus Verginius,* who are still very young. And since the nature of our life is so composed that one generation must follow on another, one should, of course, wish most of all to be able, as the saying goes, to reach the finishing-line alongside men of the same age, those with whom you began the race; [102] but inasmuch as human affairs are frail and transient, we must constantly be on the lookout for people who can give us affection and receive it in turn from us. For if affection and goodwill are taken away, every joy is taken away from life. In my own eyes, although he was suddenly snatched away, Scipio still lives and will always live. It was that man's virtue I loved, and it has not died. Not only is it continually before my eyes, as I had it always within my reach, but it will also be illustrious and celebrated among generations of the future. No man will ever shoulder with courage or hope the greater tasks of life without thinking he should keep before him the memory and example of that man.

[103] For my part, of all the good things either fortune or nature has bestowed on me, I have nothing else I can compare with Scipio's friendship. In it I found agreement on public matters, in it, advice on private business, in it also, relaxation filled with delight. Never did I offend him, so far as I was aware, even in the slightest matter, and there was never a single word I heard from him I would have wished unspoken. We had one house,* one way of life that we shared in common, and we were together not only on military service but also when we journeyed abroad or took holidays in the country.

[104] What should I say of our eagerness to be constantly investigating and learning something, in which, far from the people's gaze, we spent

all our leisure time?* If my recollection and memory of these things had perished together with him, I could in no way endure the loss of a man so close to me, so much in my heart. But those things are not dead, rather they are nourished and increased as I remember them and dwell on them in thought. And even had I been entirely deprived of them, my time of life itself would still bring me great comfort; for it cannot be that I should have to bear this loss much longer; and every trial that is brief ought to be tolerable, even if it is severe.* This is all I had to say about friendship; but for your part, I encourage you both so to value virtue, without which friendship cannot exist, that, with the one exception of virtue, there is nothing you consider finer than friendship.

APPENDIX

TWO LETTERS TO FRIENDS

Letter from Cicero to Gaius Matius (Letters to his Friends 11.27)

Tusculum, end of August 44 BC

[1] I have not yet quite decided whether I am more irritated or pleased by our friend Trebatius' visit,* though he is such an obliging fellow and so devoted to both of us. I had just reached my villa at Tusculum in the evening, and early in the morning of the next day he came to see me, despite not yet having properly regained his strength. When I took him to task over not paying enough attention to his health, he said he had found nothing harder to wait for than the opportunity of seeing me. 'Is there any news?' I asked. Then he told me about your complaint,* but before I give you my answer to that, just let me make a few points.

[2] As far as my memory allows me to go back into the past, I have no older friend than yourself. But while a number of others may claim to have some attachment to such a lengthy friendship, they cannot claim to share in its depth of affection. I formed an attachment to you the day I made your acquaintance, and my judgement told me that this affection was returned. Your subsequent departure for a long time, my interest in politics, and the difference between our chosen lifestyles* did not allow our friendly feelings to jell through time spent together. Yet your warm feelings for me I had cause to recognize many years before the civil war, when Caesar was in Gaul.* You succeeded in bringing about what you strongly believed was to my advantage, and not without advantage to Caesar himself, namely his affection and respect for me, together with a place among his intimate acquaintances. In those days there passed between us many conversations, many letters and many communications expressive of the warmest friendship, but these I pass over, as they were followed by more serious events.

[3] At the outset of the civil war,* when you were making your way towards Brundisium to see Caesar, you broke your journey to visit me at my villa at Formiae. First of all, how significant was that in itself, particularly at that time! Secondly, do you imagine that I have forgotten your advice, your conversation, your kindness? In all this Trebatius, I remember, was a participant. And I have not, of course, forgotten the letter you sent me* on the occasion of your coming to meet Caesar in the district, I think, of Trebula.

[4] There followed that time when I set out on my way to Pompey,* compelled by my sense of shame, or, it may be, a sense of duty, or mere chance. What obligation or favour did you fail to perform, either towards me in my absence or towards my family who were there? What person in the judgement of all my people was a greater friend both to me and to themselves? I came to

Brundisium.* Do you think I have forgotten the speed with which you flew from Tarentum to my side, the moment the news reached your ears? Or how you sat down beside me and spoke to me, strengthening my resolve, broken as it was by my fear of the wretched fate we all faced?

[5] Finally the time arrived when we began to live our lives in Rome.* Our friendship was in every way complete. In the most important matters I had the benefit of your counsel as to how I should behave towards Caesar, in every other respect, of your kindness; with the exception of Caesar, you paid no one else the compliment of regularly paying visits to his house and spending many hours there often in the most agreeable conversation. That too, if you remember, was the time when you urged me to write these examples of *ouvrage philosophique.** After Caesar's return you made it your primary concern that I should be on the friendliest terms with him. In this you succeeded.

[6] What, then, is the point of this oration which has gone on longer than I had meant? It is because I was surprised that you, who should know all this, ever believed I could have been guilty of any action that would disturb the harmony of our friendship. Quite apart from the facts I have spoken of, which are certified and conspicuous, I have in my recollection many others of a more private nature, which I am scarcely able to put into words. I take delight in all your qualities, but above all in the finest of all, both your loyalty as a friend, your judgement, your dignity and your steadfastness, and also in your wit, your kindness and your scholarship.

[7] And so I now return to your complaint.* On the matter of your having voted in favour of that notorious law,* my initial reaction was not to believe it; then, if I had believed it, I should never think you had done so without some valid reason. While your standing in men's eyes means that all your actions are observed, the spitefulness of the world causes some of these to be interpreted more harshly than is warranted. If such criticism fails to reach your ears, I do not know what to say; for my part, if ever I do hear such talk, I defend you as stoutly as I know you are in the habit of defending me against my traducers. This defence, however, takes two forms: there are some things that I am accustomed to deny flatly, as in the case of this very vote; there are others that I would justify as actions you have taken out of loyalty and human sympathy, such as your management of the games.*

[8] But to a man as learned as yourself it must be clear that, if Caesar was a king, as in my view he was,* it is possible to take two opposite views of your moral stance, either the one I adopt as a rule, that your loyalty and generosity of spirit in showing affection to a friend even after his death deserve praise, or the one taken by several, that the freedom of one's country is to be preferred to the life of a friend. How I wish that out of all this talk the arguments I advanced had been reported to you! But there is no man who speaks more gladly or more frequently than I about those two praiseworthy actions of yours. I refer to how you used all the weight of your authority to prevent the commencement of civil war, and, subsequently, to advocate restraint in the

hour of victory; and in this I have found no man to disagree with me. This is why I feel gratitude towards our good friend Trebatius, who gave me the excuse for writing this letter. If it fails to convince you, you will be guilty of judging me lacking in all loyalty and kindness; nothing could be a heavier burden upon me than this, or more incompatible with your own nature.

Letter from Gaius Matius to Cicero (Letters to his Friends, 11.28)

Rome, 43 BC

[1] Your letter brought me great pleasure, because I discovered that your opinion of me is what I had hoped and prayed for. Although I never doubted this opinion, still the great importance I attached to it made me strain every sinew to keep it undiminished. But I was aware that I had done nothing that could give offence to any good citizen,* and so I was the less inclined to believe that you, a man noted for so many excellent accomplishments, could have been persuaded recklessly* to any such view, especially when I considered how heartfelt and constant has been, and is, the goodwill I feel towards you. Now that I know that all is as I wished, I shall reply to those accusations which you have many times countered on my behalf,* as was to be expected in view of the exceptional goodness of your heart and the friendship we share.

[2] I know well the charges that men have levelled at me since Caesar died. They count it as a fault that I feel distress at the death of a dear friend and resentment at the fall of one I loved. They say that one's country should be preferred to friendship, just as if they have already proved that his death was of benefit to the state. But I shall not resort to any sophistry here. I admit to not having reached that philosophical level.* I did not follow Caesar, but a friend whom I did not desert in our civil discord, however much his behaviour offended me; nor did I at any time give my approval to civil war, or even to the cause of the breach, advocating most strenuously that it be stifled at its very birth. Consequently, when my personal friend proved victorious, I was not seduced by the charms of promotion or wealth, rewards which the rest indulged in without restraint, although their influence with Caesar was less than mine. What is more, my own private estate was curtailed by the very law of Caesar that enabled the majority of those who now rejoice in Caesar's death to keep their place in the community.* I was as energetic in arguing for mercy to be shown to conquered fellow-citizens as I was in securing my own life.

[3] Is it, then, possible that I, whose wish it was that all men remain unharmed, should not resent the fall of the man who granted this wish, especially when the very same men were responsible for his unpopularity as well as his death?* 'Well, you'll be sorry for it', they say, 'seeing that you dare to condemn our action.' What unheard of arrogance! To think that some are free to boast of a crime, while others may not even deplore it without suffering punishment! Yet even slaves have always had this much freedom, to entertain hope, to feel fear and happiness and sorrow as their own hearts, not

their masters, dictated; and now these privileges they are attempting to wrest from us by intimidation, these 'champions of liberty'*—the phrase they keep dinning in our ears.

[4] But they are wasting their time. No peril through its terrors will make me desert the cause of duty or what becomes a human being. Never have I thought that an honourable death should be shunned, often that it should even be embraced. But why do they have feelings of anger towards me for wishing that they regret what they have done? My desire is that Caesar's death should wound the hearts of all men. Ah, but my duty as a loyal citizen is to wish the republic safe. Well, if the life I have so far led, together with my hopes for the future, do not without words give assurance that this is my earnest wish, I make no claim to prove it by making speeches.

[5] Accordingly I ask you urgently to weigh actions more seriously than words, and, if you feel that expediency lies in doing the right thing,* to take my word for it that it is impossible to have any fellowship with men who are wicked. Am I, then, in the autumn of my years, to make a thorough revision of the principles I adhered to in my younger days, when I might have been forgiven even for a bad error of judgement, and with my own hands unpick the fabric of my life? I will not do it; nor will I venture on a course of action that would win me enemies, except that I deplore the grievous fall of one who was most closely bound to me in friendship and a man of the greatest distinction. But even if my thoughts were otherwise, I would never disclaim my actions and thereby be thought not only a villain in criminality but also a cowardly hypocrite in seeking to hide it.

[6] Ah, but I took responsibility for running the games held by the young Caesar* to celebrate Caesar's victory. Yes, but this has to do with a private obligation, not with the state of the republic. It was in any case a service I was bound to perform as a tribute to the memory and distinguished career of one I held most dear, even when he was dead, and which was impossible for me to refuse when asked by a young man of the highest promise and so completely worthy of Caesar.

[7] I have also on many occasions visited the house of Antony the consul* to pay my respects; but as for those who suppose me to be lacking in love for my country, you will find that they are constantly thronging at his door, to ask for something and carry off some privilege. But what presumption is this, that while Caesar never banned me from enjoying the company of friends of my choice, even men for whom he had no personal liking, those who have robbed me of my friend should attempt by slandering me to prevent my choosing what friends I please!

[8] I have no fear, however, either that my moderate way of life will fail to eclipse the malice of gossip in time to come, or that even those who do not love me because of my loyalty to Caesar will not prefer to have friends who resemble me rather than themselves. For myself, if my prayers are answered, I shall pass the remainder of my life in retirement at Rhodes;* but if some accident intervenes to the contrary, I shall be in Rome but only as one whose

constant desire is that things are done properly. I am most grateful to our friend Trebatius for having revealed your frank and warm feelings towards me and for having made it my duty more rightly than ever to revere and respect one whom I have always been pleased to hold in affection. A hearty farewell to you and continue to hold me in your affection.

EXPLANATORY NOTES

Unless otherwise indicated, all dates are BC.

TUSCULAN DISPUTATIONS, BOOK 1

1 *advocacy and my senatorial duties*: the ordinary courts ceased to operate under Caesar's dictatorship; C. resisted pressure to attend the senate, the spontaneous delivery of *On Behalf of Marcellus* in the autumn of 46, in response to Caesar's act of clemency, being exceptional. C. stresses the positive side of his leisure but his 'freedom' hints at the general lack of political freedom.

on your recommendation, Brutus: Marcus Junius Brutus, a nephew of the younger Cato and later a leader of the plot to kill Caesar, had, like Cicero, been pardoned by Caesar after fighting for Pompey in the civil war. In 44 he would serve as urban praetor. C.'s choice of a Republican close to the dictator was prudent, but Brutus had himself written on philosophy, though his mentor, the Academic Antiochus of Ascalon, was against the scepticism of Cicero's teacher Philo of Larissa. Brutus' book *On Virtue* apparently taught that virtue alone is sufficient for the happy life, as C. testifies at the start of Book 5, where he reaches the same conclusion. It was a literary convention to attribute inspiration for a work to the dedicatee, but *Brutus* 11 mentions a specific letter from Brutus. C. also dedicated to him the *Paradoxes of the Stoics*, the *Orator*, *On Ends*, and *On the Nature of the Gods*.

to relinquish: for C.'s early interest in philosophy, see Introduction, pp. ix–x. At 1.7 he mentions the contribution of philosophy to his success as an orator, and he notes his continued reading of it, even when politically active, in *On Duties* 2.4 and *On the Nature of the Gods* 1.6, 'I pursued it most keenly when I least appeared to do so.'

'philosophy', as it is called: the Greek word *philosophia* means 'love of wisdom', so C.'s pursuit of wisdom brings out the idea that it is a means to an end, incorporating the theory and teaching of the right way to live, something which, as he goes on to suggest in 1.2, the Roman ancestors understood by nature and practised.

Greek writings and instructors: C.'s imagined pupil has encountered Greek philosophy in writing, notably Plato, and has been to Athens to listen to philosophical lectures. In this work C. is not only writing philosophy in Latin but represents himself as teaching it.

their serious efforts: C. often notes that learned Romans thought philosophy best read in Greek (*Academic Books* 1.4–5; *On Ends* 1.1) and answers their objections by appealing to the willingness of the Romans to read Latin poets who imitated Greek models and Greek writers who imitated earlier ones. Here he goes further and claims that the inherent wisdom of the Romans and their ability to improve on others' achievements will enable them to outdo the Greeks in philosophy. In 2.6 he will argue that Roman philosophical writing, if taken up by those with the requisite education and ability, can eventually render Greek philosophical writings otiose.

2 *comparison with our forbears*: C. here celebrates the *mores maiorum*, the traditional Roman virtues and achievements deriving from nature and training, not from book learning like Greek moral philosophy (cf. Quintilian 12.2.30: 'Greek superiority in moral precept is matched by Roman pre-eminence in examples of conduct—which is the greater thing'). Like Virgil in the *Aeneid* 6.847–53, he stresses Roman excellence in government and law, and in military conquest.

3 *before Rome was founded . . . reign of Romulus*: C.'s cultural history here is in the spirit of the antiquarianism fashionable at this time. Atticus had just compiled a *Liber annalis*, which C. used for the *Brutus*: it correlated events in Roman history with happenings in the Greek world. The canonical date of the foundation of Rome, fixed by C.'s contemporary Varro, was 753, when Romulus became king. Archilochus is usually dated to the seventh century.

Livius . . . Naevius: regarded as the first Latin author, Livius Andronicus was a freed slave who translated the *Odyssey* and adapted some Greek plays. The date referred to here is 240, and the subject of 'who was older' is Livius, who was older than Naevius, author of a lost epic on the First Punic War, and Plautus, the writer of extant comedies, and his younger contemporary Ennius, epic and dramatic poet, born in 239.

It is stated . . . piper: the *Antiquities* (*Origines*) was the first historical work in Latin, in which the Elder M. Porcius Cato dealt with the early history of Rome and Italian towns. Consul in 195 and censor in 184, he was a renowned orator. C. knew 150 of his speeches. Cato was famous for his opposition to the importation of Greek culture, though he knew the language and literature well. The statement, which may come from the prologue to Cato's work, is mentioned again in 4.3. Here it has to be discounted as counter-evidence to early Roman contempt for poetry.

Nobilior . . . Ennius to Aetolia: M. Fulvius Nobilior conquered the Aetolians in 189 as consul and brought back statues of the Muses, which were housed in the temple of Hercules. Ennius celebrated his exploits and was a prolific writer. His epic about Rome, the *Annals*, was written in Greek hexameter metre, whereas Livius and Naevius had used the native Saturnian verse. Cato may have contrasted the poet-clients of his day with an ancestral song culture (Gildenhard 2007, 136, n. 144).

4 *Fabius Pictor . . . Polyclitus and Parrhasius*: C. Fabius Pictor decorated the walls of the Temple of Salus in 302. As an aristocrat, he would wish to be regarded as an amateur. Polyclitus and Parrhasius were (respectively) a famous Greek sculptor and painter of the late fifth century.

Epaminondas . . . deficient in culture: Cornelius Nepos, in his *On Illustrious Men*, also comments on the different Greek attitude to musical accomplishments among the elite. Epaminondas was a Theban general of the early fourth century, Themistocles a leading Athenian statesman of the fifth century and architect of the victory at Salamis against the Persians.

5 *the orator, not at first the learned one*: C. here distinguishes between the Elder Cato, whose oratory was not based on Greek theories of rhetoric, and the orators in the later second century, such as Ser. Sulpicius Galba (consul 144), Scipio Africanus the younger and his friend Laelius (consul 140), C. Papirius Carbo (consul 120), and the two tribunes, Tiberius and Gaius Gracchus. Cicero's recent work, the *Brutus*, had given a history of Roman oratory.

Philosophy . . . any illumination in Latin literature: C.'s fails to mention the great Epicurean poet Lucretius, whose hexameter poem *On the Nature of Things* he praises in a letter to his brother (*Quint. fr.* 2.10(9).3), but only for its poetic quality. Nepos, in his *Life of Atticus*, seems to regard Lucretius simply as a poet.

any service . . . now that I am at leisure: C. makes it clear that service to his countrymen is the aim of his adding philosophy to the achievements of Latin literature, though this service is second best to that of active life. This establishes the difference between his enforced leisure and the chosen way of life of Epicurean writers discussed next.

6 *the same freedom in writing*: cf. 2.7, where C. identifies these careless writers as Epicureans, and says explicitly (what here he simply implies by 'they say') that he has not read their books. The authors are named in *Academic Books* 1.5 as Amafinius and Rabirius by 'Varro', who says that Epicureanism is a simple philosophy that can be written about in non-technical language (cf. 4.6–7 on Amafinius). Epicurus himself is called a careless writer in *On the Nature of the Gods* 1.125. The Epicureans were regarded as particularly dogmatic about, and uncritical of, their founder's teachings (*On Ends* 5.3; Seneca, *Epistles* 33.4). C. here contrasts their appeal only to their own coterie with his use of rhetoric to reach a wider public, but in 4.6 they are credited with taking Italy by storm.

7 *Aristotle . . . to combine wisdom and eloquence*: Aristotle's teacher Plato had attacked rhetoric in the *Gorgias*. His own combination of eloquent philosophical teaching and instruction in rhetoric paid off in his being hired to teach Philip of Macedon's son Alexander. C. gave a full account of Aristotle's rivalry with Isocrates in *On the Orator* 3.141, a work designed to show how rhetoric and philosophy reinforced each other.

greater and more fruitful art: C.'s elevation of philosophy above oratory started in 46 with the *Orator* 148. However, in 2.9 C. says that, on occasion, he followed the practice of Philo of Larissa in doing rhetorical exercises at one time of day and philosophical disputation at another.

set discourses in the manner of the Greeks: usually C. and his speakers are keen to avoid the appearance of lecturing like professional Greek teachers of philosophy and rhetoric (*On the Orator* 2.22; *On Ends* 2.1). In the next paragraph, he explains that each of the five books represents the discourse of one day.

7 *declamation of my old age*: 'declamation' was the term for rhetorical exercises normally practised in youth. Examples are preserved in the Elder Seneca's collection of *controversiae* and *suasoriae*.

8 *the old Socratic method . . . another person's view*: at the end of 1.7, C. seems to adopt the teaching method ascribed in *On Ends* 2.2. to the sophist Gorgias—namely, that someone states a subject he wants to hear about and the speaker expounds it. But in 1.8, C. adopts the method ascribed in the same passage to the New Academy, whereby the would-be learner states an opinion in order to elicit a lecture to the contrary, except that C.'s pupil really believes what he states. This sounds like the method ascribed to Arcesilas in the same passage of *On Ends*, but Arcesilas, like Socrates, invited a real defence of the original opinion, whereas that hardly happens in the *Tusculan Disputations*. Nor does the truth emerge here from arguing on two sides of the question — the method ascribed in 2.9 to the Peripatetics and the Academy. The actual discussions could not have been very different in form, as C. says that he is re-enacting what happened (see next note).

dramatic exchange: C. decides not to recount the occasion, in his own voice, but to present the discussions as a drama that the reader witnesses.

9 *A. . . . M.*: the indications 'A.' and 'M.' are not Cicero's but were added later by scribes and are often interpreted as *auditor* or *adulescens* and *magister* (teacher). A. is minimally characterized as a young man who has studied philosophy in Athens (2.26), knows some Greek literature (1.15), and has been inducted into the Eleusinian mysteries (1.29).

both those . . . are wretched: C. has A. distinguish between the case of those who are dead and that of those who will eventually die, and deals with the first category in 1.10–15.

10 *Cerberus . . . Minos and Rhadamanthus*: C. raises the question of punishment after death as the most obvious reason for thinking that the dead are wretched. Cerberus is the three-headed dog who guards the entrance to the underworld; Cocytus and Acheron are rivers there. Tantalus, king of Sipylus, and Sisyphus, king of Corinth, were punished for offences against the gods, the first by having water and grapes kept eternally just out of his reach, the second by being made to push a stone uphill which kept rolling down again. The quotations are, respectively, from an unknown Latin tragedy and possibly from Ennius. Minos and Rhadamanthus are traditionally judges in the underworld.

Lucius Crassus or Marcus Antonius: the great orators of the generation before Cicero, who made them the principal speakers in *On the Orator*. They are described in his *Brutus* 139–65, where C. regards the fourth-century Athenian orator Demosthenes as the greatest of the Greek orators (35).

11 *philosophers who argue against those very notions*: C. means the Epicureans who argued against belief in punishment after death as part of their

campaign against the fear of death. C., in this work (1.48) and elsewhere (*On the Nature of the Gods* 2.5), describes their teaching as otiose, since not even old women believe in these stories (cf. also Horace, *Odes* 1.4.16 and Seneca, *Epistles* 24.18). The attacks by Lucretius on these beliefs might suggest that such superstition still existed in some quarters (cf. C. in *On Divination* 2.148), but it has been suggested that the poet was just combating belief in divine control of the world in a colourful way.

12 *Marcus Crassus . . . of such great fame*: C. mentions two members of the so-called First Triumvirate, both of whom had died, M. Licinius Crassus in 53 fighting the Parthians, and Pompey the Great murdered in 48 by the Egyptians after his defeat by Julius Caesar. Crassus was known for his wealth and Pompey for his military conquests.

If they are wretched, they must be: C. deliberately conflates the two senses of the verb 'to be', copulative and existential. But though it is possible to predicate qualities of a subject who is fictitious or non-existent, A. here is clearly interested in real people who once existed but no longer do.

13 *Capenan Gate . . . the Metelli*: Marcus Atilius Calatinus was a distinguished general in the First Punic War. The others are well-known Roman families, who also had elaborate tombs along the Appian Way, which was reached by the Porta Capena.

'wretched Marcus Crassus': in Latin *miser M. Crassus* would normally mean 'M. Crassus is wretched', the verb 'to be' often being understood, rather than expressed. So this is a desperate attempt by A. to avoid M.'s sophistic logical point.

15 *Epicharmus*: a fifth-century writer of comedies. C. comments elsewhere on Sicilian wit (*Letters to Atticus* 1.18.8; *Against Verres* 2.4.95).

speak Greek . . . speak Latin in a Greek one: C.'s letters often include remarks and quotations in Greek. In his speeches he avoids Greek, so as not to alienate his less educated hearers. But in the philosophical works, C. translates Greek, as with *axioma* in 1.14, or explains the term in Latin, partly to show that it can be done.

16 *more ambitious project*: in switching to his second category—those who have to die—discussed in 1.16–23, C. looks ahead to the later discussions in 1.24–76 of whether death is not only not an evil, but actually a good thing.

thorny: the interlocutor uses language applied elsewhere (*On Ends* 3.2) by C. himself to the Stoa's reliance on dry, logical argument.

compels me to agree before I am convinced: the Latin for 'I am convinced' translates the Greek term *sugkatathesis*, the Stoic term for giving rational assent to a presentation by the senses.

continuous speech: this marks the end of C.'s pretence to be practising Socratic dialectic.

17 *seeing what resembles the truth . . . capabilities*: agreeing to expound, C. stresses that, as a sceptical Academic, he cannot guarantee the truth of what he says: it is only probable or an approximation of the truth.

17 *known for certain . . . being wise*: C. first compares his scepticism to the
certainties of the Stoics. He alludes in 'known for certain' to the *phantasia
kataleptike*, an impression from the senses that carries the unmistakable
mark of truth. The Stoic philosophers did not, however, claim to be
wise men. According to C. (*On Ends* 5.73, cf. 2.7), only Epicurus made
that claim.

18 *what the soul is . . . considerable dispute*: on the nature of the soul, C. now
gives a list of philosophical views—that is, a doxography. His ultimate aim
is to show that, on any of these views, the answer to the important question
whether death is an evil turns out to be the same: either it is extinction or
a good thing (1.23).

   actual heart [cor] . . . shrewd Aelius Sextus': C. is following an idea of the
Stoic philosopher Chrysippus when he finds, in such adjectives as follow,
popular support for the idea that the heart is the seat of the soul. He goes
on to adduce Roman nicknames applied to P. Scipio Nasica (consul 162
and 155) and Sex. Aelius Catus (consul 198). The line of verse is from
Ennius' *Annals* (1.329, ed. O. Skutsch (1985)).

19 *Empedocles' view*: Empedocles was a pre-Socratic philosopher and poet
from Sicily who lived *c.*493–433.

   Zeno believed . . . soul is fire: Zeno of Citium, founder of the Stoa (334–
262). Strictly speaking, the soul for the Stoics was fiery breath (*pneuma
enthermon*), which at 1.42 C. gives as the view of the later Stoic Panaetius.

   Aristoxenus: born *c.*370 at Tarentum, he studied with the Pythagoreans
(see nn. to 1.38), and then with Aristotle.

   'harmonia': not the modern concept of harmony as the simultaneous sound-
ing of notes, but the sequence of notes in a scale or mode. Aristoxenus was
concerned more with the effect on the ear of certain scales than with the
mathematical relation between the notes.

20 *Plato*: he actually rejected this view of the soul in *Phaedo* 86B.

   Plato imagined the soul to be tri-partite: Plato's view is developed in the
Timaeus 69D. 'Passion' or 'spirit' had the function of carrying out the
instructions of reason against the desires.

21 *Dicaearchus*: Peripatetic philosopher (320–300), pupil of Aristotle, well-
known to Roman readers for his advocacy of the mixed constitution, which
had been applied to Rome by Polybius and Cicero.

   Deucalion: mythical survivor of a flood sent by Zeus, who became king of
Phthiotis in Thessaly. He is often compared to Noah.

22 *Aristotle . . . four well-known elements*: Aristotle (384–344) is mentioned
out of chronological order as a climax. The four elements are hot, cold,
wet, and dry.

   a fifth nature: this is *aether* (C., *For Marcus Caelius* 270a), and it was
not invented by Aristotle, as C. claims at 1.65. Aristotle distinguished
the mind from the soul, of which it is the aspect that is peculiar to
humanity.

endelecheia: C. is not unique in confusing the Greek word for 'continuity', which implies movement, with Aristotle's word *entelecheia*, which is the perfect state of a thing, or its 'form' as opposed to its 'matter', so that the soul does not exist in separation from the body (with the exception of the rational faculty of human beings). Aristotle denied that the soul had movement.

Democritus: fifth-century (*c*.460) philosopher from Abdera in Thrace. He is best known for his version of the atomic theory, which was taken over by Epicurus and Lucretius. It was used by the Epicureans to show that the soul did not survive after death, which was therefore not to be feared.

23 *most likely to be true*: this is as far as an Academic Sceptic like C. can go in asserting an opinion.

24 *returning to their home*: the Pythagoreans and Plato thought that the soul inhabited the body for only a short time before returning to its true home (*On the Republic* 6.29).

if it were not true: cf. *On Old Age* ¶85.

that book of his on the soul: C. means Plato's *Phaedo*, in which Socrates develops the idea of the soul's return to its heavenly home.

25 *compelled me to it*: in 1.16, the interlocutor expressed disquiet by saying he felt compelled to agree. In 1.26, he explains his reluctance to agree by pointing out that the lack of sensation may mean the dead are not wretched, but the fear of losing sensation can make those who will die wretched.

26 *death is free from any evil*: the two questions the interlocutor asks C. to consider give the structure of the rest of the book: in 1.27–81 the case for the immortality of the soul is treated; from 1.82 on that death is free from evil even if the soul perishes.

but to have to lack sensation: C. never really engages with this point even when he returns at 1.82 to considering the case when the soul perishes.

the greatest weight: the argument from authority sits ill with C.'s scepticism, as even a widely held belief can be ill-founded. In *On the Nature of the Gods* 1.62 the sceptical Academic argues against it, but on the factual grounds that such a widespread consensus does not exist (see n. to 1.30).

27 *casci*: according to Varro, *On the Latin Language* 7.28, the word means 'old' in the Sabine dialect. The line of Ennius is *Annals* 1.22, ed. Skutsch.

pontifical law . . . burial: the pontifical priesthood, originally the sole legal authority, still had jurisdiction over legal matters of religious significance, such as marriage and burial (C., *On the Laws* 2.55, cf. 22). C. gives, as the motive for concern with proper burial, the wish of the ancestors to include the dead (*di manes*) among the gods of the underworld.

it: grammatically, the pronoun refers to 'migration and changing of life' but the reader naturally supplies 'soul' as the subject.

held down to ground level: C. here annexes to Roman notions enshrined in pontifical law, ideas from Plato, already adopted in the *Dream of Scipio* at the end of *On the Commonwealth*, about outstanding souls going to heaven and others wallowing about near the earth. At this stage of the argument he is concerned only with the natural human consensus in some kind of survival after death (see 1.36).

28 *This is why . . . with the human race?*: in fact, C. has been talking about the men and women of distinction who go to heaven, not about all humans who die. Romulus, despite having killed his brother, was thought to have been deified as Quirinus. The Ennius passage is *Annals* 1.110, ed. Skutsch. With Hercules, C. switches to Greek examples adopted by the Romans: Heracles—Hercules; Bacchus—Liber; Dioscuri—Castor and Pollux; Ino—Matuta. The Greek examples were not promoted mortals but half-mortals, as Zeus was the father of all of them, while Liber and Matuta were deities.

29 *gods . . . of the highest standing*: C. alludes to the view of Euhemerus, *c.*300, who thought that even the great Olympian gods were mortals deified because of their benefits to mankind. The theory was popular with Christian apologists for whom it explained the true nature of the pagan gods.

whose tombs: C. is thinking of such tombs as that of Zeus in Crete, of Asclepius in Arcadia, of Dionysius at Delphi.

the revelations . . . mysteries: C. must mean the Eleusinian Mysteries and clearly hints at the idea that the initiated receives preferential treatment after death (cf. *The Hymn to Demeter* lines 480–2). This passage provides a rare biographical detail about the interlocutor (see n. to 1.9).

only such convictions . . . instruction of Nature: C. prepares the reader for the distinction in 1.35–6 that the consensus of humankind, unexamined by reason, can be trusted only for the most general notion that the soul survives.

visions: C. choice of dreams as an instance of the instruction of nature fits with the idea in *On Divination* 1.12 that dreams and prophecies are natural forms of divination as opposed to divination using techniques such as augury.

30 *a law of nature*: that human consensus in the belief that the gods exist is based on nature is presented in *On the Nature of the Gods* (which C. was preparing to write at this time) by the Epicurean (1.44) and Stoic (2.5, 12) spokesmen. Human conventions, institutions, and laws can inculcate more specific ideas, such as what the gods are like or where the souls of the dead dwell and in what form, and these ideas must be examined critically by reason. C. is alluding to the Greek *nomos / phusis* (convention vs. nature) distinction.

the loved one . . . is aware of this: C.'s principal point is that the universal belief that the dead are aware of the loss of life's comforts means that everyone believes in survival after death. There is perhaps a hint in the next sentence, that, with reasoning and learning, we would retain only the latter as trustworthy belief, and in 1.87 he rejects the idea that the dead can lack the good things of life.

31 *overriding proof . . . all men feel anxiety*: with the arguments from human concern for future generations and the concern of the best specimens for future fame in 1.31–4, summarized in 1.35, the proof of the soul's immortality based on consensus reaches its climax.

Synephebi: Greek title of a comedy by the Latin playwright Caecilius Statius (early second century). C. gives the same quotation in *On Old Age* ¶24. Ephebes were young men of 17–20 undergoing compulsory military service.

the continuation of a name, adoption of sons: C. carefully distinguishes between the adoption of sons and the continuation of one's name. Under Roman law one could make it a condition of receiving an inheritance that one took the family name of the deceased. This did not amount to legal adoption, and women could make such a condition, though they could not adopt. Julius Caesar's will was to make such a provision for his great-nephew C. Octavius, the later Augustus.

future . . . in our thoughts: C. implies that we expect to be aware and to see the fruits of our efforts in the future. Of course, concern for family continuity and the survival of the commonwealth does not need such additional motivation, as C. will explain in 1.91.

32 *lost their lives for their country*: C. can expect his Roman readers to feel sceptical on the attribution of selfish motives to the greatest heroes from Hercules on, especially to the Roman patriots who gave their lives for their country. This prepares his readers for the importance of reason in 1.36.

33 *Themistocles*: fifth-century Athenian statesman and general at the time of the Persian War, who was responsible for the great victory at Salamis.

Epaminondas: fourth-century Theban statesman and general, famous for his victories over Sparta at Leuctra and Mantinea.

I myself: C. puts himself in the ranks of leading statesmen, but also confesses to being motivated by the desire for fame, a motive of which he will be critical at 2.63–4; 3.3–4, 45–6, 103–5.

34 *these lines . . . mouth of men*: from Ennius, *Epigrams* 15–18V; 7–10W. The words in brackets are not in the best manuscripts, but are given by C. in a full quotation at 1.117.

Phidias . . . shield of Minerva: on the shield of the gold statue of Athena, the sculptor Phidias, whom Pericles had appointed to oversee the building projects on the Athenian Acropolis, put a figure resembling himself and one of Pericles (Plutarch, *Pericles* 13, 31).

36 *This led men to believe . . . by the poets*: C. gives examples of belief in the underworld, a belief already dismissed by his interlocutor at 1.10–11 as inventions of poets and painters. In the next paragraph he shows how irrational it is to think that souls suffer the kind of things that require bodies, even after cremation.

37 *'Here am I . . . endures'*: lines from an unknown tragedy.

37 *dispensed with*: C. often (1.48; *On the Nature of the Gods* 2.5) says that no
one believes these stories any more. Yet the necromancy practised by his
contemporaries Appius Claudius and Vatinius (*Against Vatinius* 14) meant
calling up from the underworld the spirits of the dead to speak, for which
bodily parts are required. But C. says that Appius was ridiculed for his
credulity (see n. below, *my friend Appius*).

Homer's entire Nekuia: in the *Odyssey* Book 11, Odysseus visits the ghosts
in the underworld.

my friend Appius: Appius Claudius Pulcher (consul 54), a fellow member
of the augural college, had dedicated a work on augury to C. in 51 (*Letters
to his Friends* 3.4.3; 3.9.3). Although he had greatly irritated C., as his
predecessor in governing Cilicia, C. regarded him as a good augur
(*On Divination* 1.29; *Brutus* 267), but says that his colleagues in the augural
college ridiculed him for believing that there really were significant signs
that could be read by augural techniques (*On Divination* 1.105; *On the
Laws* 2.32–3). He died in 48.

Lake Avernus: a lake in Campania. The appearance of the place, a former
volcanic crater, led to its being thought of as an entrance to the underworld. The lines of poetry that follow are by an unknown author.

38 *separate the mind . . . from mere habit*: C. explains that it took the ability
to separate thought both from the senses and from tradition to conceive of
a soul that was itself separate from the body, but that before Plato the view
was not supported by reasoned argument.

when my kinsman . . . pupil Pythagoras: C. knew that his family, the Tullii,
were not really descendants of King Servius Tullius, who reigned 578–535
and was alleged to be the son of a slave woman. Pherecydes of Syros was
reputed to be the first Greek prose writer and, because of his belief in the
transmigration of souls, a teacher of Pythagoras.

Tarquin the Proud: the last of the Roman kings, expelled in 510.

Magna Graecia: that is, Great Greece, the name given to the Greek cities of southern Italy. A community of Pythagoreans was established in
Croton.

For many generations . . . as learned: in *On the Commonwealth* 1.16, the
influence of Pythagoras behind Plato's interest in arithmetic, geometry,
and harmony is mentioned; in the *Tusculan Disputations* 4.10, Plato is said
to be indebted to his view of the parts of the soul. The Elder Pliny (*Natural
History* 34.26) speaks of a statue of Pythagoras in the Roman forum in the
fourth century, and there was a neo-Pythagorean movement in Rome and
elsewhere in the first century. Ultimately Pythagorean ideas fed into
neo-Platonism.

39 *Plato came to Italy*: in *On the Commonwealth* 1.16, C. had spoken of a tradition that Plato visited the Pythagoreans in Italy.

40 *I should be happy . . . that same thinker*: Gildenhard 2007, 253, regards this
statement of support for authority as ironic. Certainly C. immediately

embarks on the exposition of philosophical arguments for the immortality of the soul, which continues through 1.75.

kentron: the Greek word appears in Plato, *Timaeus* 54E. C. here subscribes to the usual ancient view that the earth was the centre of the universe. The Pythagorean Pitholaus thought that the earth was just one heavenly body circling round an invisible central fire and was therefore claimed by Copernicus as a predecessor.

souls . . . carried up on high: C. reviews, in 1.40–2, the theories about the nature of the soul given in 1.19–22, ruling out those that cannot be made compatible with survival after death, notably the view of the soul as physical like the body (heart, brain, blood, dispersible atoms, even hot airy ones). His preference seems to be for fiery air—the view of the Stoic philosopher Panaetius (1.42)—though he accommodates Xenocrates' notion of number and Aristotle's fifth element (1.41).

41 *Greek proverb . . . art he knows*: found in Aristophanes' *Wasps* 1431. C. had already suggested (1.20) that Aristoxenus thought more as a musician than as a philosopher.

42 *air . . . nearest to earth*: the earth's immediate atmosphere, where there are clouds, storms, and winds (1.43), is different from the aether above it. The soul is akin to the hot and clear upper air and is described by C. in *On the Commonwealth* 6.15 as derived 'from the everlasting fires which you call stars and planets' (cf. 1.43 end).

44 *the firebrands in our bodies*: physical desires and jealousies. In *Phaedo* 66C, these are among the features of the body that hinder pursuit of the truth.

longing to discover the truth: C. in *On Duties* 1.13 finds in this drive the roots of the virtue of *sapientia* or wisdom. The notion of contemplation as the life of the soul when freed from the body stems from Plato's *Phaedo* 65E–66A and Aristotle's *Protrepticus* frag. 78.

45 *Theophrastus*: *c*.370–285. He was Aristotle's successor as head of the Peripatetic school.

'Argo . . . Libya': a passage from Ennius' *Medea*. The name of Jason's ship was derived by the poet from 'Argives', but it could come from the Greek *argos*, meaning 'swift, fast'.

manner of sight: in the *Dream of Scipio* (*On the Commonwealth* 6.20–1) the younger Scipio sees the earth with its five zones from above.

46 *by natural philosophers . . . and nostrils*: the 'natural philosophers' are principally the pre-Socratic philosophers of the sixth and fifth centuries, who relied on theory and analogy. Even the medical men did little by way of dissection of human corpses, though some looked at animals. The pathways from the soul to the sense organs may refer to the arteries which in dead humans and animals are empty and were thought to carry air or breath. The seat of the soul was usually thought to be the heart (Aristotle and the Stoics) or the brain.

47 *fenced in*: Plato argued in *Phaedo* 65A–68B that the soul will only find pure wisdom, freed from the senses, in the other world when he will see the forms with his reason.

48 *some philosophers . . . as if he were a god*: C. means the Epicureans: see Lucretius 5.8 on Epicurus as a god.

   tyrannous masters: the gods themselves, as conceived by non-Epicurean believers: see Lucretius 2.1090–2; 5.87.

   What fear?: see 1.11.

   '*Hell's lofty sanctuaries . . . murky cloud*': usually thought to come from Ennius' *Andromacha* because of its similarity to a quotation by Varro in *On the Latin Language* 7.6.

50 *soul without body*: see n. to 1.38.

51 *it . . . resides in the body*: C. thinks the difficulty people find in conceiving of the soul without the body is its invisibility, and argues that that problem already exists when the soul is in the body. He goes on to note that invisibility is clearly no obstacle to forming a conception of God.

   Dicaearchus and Aristoxenus: for their views, see 1.19 and 1.21.

52 *Apollo's injunction . . . to know himself*: the famous instruction in Apollo's shrine at Delphi, *gnōthi seauton* ('Know thyself'). The idea that the soul is the real person is found in Plato, *Alcibiades I* 130D.

54 *Whatever is produced . . . would not be an origin*: C. translates Plato's *Phaedo* 245D–246A accurately, except for this sentence, where the original reads, 'for if an origin were produced from anything, it would not be produced from an origin'. Since C.'s Greek was excellent, we must assume that he may have deliberately simplified Plato or was using a Greek text different from ours.

55 *those who disagree with Plato and Socrates*: C. probably means the Epicureans, as the other schools all claimed descent from Socrates. On Epicurean lack of elegance, see n. to 1.6.

56 *blood, bile, phlegm*: the first three components of the body mentioned are the 'humours' (i.e. fluids), usually numbering four, with yellow and black bile distinguished; their correct balance was regarded as important to health.

   the soul itself: the notion that all living things possess soul and that there is a hierarchy of forms of the soul ranging from the minimal or nutritive in plants, through the sensitive soul in animals who perceive and desire, to the human soul which has the faculty of reason, each form including the functions of the preceding form or forms, is Aristotelian and is expounded in Aristotle's *On Soul* 413a21–413b3; 414a29–415a12.

57 *Socrates claims . . . recollection*: C. does not endorse Socrates' claim that the episode in Plato's *Meno* 82A–86A, in which one of Meno's slaves who has never studied geometry is led, with the help of diagrams, to construct a square doubling the area of a previous one, demonstrates that the soul has prenatally acquired knowledge. What is actually demonstrated, of

course, is that mathematical knowledge is *a priori*—that is, independent of sense experience.

that discussion . . . departed this life: *Phaedo* 72C–77A, where Plato extends the notion of recollection to cover the *a priori* knowledge we have of the *ideai* or forms, which include not only mathematical entities but also moral qualities. The idea of knowledge before birth, temporarily lost and then recollected, is there primarily an argument for the pre-existence of the soul before birth.

59 *in my case . . . memory*: C. now turns from Plato's theory of recollection, which aimed to show the soul's capacity for disembodied existence, to his own argument that the actual human ability to remember shows that the soul is divine. For an orator like C., a naturally good memory was essential (*On the Orator* 2.355–6).

Simonides: of Ceos, poet, *c.*556–468. C. tells the story of his invention of the art of mnemonics in *On the Orator* 2.351–4.

Theodectes: of Phaselis, *c.*375–334, orator and poet, who had a work on rhetoric named after him by Aristotle.

Cineas: an envoy of King Pyrrhus in 280. His remarkable memory for names and faces was celebrated by the Elder Seneca (*Controversies* 1. pref. 19).

Charmadas: Academic philosopher of the second century, a pupil of Carneades and associate of C.'s contemporary Philo of Larissa, whose views on rhetoric C. mentions in *On the Orator* 1.84, and whose powerful memory and contribution to the art of mnemonics he attests at 2.360 (cf. the Elder Pliny, *Natural History* 7.89).

Metrodorus of Scepsis: a fellow pupil with Charmadas of Carneades, also celebrated in *On the Orator* 2.360 for his memory and contribution to the art, and described at 3.75 as a professor of rhetoric in the Academy.

Hortensius: C.'s older contemporary Gaius Hortensius Hortalus, consul in 69, and C.'s great rival as an orator. His unparalleled memory is mentioned in *On the Orator* 3.230 and *Brutus* 301.

61 *the power . . . discovery and research*: C. moves from memory to other powers of the mind or soul to back up his idea that it is divine. This common style of giving the history of civilization sees it as a record of individual inventions (cf. the Elder Pliny, *Natural History* 7.191–215). The Epicureans preferred to credit mankind as a whole with creative reactions to natural phenomena (see Lucretius, *On the Nature of Things* 1440–57). Progress is all set in the past with no hint of continuation in the future. C. first lists the social arts of language, government, and practical astronomy, then goes back to the basic discoveries essential to human survival, and on to the finer arts of music and theoretical astronomy.

62 *the man . . . with names*: one thinks of the naming of animals by Adam in Genesis 2.15–21.

written characters: the alphabet, derived from the Phoenicians, was traditionally thought to have been brought by Cadmus to Thebes.

62 *'wandering'*: the Greek *planētai* means 'wanderers' and was intended to differentiate the planets from the fixed stars. C. makes it clear that their movements were not random, but systematic (cf. *On the Nature of the Gods* 2.51). As 1.63 shows, he knew of five planets: Mercury, Venus, Mars, Jupiter, and Saturn.

63 *Archimedes*: the famous Greek scientist, 287–212. The creation of the sphere, which demonstrated how the movements of the heavenly bodies worked, is more favourably compared with the creation of the heavens here than in *On the Nature of the Gods* 2.88. It was taken to Rome after the capture of Syracuse by Marcellus in 212 (*On the Commonwealth* 1.14).

   Timaeus: particularly 21B–42E.

64 *eloquence . . . greater power*: that poetry came from divine inspiration rather than human reason was a common view in antiquity. C. here elevates oratory to virtually the same status.

   as Plato holds: in *Timaeus* 47B.

   drove from our minds . . . the darkness: five virtues are alluded to: piety, justice, temperance, courage, and wisdom. Philosophy here is not wisdom but the inculcator of the five.

65 *Homer . . . divine characteristics to us*: the moral weaknesses of the Homeric gods had long been a target for criticism, even before Plato, *Republic* 377A–383C.

   the soul . . . free from earth and moisture: C. expresses the same view in 1.40 (see n.), but in the *Consolation*, written earlier in the year, after Tullia's death, and quoted below in 1.66, he had rejected the idea that soul is composed of any of the four elements.

   there exists . . . Aristotle first mooted: the claim, made earlier, at 1.22, is not true but Aristotle was the most important champion of the notion.

66 *'No origin . . . everlasting motion'*: in this passage, C. combines Aristotle's view of the fifth element with the Platonic view of God as self-moving rather than unmoved.

68 *the same sphere . . . twelve divisions*: the constellations of the zodiac.

   'set beneath . . . freezing snows': from Accius' *Philoctetes* (see n. to 2.13).

   antichthon: Aristotle (*On the Heavens* 293a 23–6) criticizes the Pythagoreans for inventing a counter-earth solely on the basis of the *a priori* principle of symmetry, which is all the ancients had.

69 *'the sky to shine . . . in grasses'*: the authorship of this passage from a Latin tragedy is unknown.

70 *work of construction*: C. alludes to Plato's *Timaeus* and Aristotle's *On the Heavens*.

   in the head: cf. 1.20.

71 *he refused*: C. refers to Socrates' speeches in the *Apology*, the *Phaedo*, and the *Crito*.

72 *substance of his discourse*: C. paraphrases Plato's *Phaedo* 80D–85D, adding the reference to public conduct, in the true Roman spirit.

73 *swans*: the Elder Pliny, *Natural History* 10.63, denied the truth of the story that the dying swan sings.

74 *But when the god . . . in Cato's*: C. draws a parallel between the suicide of Socrates, which was really execution, and the recent suicide of Cato at Utica, who killed himself rather than surrender to Caesar after defeat (full account in Plutarch, *Cato Minor* 66–70). Cato himself marked the parallel by reading the *Phaedo* on the night he died. The real parallel was via martyrdom—retaining the courage of one's convictions unto death: Socrates refused, as C. explained in 1.71, to take any steps to avoid conviction or to escape from prison; Cato refused to recognize Caesar's authority to pardon. C. here, however, seems to adopt the Stoic internalization of Socrates' divine necessity, in which a man's reason interprets circumstances as a divine hint: thus Zeno, founder of the Stoa, after a fall in which he broke one of his digits, said, 'I come; why do you call me?', held his breath, and died.

'The entire life . . . a careful preparation for death': Plato *Phaedo* 64A, 67D–E, 80D; Seneca, *Consolation to Marcia* 23.2.

76 *what I have just heard*: cf. 1.24, where A. says that Plato's *Phaedo* does not produce in him a lasting conviction of the immortality of the soul. C. goes on to mark the contrast between A.'s current longing for death and his original belief that death was an evil. C.'s philosophical teaching has had its effect: all the philosophical schools faced the problem that they made death seem preferable to life (Lucretius 3.79f.; Seneca *Epistles* 24.24–5; Epictetus 1.9.12).

if . . . we . . . become gods ourselves: having established that the soul is divine (Plato *Laws* 10.899B actually called the soul a god), C. presumably bases his first alternative on the idea that the mind or soul is the real person (*On the Commonwealth* 6.26). But in his *On Duties* 3.44 C. has God giving the soul ('the most divine thing') to man.

or . . . the gods' company: that a lacuna follows is clear. The missing matter must have carried the suggestion to examine some other views of the soul that do not regard it as immortal.

77 *Mytilene*: the chief city of the island of Lesbos.

The Stoics . . . but not for ever: Cleanthes said that souls survived until the next of the periodic conflagrations in which the universe is destroyed and then recreated. Chrysippus said that only the souls of the wise survive. Crows were proverbially long lived.

78 *questions that are comparatively clear*: C. retains the stance of a sceptical Academic.

A good criticism: C. marks the progress of A. in producing a good argument.

79 *this one view . . . he rejects*: Panaetius was a Rhodian aristocrat who lived *c.*180–109, visited Rome, and was the intellectual companion of Scipio

Africanus Aemilianus (see n. to 1.81). He became the head of the Stoic school in Athens in 129. C. was to use a work of his as his principal guide in writing *On Duties*. His philosophy was influenced by Plato.

80 *separated . . . from the mind*: C. deals first with Panaetius' second argument about pain: it was not new with him, as Empedocles and Carneades are credited with it. Plato's soul had parts, and the emotions were not in the rational part. The orthodox Stoic position was that the soul was a unity and that error was the basic cause of the bad emotions, or passions.

Aristotle says: in *Problems* 30.1 953a–955a.

81 *Africanus' great nephew . . . the worst*: P. Cornelius Scipio Africanus Aemilianus, the friend of Panaetius, was a son of L. Aemilius Paulus and the natural brother of Q. Fabius Maximus Aemilianus (consul 145), who had been adopted into another family as he had been into the Cornelii Scipiones. His brother's son Q. Fabius Maximus Allobrogicus was a good general, but his grandson was known for his luxurious living, which led to his being disinherited.

grandson of Publius Crassus: Publius Licinius Crassus Dives (consul 205) had a grandson, Publius Licinius Crassus Dives, praetor in 57, who went bankrupt and was taunted with the name 'Dives' or 'rich'.

82 *sensation . . . after death*: the slight evidence for this belief was the occasional growth of hair on corpses.

Democritus: see n. to 1.22.

83 *to bring myself consolation*: see n. to 1.65, *earth and moisture*.

Hegesias of Cyrene: the head of the Cyrenaic school of philosophy founded by Aristippus. He taught that avoidance of distress was the highest good, and stressed the evils of life to such an extent that he was nicknamed 'Death-Persuader'.

King Ptolemy: Ptolemy I Soter, the king of Egypt, of which Cyrene was a dependency at that date.

84 *Callimachus*: early third-century Alexandrian poet. The epigram survives (*AP* 7.471).

Apokarteron: 'the Starver'. Starvation was a common form of suicide, especially among the elderly.

death . . . not from good: see Introduction, pp. xvi–xvii, for C.'s plight at the time of composition.

85 *Metullus had four . . . sons*: of the sons of Q. Metellus Macedonicus (consul 145), three became consuls, one of whom was also censor, and one reached the praetorship.

Priam had fifty: Homer's *Iliad* 6.244 and 24.496 also gives this number of sons to Priam, king of Troy, but says nineteen (rather than C.'s seventeen) were with his wife, Hecuba. Priam was killed by Neoptolemos the son of Achilles, after the events narrated in the poem.

'*with barbaric . . . richly carved*': this and the following quotation come from Ennius' *Andromacha*. The passage is given more fully at 3.44.

86 *My friend Pompey . . . Naples*: C. had joined Pompey's side in the civil war with Caesar, partly because of his personal relationship with him. The illness was in 50 at Naples, a Greek city.

fallen . . . to . . . armed slaves: Pompey was assassinated when he landed in Egypt. His head was cut off and presented to Caesar on his arrival there, who was not pleased.

88 *Tarquin*: the last king of Rome, expelled in 509 by Lucius Junius Brutus (whose death the next year at the hands of Tarquin's son is mentioned in 1.89). This remark has been taken as a hint for the dedicatee Brutus to emulate his ancestor (cf. *Brutus* 331–2).

89 *Decius . . . weapons of the enemy*: the Decii were renowned for performing *devotio*, the sacrifice of oneself in battle in hopes that the gods would spare one's country. Usually two are mentioned on different occasions (*On Old Age* ¶75).

Spain . . . selfsame war . . . Gracchus: the war referred to is the Second Punic War of 218–202. Publius and Gnaeus Cornelius Scipio were killed fighting the Carthaginians in Spain in 212; Lucius Aemilius Paulus and Cn. Servilius Geminus at Cannae in 216; Marcus Claudius Marcellus at Venusia in 208; Lucius Postumius Albinus in the Litana forest near Modena in 215; and Tiberius Sempronius Gracchus in Lucania in 212.

90 *King Agamemnon . . . in that man's lifetime*: C. assumes that the Homeric characters are historical and once existed, as opposed to mythical creatures like centaurs—half human, half horse—who never existed. Marcus Furius Camillus, in the fourth century, completed the conquest of Veii but was unable to prevent the capture of Rome by the Gauls *c.*390.

91 *the man . . . does not pursue it*: C.'s argument in 1.89 was leading to the conclusion that, since death is annihilation of soul as well as body, the future means nothing to us. But he then turns to consider our care for the future of our country and our loved ones, and some of us being prepared to risk our lives in heroic deeds. C. rejects the Epicurean solution that, according to the calculus of pleasure, the fame of heroic deeds is to be pursued even at the price of safety and security, and accepts the Stoic idea of virtuous action being intrinsically valuable as the highest (and only) good, fame and glory being at best one of the positive indifferents (things neither good nor bad, but normally worthy of selection as being in accordance with nature): see n. to 1.109.

92 *anyone would wish . . . sleep for the remainder*: the comforting argument that death is like sleep, in which we have no sensation, seems undermined by C.'s initial point that no one would choose to sleep even one-third of his lifetime away; but C. may want to concentrate on the idea that they are parallel in lack of sensation, so death is not alarming, without going back on his argument in *On Ends* 5.55 (where Endymion appears again) that human beings are designed by nature for activity.

93 *Troilus*: one of Priam's sons killed by Achilles (*Iliad* 24.257). The argument is difficult. The point Callimachus (see n. to 1.84) made runs counter to the argument that having more of life is better than having less. Similar negative points occur in 1.94: increasing old age gets worse; wisdom may be left but other things are gone.

94 *the river Hypanis . . . a single day*: the river is the Bug in Russia. Aristotle says this in *History of Animals* 5.19, 552b.

95 *the Chaldaeans*: astrologers who may be predicting future good fortune.

96 *How I admire . . . pass the cup*: the story of Theramenes' death is told by Xenophon in *Hellenica* 2.311–56, but there is no mention of the loving cup. Critias, an associate of Socrates who features in several of Plato's dialogues, was, like Theramenes, one of the Thirty Tyrants who ruled Athens in 404–3 after her defeat by Sparta in the Peloponnesian War. Critias was in favour of repressive measures, whereas Theramenes was not. Theramenes threw the last drops of hemlock out of his cup, like a man playing *kottabos* who throws the last drops of wine into a bronze vessel, often pledging the name of his beloved.

97 *Socrates, condemned by a jury*: Socrates was tried in 399 before the assembly of the restored democracy, acting in its judicial capacity. No doubt his association with men like Critias did not help his case, but the charge was impiety—introducing new gods and corrupting young men.

    that man's speech . . . passed on him: C. translates here Plato's *Apology* 40C–41D accurately but with some abridgement.

    called judges . . . Rhadamanthus: see n. to 1.10.

    if I met . . . verdict that was unjust: Palamedes was stoned by the Greeks at Troy, after being wrongly condemned for treason; Ajax committed suicide after being defeated by Odysseus in a contest for the arms of Achilles, which were meant to pass after his death to the bravest of the Greeks.

    the supreme king: Agamemnon.

99 *final words*: in Plato's *Apology* 42A.

    he maintains . . . nothing to be certain: C. speaks of Socratic irony—the claim that he knew nothing except that he knew nothing—in *Academic Books* 2.74.1. But here C. assumes that it was a technique, as the followers of Antiochus are made to say in *Academic Books* 2.15, cf. 1.16.

100 *A man . . . proud of*: the story in Plutarch, *Apophthegmata Laconica* 221F, gives him the name Thectamenes. Lycurgus was by tradition the lawgiver who gave Sparta her idiosyncratic system of government and institutions.

101 *Cato*: see n. to 1.3 for the *Antiquities*; cf. *On Old Age* ¶75.

    'Why, then, . . . in the shade!': the retort is attributed by Herodotus (7.226) to a man from the town of Trachis near Thermopylae.

102 *Lysimachus . . . with the cross*: Lysimachus was one of the bodyguard of Alexander the Great, who controlled Thrace and part of Asia Minor after

Alexander's death. The story of his threat to Theodorus is referred to again in 5.117.

stated . . . in the book: Plato's *Phaedo* 115C–E.

104 *unburied*: Diogenes of Sinope, *c.*400–320, was the founder of the Cynics, who attacked conventional behaviour and beliefs, aiming to shock people into believing that only virtue mattered.

'*No need . . . you start from*': Anaxagoras, one of the pre-Socratic philosophers interested in physics and the natural world, was a close associate of Pericles and was banished to Lampsacus for impiety. He is regarded by David Sedley as the first 'creationist', someone who believed that the world can be adequately explained only by assuming a divine designer or designers (Sedley 2007, ch. 1).

105 *the poor woman laments . . . team of four*: Homer *Iliad* 22.395–404 describes the treatment of Hector's corpse. The lament of his wife, Andromache, probably comes from Ennius' *Andromacha*.

makes Achilles . . . taken away: the fragment is unassigned.

106 '*Mother . . . your son burial.*': the fragment of verse is from a tragedy by Pacuvius, often performed in Cicero's time. The speaker is Deiphilus, whom his father, Polymestor, king of Thrace, killed by mistake. His mother was Iliona. According to Horace (*Sermones* 2.3.60) the audience joined in a cry of 'Mother' in an attempt to wake the actor playing Iliona, who had fallen asleep on stage.

107 *Pelops . . . educating his son*: Pelops was the father of Thyestes and Atreus. The latter served his brother a dish of the flesh of his own children in revenge for Thyestes' seduction of his wife.

108 *embalm their dead . . . in the house*: according to Herodotus 2.86–8, this was the least expensive way of storing a mummy.

the Magi: a priesthood in the Persian Empire, charged with religious functions. On the two methods of burial used in Persia, see Herodotus 1.140.

Chrysippus: *c.*280–207. Known as the second founder of the Stoic school, because of his voluminous writing, he became the principal authority for Stoic doctrine. This collection of burial practices clearly exhibited his usual thoroughness and also the Cynic strain of language he sometimes employed.

109 *follows virtue like a shadow*: at 1.91 C. said that heroes do not face death from a desire for fame, since they will not be conscious of it, but here he seems to use glory as a comfort if the idea of lack of consciousness is not enough to make death acceptable. This paragraph and the next are Stoic in thought: the highest good is virtue and that is exercised in the performance of our duties. Glory is not worth seeking for Chrysippus, but later Stoics accepted it as a positive indifferent (see n. to 1.91), provided it was 'true glory' based on virtuous action and accorded by good men, rather than 'false glory' accorded by the ignorant and based

on popular but unworthy actions (*On Ends* 3.56–7; *On Duties* 1.83, 2.43, 2.88).

110 *Lycurgus . . . political organization*: for Lycurgus, see n. to 1.100. Solon, archon in 594–3, was regarded as the great lawgiver of Athens, so that many subsequent laws were credited to him.

Themistocles . . . military excellence: for Themistocles and Epaminondas, see nn. to 1.4 and 1.33.

Curius, Fabricius, Calatinus: Manius Curius Dentatus (consul 290, 275, 274) won the battle of Beneventum against the invader Pyrrhus in 275. Gaius Fabricius Luscinus (consul 282, 278) was a successful general in the wars in which Rome completed her conquest of the Italian peninsula. Both were known for their austerity and incorruptibility. On Calatinus see n. to 1.13.

the two Scipios . . . countless others: see n. to 1.89 for Publius Cornelius Scipio Africanus Aemilianus. The Elder Publius Cornelius Scipio Africanus, his adoptive grandfather, was the general who defeated Hannibal in the Second Punic War at the Battle of Zama in 202. On Marcellus, see n. to 1.89: he was famous for the conquest of Syracuse in 168; Lucius Aemilius Paulus was the conqueror of Perseus of Macedon in the same year. Marcus Porcius Cato the Elder (see n. to 1.3) and Laelius (see n. to 1.5) were competent generals, but their fame was based on their political and cultural achievements.

The man who lays claim . . . cause vexation: the problem for the Stoics of setting a value on glory shows up well here. The 'good things'—here successes—being only positive indifferents, do not affect happiness, as C. says. But, as a Roman, he finds it impossible not to value good repute, as he says in the next sentence. And the last sentence of the paragraph attaches more importance to indifferents (see n. to 1.91) than Stoicism allows.

111 *Diagoras . . . ascend to heaven*: Diagoras of Rhodes won an Olympic victory for boxing in 464. The victories of his sons brought him to the peak of human felicity.

It is a suspicion . . . out of myself completely: C.'s most explicit statement that writing on the subject of death has a therapeutic value in helping him to cope with the death of his daughter Tullia earlier in the year (see Introduction, pp. xvi–xvii).

112 *we have no need . . . this art entirely*: C. brings us back to the fact that he has been recording the philosophical discourses in the Greek style, combining philosophy with eloquence (see n. to 1.7), that took place in his villa—the declamation of his old age.

113–14 *In the schools of rhetoric . . . as soon as possible*: teachers of rhetoric often used philosophical themes as exercises, so C. here treats his material openly in that fashion. The well-known tale of Cleobis and Biton comes from Herodotus 1.31; that of Trophonius and Agamedes from the poet Pindar; and that of Silenus from Herodotus 8.138.

115 *Euripides . . . Cresphontes*: the play is lost.

   Crantor: of Soli in Cilicia, *c.*335–275, joined the Academy. He was credited
   with inventing the literary form of consolation, and C. said that he took
   his work *On Grief* as a guide when writing his own *Consolation* (*Cicero:
   Consolationis fragmenta*, ed. C. Vitelli (1979), 4).

   Terina: in Bruttium in southern Italy.

116 *Alcidimas . . . famous rhetorician*: C. shifts from the gods giving their judgement on death by inflicting it, to rhetoricians who praise it. Alcidimas was
   a pupil of the sophist Gorgias, immortalized by Plato in his dialogue of
   that name.

   Erechtheus . . . sacrificing their own: Erechtheus was a legendary early king
   of Athens, who was promised victory in battle if he sacrificed one of his
   daughters; whereupon they all killed themselves.

   Codrus . . . would be victorious: Codrus was another legendary king of
   Athens and the enemy were the Dorians.

   Menoeceus . . . oracle was delivered: Menoeceus was the son of Creon who
   killed himself at the gates of Thebes.

   Iphigenia . . . : the verse is from Ennius' play of that name, in which
   Agamemnon's daughter willingly sacrificed herself, so that the Greek fleet
   could have a favourable wind to sail to Troy. In some versions she was
   deceived into going to Aulis.

   Harmodius . . . Epaminondas: Harmodius and Aristogiton were often credited with the slaying of Athens's tyrant Hippias in 514, when in fact it was
   his brother Hipparchus whom they killed. They were executed by Hippias
   who was expelled from Athens only in 510. Leonidas was the Spartan king
   (see 1.101) who led the three hundred and died at Thermopylae. On
   Epaminondas, see n. to 1.33.

117 *Ennius . . . better than Solon*: on the lines of Ennius, see n. to 1.34; on
   Solon, see n. to 1.110: he was a poet as well as a statesman.

118 *a sentence passed by the god*: see n. to 1.74.

119 *anxieties, fears and desires*: the topics that C. will cover in Books 3 and 4,
   but C. here omits mention of the subject of physical pain (*dolor*), which
   occupies Book 2. C.'s decision to treat *aegritudo* (mental pain) first and separately from the other emotions may be connected with his bereavement;
   see Graver 2002, p. xvi.

TUSCULAN DISPUTATIONS, BOOK 2

1 *Neoptolemus in Ennius' play*: Neoptolemos was the son of Achilles. The
   play of Ennius mentioned is probably the *Andromeda*. See n. to 1.3.

2 *that discussion . . . mind from fear*: C. claims that the discussion of death in
   Book 1 has freed the mind from the worst fear. In 4.12 C. gives the Stoic
   division of the passions into four: attitude to present presumed good

(pleasure); attitude to future presumed good (desire); attitude to present presumed evil (pain); attitude to future presumed evil (fear).

3 *from which the 'Attic style' had arisen*: C. discusses the criticisms of his lush style in the *Brutus*. His dedicatee there and here had sympathies with the 'Atticists' who claimed to be imitating the best of the Athenian orators, while C. believed they were ignoring the example of the greatest Athenian orator, Demosthenes (*Brutus* 28.4–29), who could, like himself, use different levels of style.

4 *the four books of the Academics*: the *Hortensius* was a general defence of the value of philosophy; the *Academic Books* was originally in two books entitled *Lucullus* and *Catulus*, named after the speakers who debate with C., but was later changed to four books, in which C. debates with Varro, while Atticus is a minor speaker.

5 *forms of distinction . . . that were desirable*: cf. 1.4–5 where C. explains Rome's early neglect of poetry and cultivation of oratory. Here he thinks presumably of Latin prose indebted to oratory, such as history.

out of these times: C. means Caesar's dictatorship under which oratory could not flourish because it requires freedom of speech.

be refuted without loss of temper: a testimonial to C.'s preferred school of philosophy, the New or Sceptical Academy in the form taught by Philo of Larissa—i.e. acceptance of the probable view on each occasion. In the *Tusculan Disputations* it is the Stoic position on grief and other emotions that C. finds convincing in Books 3 and 4 (see Graver 1992, pp. xii–xiv, on his need to put on a brave face after the death of Tullia), though he is critical of the Stoics' views on pain in Book 2 (e.g. 2.42), and follows Plato in Book 1 on the immortality of the soul.

7 *avoid . . . a polished style*: cf. 1.6. C. means the Epicureans. In the *Academic Books* 1.5 he has Varro claim that Epicureanism can be expounded in much simpler language than other philosophies. C. often stresses stylish writing as his contribution to philosophy.

8 *Plato and the other Socratics*: Socrates did not write anything himself, but he was portrayed in dialogues, not only by Plato but by Xenophon and Aeschines.

Metrodorus: of Lampsacus was one of Epicurus' followers who wrote extensively on his philosophy.

9 *practice of the Peripatetics . . . training in expression*: C. often notes (e.g. *Brutus* 119–20) that the Peripatetic and Academic schools of philosophy offered the best practice for the orator, since they presented their views eloquently, not sloppily like the Epicureans, or sharply like the Stoics. But he sometimes (e.g. *On Ends* 5.10) distinguishes their approach to argument, saying that the Peripatetics favoured arguing both sides of a case, while some Academics preferred destroying a proposed thesis, much as in the *Tusculan Disputations*.

Philo . . . regularly attended: Philo of Larissa in Thessaly, was head of the Academy in Athens, succeeding Carneades and Clitomachus in

110–109. When Philo came to Rome in 88, C. was one of his pupils (*Brutus* 119).

into my Academy: the lower of the two gymnasia in C.'s Tusculan villa, named after Plato's school in Athens. The upper one was called the 'Lyceum' after Aristotle's school (*On Divination* 1.8). The Greek gymnasium was a place for physical exercise but, being a public space where the young gathered, was also a setting for philosophical discussions.

13 *Accius' saying*: in his play *Atreus*. Accius was a Latin playwright and literary scholar of the second century. He wrote a great many tragedies of which over forty titles survive.

14 *pain . . . greatest of all evils*: this is clearly related to the Epicurean belief that the highest good is pleasure, which consists in the absence of pain; but C. has M. take 'pain' to mean only physical pain and treats dishonour and shame, which the Epicureans thought were evils because they cause mental pain, as separate evils.

15 *the Socratic Aristippus*: the older Aristippus, whose grandson of the same name, had the same view. This one was a contemporary of Socrates and is represented by Xenophon in the *Memorabilia* 3.8 as a champion of luxurious hedonism.

Hieronymus of Rhodes . . . highest good: a philosopher of the third century. Originally a Peripatetic, he defected and defined the goal of life as freedom from pain.

Zeno, Aristo, and Pyrrho: Zeno was the founder of Stoicism and held virtue to be the highest good and the goal of life. Aristo rejected the Stoic distinction among 'indifferents' as 'preferred', 'rejected', and 'absolutely indifferent' (see n. to 2.29, *rejected*). Pyrrho, the founder of Scepticism, regarded certain knowledge as impossible and so left ethical priorities to custom.

16 *no one can be happy*: achieving happiness in the view of ancient philosophers meant achieving a stable and secure condition of well-being, so that vulnerability to the greatest evil would prevent happiness.

17 *Metrodorus*: see n. to 2.8.

inside Phalaris' bull: this legendary tyrant of Acragas in Sicily in the early sixth century was famous for punishing people by roasting them inside a brazen bull. C. says that the bull was captured from the Carthaginians and restored to Acragas by the Romans (*Verrine Orations* 2.4.73).

'How sweet . . . troubles me!': the quotation from Epicurus is not found in what survives of Epicurus' writings, but it sounds like an exaggeration of his idea that, by invoking reliable pleasures like those remembered, one can keep the balance of pleasure and pain positive.

pain is the only evil: this too seems to be an exaggeration of what Epicurus taught.

19 *Philoctetes . . . ruin on my soul*: the Greek hero Philoctetes was abandoned on the island of Lemnos because of a wound on his foot caused by a snake.

To capture Troy, however, the Greeks needed him because he had the bow and arrows of Hercules. The quotation is from a Latin poet, probably Accius.

20 *Hercules . . . his goal of immortality*: Hercules was to become a hero or demi-god after death.

Deianira: Hercules' wife, whom he married after rescuing her from being raped by the centaur Nessus, who told her falsely that his blood was a love-potion.

grim Eurystheus: king of Mycenae, he imposed the twelve labours on Hercules at the request of Juno, who knew him to be the son of her husband, Jupiter, and Alcmena, a mortal woman.

Centaur of double form: half-horse, half-man. C. adds the specification 'Centaur' to line 1059 of the *Women of Trachis* (the *Trachiniae*), probably wrongly.

Son of mine: the son addressed in the *Women of Trachis* 1046–102, is Hyllus.

22 *your strong grip . . . Nemean lion gasp out his final breath*: the Nemean lion was a man-eating beast that could not be killed with weapons but was strangled by Hercules.

Lerna . . . loathsome serpent: the Argolid home of the many-headed Hydra whom Hercules finally killed, dipping his arrows in the poisonous blood.

lay low the twin-bodied band: the Centaurs whom Hercules helped Theseus to defeat in their battle with the Lapiths.

Erymanthus: a plain in Arcadia where Hercules captured the lion.

triple-headed hound born of the Hydra: Cerberus is the hound who guards the gates of the underworld. The usual version, adopted by Sophocles, had Cerberus and the Hydra both children of Echidna.

gold-bearing tree: the Golden Apples of the Hesperides at the western end of the Mediterranean.

23–5 *Let Aeschylus . . . a Pythagorean as well*: C. clearly does not believe Aeschylus to have been a Pythagorean.

In his play . . . Jupiter most high: the quotation, in Latin, is in fact from Accius' play *Philocteta Lemnius*.

Mulciber: an alternative name for Vulcan, the god of fire and metalwork.

these words . . . Caucasus: the quoted passage is C.'s own translation into Latin from the lost play *Prometheus Freed* by Aeschylus.

26 *Dionysius the Stoic*: this philosopher, clearly contemporary with both the younger and the older speaker here, cannot be further identified. The criticism is typical of C.'s attitude to the Stoic presentation of their philosophy.

Philo: of Larissa, see n. to 2.9.

27 *Plato . . . political constitution*: C. alludes to Plato's *Republic* 395D–398A.

28 *to endure pain*: having used the poets to show that pain is not 'sweet' (the view of Epicurus, according to C.), C. now attacks them for representing

pain as overcoming even great heroes and defeating virtue. But it is even worse when a philosopher (Epicurus) says that pain is the greatest evil, greater even than dishonour. C. proposes to move on to the subject of how to endure pain.

29 *the Stoics . . . foolish syllogisms*: such a syllogism might be:

nothing is evil unless it is base and wicked
pain is not base or wicked
pain is not an evil

Even a Stoic like Seneca thought Zeno's attempt to combat emotional reactions with syllogisms was useless (e.g. *Epistles* 82).

to be rejected: the Stoics believed that the only good is virtue, the only evil is vice, but, in order to provide a basis for choice and action, they classified things that were strictly speaking 'indifferent' into 'positive indifferents' or 'things to be preferred' and 'negative indifferents' or 'things to be rejected', the grounds for preference being their accordance with nature in promoting life and health.

30 *It would be better and truer to say . . . the evil of immorality*: what follows to the end of the paragraph is the Peripatetic view that was also adopted by the founder of the 'Old Academy', Antiochus of Ascalon, C.'s older contemporary.

31 *exercise of your mind*: the use of reason gives one the right evaluation of pain in comparison with virtue and vice.

32 *Corinthian vases*: made of an alloy of gold, silver, and copper, they were particularly valuable.

if you lose one virtue . . . possess none: it was a distinctively Stoic view that to possess one virtue is to possess all. There were also Stoics who held that virtue could not be lost.

33 *I prefer not . . . an example here*: presumably intended as a polite way of considering his interlocutor as a typical man—that is, not a particularly brave one.

'in a damp hut . . . tearful sounds': the Latin quotation is probably again from Accius (cf. 2.19).

present your throat: like a defeated gladiator whom the crowd has condemned.

Vulcan's armour: C. is thinking of the shields made by Vulcan for Achilles in the *Iliad* and for Aeneas in the *Aeneid*.

34 *Minos*: a legendary king of Crete.

Lycurgus: legendary lawgiver of Sparta, credited with its constitution and peculiar way of life. Sparta's institutions were said to be based on the Cretan ones (Aristotle, *Politics* 127b22f.).

such a hail . . . in streams: the altar is that of Artemis Orthia. C. notes this as a contemporary custom and it is attested even later. The Latin verse is presumably from a Roman tragedy.

34 *when I was there*: C. studied philosophy and oratory in Greece in 79–77.

35 *Consequently . . . abound in always*: C. apparently thinks that Greek has only one word (*ponos*) for both labour and pain. This gives him the opportunity to say that the Greeks are not always richer in vocabulary than Latin, often a topic of complaint with him.

   Gaius Marius' varicose veins: see 2.53 n.

36 '*in Spartan maidens . . . barbarian fertility*': the obvious contrast with the Spartan woman exercising in public is the Athenian woman who largely stayed in the woman's quarters. Even the Spartan woman, however, did not engage in warfare, contrary to what the unknown Latin author says here. The Greeks called non-Greek peoples 'barbarian', especially after the Persian Wars when the Greeks united in defence of their country.

   Eurotas: river near Sparta.

38 *as we have found*: in the recent civil war between Caesar and Pompey.

   Surely . . . Eurypylus: the visit of Eurypylus to the tent of Patroclus and Achilles is in *Iliad* 11.804–48. The dialogue here and in the following paragraph comes from a Latin play.

39 *say nothing more . . . Aesopus could not*: an actor in C.'s day who played Eurypylus; as an actor in a play, he could hardly say nothing.

40 *Indians . . . burnt*: at 5.78, C. describes the custom of suttee where the favourite wife joins her dead husband on the funeral pyre.

   boxers . . . gloves: C. refers to the Roman boxing glove made of hard leather thongs sometimes reinforced with metal.

41 *Olympic victory . . . consulship of old*: C. means the highest office in Rome when it was elective and not in the gift of Caesar the dictator. An Olympic victor seems an odd example to give of endurance when, in the paragraph before, such an athlete is an example of weakness caused by habit.

   '*the Samnite . . . life and place*': a Samnite was a gladiator armed in traditional fashion with a short sword, a helmet with a visor, and a long shield. The quotation is from the Roman satirist Lucilius.

   gladiatorial show . . . as conducted these days: this is the earliest extant objection to gladiatorial games on grounds of humanity, but C. approves of them when the combatants were condemned criminals, not slaves and volunteers, as they helped to inure the spectators to pain and death. Seneca objects more strongly (*Epistles* 7.2–5).

42 *turn our attention to Reason*: as noted by Gildenhard 2007 (263, n. 136), C. uses a brief exchange with the interlocutor, as in the first disputation (1.9–17), to mark the turn in the argument from Roman common sense to the insights of reason.

   leave it to the Stoics . . . or not: they held that the passions rested on false beliefs that things other than virtue could be good and things other than vice bad. Thus pain or grief sprang from belief in present evil, and pleasure from belief in present good. Since the beliefs are false, the feelings should be rejected. For C. such teaching does not rid us of our feelings, and we must concentrate on enduring pain, not on defining it out of existence. The criticism of Stoic style that follows is typical of C. (cf. 2.26).

43 *shameful . . . to shrink from . . . pain*: the verb translated here as 'shrink from' is *extimescere* meaning 'to dread' or 'to be afraid'. This makes C. sound more sympathetic to the Stoic view (see n. to 2.42), when he is supposed to be concentrating on the endurance of pain.

named after the one virtue: the older meaning of the Latin *virtus*, 'manliness and bravery', still occurs in the golden shield presented by the senate in 23 to Augustus, where he is praised for four virtues—the other three being clemency, justice and piety. Clearly *virtus* here is not the generic term but the single virtue of bravery. C.'s etymology is correct.

philosophy . . . possesses such a cure: for the fear of death and intolerance of pain.

44 *Epicurus . . . his intelligence*: cf. 3.46, where C. contrasts Epicurus' poor intelligence with his admirable morality.

45 *another ten atoms greater*: C.'s joke is based on the Epicurean physical theory, taken over from Democritus, according to which everything, including the human body and soul, is composed of tiny indivisible particles of matter. The Epicureans did not think pain was a disturbed state of the atoms, but an incorporeal condition resulting from it.

stomach gripes . . . passing water: C. alludes to Epicurus' deathbed letter to Idomeneus: 'My continual sufferings from strangury and dysentery are so great that nothing could augment them; but over against them all I set gladness of mind at the remembrance of our past conversations.'

those who regard . . . the greatest evil: C. means the Stoics.

46 *describe . . . the only . . . the greatest good*: C. means that he would rather adopt the extreme Stoic view that virtue is the only good, than give up the Peripatetic view that it is the greatest among other goods.

47 *the soul . . . two parts*: as C. has said at 2.10, Plato himself believed in a threefold division of the soul into rational, spirited, and irrational, but his view was not influential even in his Academy. At 4.10 a twofold division is attributed to Plato—that is, rational and irrational—which could go back to *Republic* 439E–441C, where the threefold division arises as a refinement of that bipartite division, the irrational part being divided into two.

48 *guardianship of friends and relatives*: in Roman law the head of a household was supposed to restrain a lunatic member of the family, no doubt with the help of friends and relatives.

The Bath: a play by the Roman poet Pacuvius about the return of Ulysses to Ithaca, the bath being that in Homer's *Odyssey* 19.349–68. The wounding is what caused the death of Odysseus, when Telegonus, his son by Circe, shot his father by accident with the bone of a sting-ray.

49 *Pacuvius improves on Sophocles*: in his lost play *Odysseus Akanthoplex*; another lost play of Pacuvius, the *Niptra*, dealt with Odysseus' homecoming.

51 *the man . . . before now*: C. means the Wise Man whom philosophers, particularly the Stoics, were always describing, despite admitting he had never existed. Cato the Younger was often cited as the nearest approximation. The allusion to weaker parts of the soul shows that Stoicism, whose founders believed in a unitary soul, is not in his mind.

52 *Zeno of Elea*: this pre-Socratic philosopher, who lived in the first half of the fifth century, was famous for his paradoxes about motion, such as Achilles and the tortoise. In *On the Nature of the Gods* 3.82, C. tells us that the tyrant's name was Nearchus.

   Anaxarchus . . . torture: a friend of Alexander the Great, who was pounded to death in a mortar.

   Callanus—the Caucasus: another companion of Alexander. 'Caucasus' is used here of the Hindu Kush.

53 *Gaius Marius . . . surgeon's knife*: the story of the great general's operation for varicose veins is preserved in Plutarch, *Marius* 6.

   belief, not nature: a Stoic contrast much used in Books 3 and 4 of this work.

54 *the soul . . . own tension*: there may be, in this mention of the soul's tension, an allusion to the Stoic idea of *tonos* whereby the soul needs to have good tone and strength to give rise to good judgement and good deeds. The soul as breath is characterized by its tensile motion.

55 *keening . . . at funerals*: the earliest Roman law code, the Twelve Tables, forbid excessive displays of mourning, as C. reports in *On the Laws* 2.59 and 2.64.

57 *Marcus Antonius*: consul in 99. He and Marcus Licinius Crassus were the leading orators in the generation before C., who celebrated them in his *Brutus* and *Orator*.

   defence under the Varian law: the Varian law was passed after the outbreak of the Social War in 91 between Rome and some of her Italian allies to punish those who were accused of fomenting the war. They seem to have been required to speak in their own defence.

58 *to bear pain . . . to do so*: C. indicates by the phrase 'as the saying goes' that this is a proverbial phrase, and does not commit himself to where thinking actually takes place.

   place of honour: C. elides the two ideas of withdrawal from one's place in the battle line and loss of face.

59 *the Decii*: see n. 1.89 n.

   Epaminondas: the Theban general killed at Mantinea in 362 at the moment of victory for the Thebans, who were fighting for their freedom from Sparta's Peloponnesian League.

60 *Dionysius of Heraclea*: on the Pontus. He was a pupil of Zeno and hence a fellow student of Cleanthes, who succeeded Zeno as head of the Stoic school. He later went over to the Cyrenaic school, which held that pleasure is our proper goal.

the Epigoni . . . teaching: this translation from a lost play of Aeschylus could be by C. himself. Amphiaraus was a seer who accompanied the expedition of the Seven against Thebes and was swallowed up by the earth.

61 *our own Posidonius*: born in Apamea in Syria, he settled in Rhodes and was the head of the Stoic school in C.'s day. C. knew him personally, having studied with him on his eastern tour of 79–77. Posidonius wrote many philosophical works and a history that ranged widely over the Mediterranean world.

Pompey . . . a visit: Pompey's visit to Posidonius took place on his return from the Mithridatic War.

62 *in earlier days*: see n. to 2.5, *out of these times*.

high rank . . . easier to bear: the reference is to Xenophon's *Education of Cyrus* 1.6.25.

63 *foolish people*: the Stoics held that virtue was a matter of correct judgement about good and bad and that all who did not have this knowledge were complete fools. At 3.2–4, C. discusses true honour or glory as opposed to that resting on the approval of the majority. Real glory is the unanimous praise of good people who recognize excellence of character, whereas popular acclaim frequently goes to misdeeds and faults and can mislead people who mistake it for the real thing.

as for you: C. moves abruptly to the conclusion which takes the form of direct advice to A.

judgement . . . is your own: C. remains true to his New Academy which set a high value on independent judgement.

65 *tension of the soul*: see n. to 2.54.

bear sickness . . . as humans ought: that is, through reason and wisdom. C. does not take the opportunity to rate the Romans above the Greeks for their rational courage, because he is interested in the stronger comparison with the barbarians.

66 *pain is . . . of such insignificance*: the view that C. here seems to accept as an alternative to the belief that pain is an evil—namely that pain is a trivial evil eclipsed by virtue (which is sufficient for happiness on its own)—is at 5.29–30 attributed to his dedicatee's teachers (Antiochus and Aristus), as well as to Aristotle and the Peripatetics and emphatically rejected.

our discussion yesterday: at *Tusculan Disputations* 1.74, 118.

67 '*Throw yourself . . . Arion of Methymna found*': a seventh-century poet from Lesbos, who was thrown into the sea from a ship but was rescued by a dolphin.

horses . . . aided Pelops: Neptune gave Pelops horses to help him beat Hippodamea's father in the race in which victory would bring marriage with her.

refuge you must seek: C. groups suicide here with forms of divine rescue because he is thinking that here too there is a divine command (see n. to 1.74).

67 *water-clock*: used to time public speeches, it could also be used in private oratorical practice.

TUSCULAN DISPUTATIONS, PREFACE TO BOOK 3

1 *Brutus*: see n. to 1.1.

the immortal gods: the art of medicine was credited to Apollo and, particularly, to his son Asclepius, variously thought of as a god or hero. Medical schools named after him were attached to his sanctuaries on Cos and Epidaurus.

2 *seeds of virtue . . . with its own hand*: C.'s metaphors involving sparks and seeds allude to the designing fire that the Stoics thought gave the world its form and to the seminal principles implanted in us by Nature.

our upbringing begins: literally 'we are raised up'. There is no ancient evidence for the custom often adduced of the father raising the new infant off the ground to acknowledge it as his.

returned to our parents: that is, from the wet-nurse.

3 *the poets*: for C.'s allusions to Plato's attack on the bad influence of poets, see n. to 2.27 n.

shadowy . . . echo: C. gives us a complicated set of metaphors. There seems to be a comparison between sculpture, with its rounded forms, and drawing, which produces outlines, but there is also the notion of glory as a real thing vs the shadowy image of it as in Plato's image of the cave in *Republic* 7.514A–516D. Finally, glory as a real thing is itself only an echo of virtue.

4 *makes men blind . . . their own ends*: C. clearly has in mind here Caesar and Pompey, particularly the former.

not wilfully . . . wrong turning: for the Stoics, all misdeeds are wilful in that they spring from wrong judgements as to what is good and bad. So C.'s distinction between will and errors is not strictly compatible with Stoicism, his main philosophical guide in this book.

madness: in the Stoic view, being subject to passions such as distress and desire (see 3.5 below) is technically the unsound condition of mind that constitutes insanity.

5 *Ennius*: see n. to 1.3, *Livius*.

diseases of distress and desire: the medical analogy of body and soul is often pressed to render the passions or emotions as diseases.

6 *the Hortensius*: C.'s first philosophical dialogue in the late series of 45–44. It was an exhortation to the study of philosophy, which St. Augustine said turned him from worldly to serious matters (*Confessions* 3.4.7; 8.7.17).

the most weighty subjects: the *Academic Books* concern logic and epistemology; *On Ends* covers different theories of ethics.

7 *our Academy*: see nn. to 2.9.

TUSCULAN DISPUTATIONS, PREFACE TO BOOK 4

1 *from Greece*: C. reverts to the theme of the preface to Book 1 on the late reception of the Greek arts of poetry and oratory.

   under the kings, and . . . by the laws: in *Digest* 2.2.2, Pomponius says that Romulus and his royal successors had laws passed by the people.

   For although . . . defying belief: C. in this sentence celebrates the good side and then the bad side of Roman kingship, the liberation from tyranny being a compliment to his addressee (4.2).

   on the commonwealth: C. excuses the length of his digression on the political development of Rome and notes his treatment of the subject in the six books *On the Republic*, written in 54–51.

2 *learned studies . . . why these also*: in speaking of 'learned studies' that, like poetry and oratory, also came from Greece, C. is thinking of Roman practical wisdom, a forerunner of real philosophy, which arrived only in the mid-second century, as C. says in 4.5–6.

   Pythagoras: see n. to 1.38.

3 *King Numa . . . student of Pythagoras*: in *On the Republic* 2.28–9, C. has Scipio Africanus expose this legendary meeting as a fiction, but, in contrast to this passage, gave little credit to Pythagorean influence on the early Roman Republic.

   in his Antiquities: see n. to 1.3.

4 *the poem . . . Pythagorean*: Appius Claudius Caecus was censor in 312. We do not know why C. found the poem Pythagorean. Quintus Aelius Tubero, the nephew of the younger Scipio Africanus, was a Stoic and friendly with the Stoic philosopher Panaetius and his pupil Hecato (Cicero, *On Duties* 3.63). The letter Panaetius wrote to him was on the subject of enduring pain (*On Ends* 4.23).

5 *the Stoic . . . as ambassadors to the senate*: in 155 the Athenians sent an embassy consisting of three philosophers, to ask for remission of a fine imposed on them for sacking Oropus: the third, with Diogenes and Carneades, was Critolaus the Peripatetic. Their lectures at Rome attracted great attention among the young and were disapproved of by the Elder Cato as purveying ideas contrary to Roman tradition.

   Cyrene . . . Babylon: Carneades came from Cyrene; Diogenes was from Seleuceia, but acquired the nickname 'Babylonian' from the nearby city of Babylon.

6 *the same notions . . . in different languages*: critics of the Stoics, notably Carneades and later Antiochus of Ascalon, held that the Stoics held the same moral views as the Peripatetics but changed the vocabulary, calling what the Peripatetics allowed to be 'good', such as health and wealth, 'positive indifferents' (*On Ends* 4.22)—that is, possessing a certain value but not contributing to happiness.

   the Academic school: C. refers to the Academy in its sceptical phase, to which he adhered.

6 *Gaius Amafinius*: one of the expounders of Epicureanism in Latin, of whom C. had a low opinion (see nn. to 1.6 and 2.7).

7 *seek . . . solution to every difficulty*: as in 3.50–1 and 4.47, C. makes clear his adherence to the sceptical Academy, avoiding dogmatism and not laying claim to certain knowledge, but acting on what he thought probable. This was the tradition of Arcesilaus, Carneades, and Clitomachus, softened somewhat by C.'s teacher Philo of Larissa.

the lower gymnasium: see n. to 2.9.

TUSCULAN DISPUTATIONS, BOOK 5

1 *that book which you wrote*: Brutus' own work *On Virtue* (see *On Ends* 1.8; Seneca, *Consolation to Helvia* 9.4). The view adopted there (5.12) that virtue was sufficient for the happy life was common ground between the Stoa and the 'Old Academy' of Antiochus of Ascalon, to which Brutus adhered, but the latter thought that the things fortune provided could enhance or diminish happiness, whereas the former thought they were only 'indifferents', 'positive' and 'negative', and did not affect happiness.

2 *those who first . . . philosophy*: for problems in the argument here, see Douglas 1990, 144. C.'s idea that morality and the happy life were the prime concerns of philosophy from its inception clashes not only with his later statement that the name philosophy was not originally used for what was just part of wisdom, but also with his account of the history of philosophy in 5.7–10 where it is Socrates who first brought philosophy down from heaven to enquire about life and morals.

virtue . . . brought to maturity: C. seems to elide the quality of virtue with the study of virtue.

saying our prayers: the self-reliance of human beings is a basic assumption of Greek and Roman ethics.

3 *those misfortunes*: notably the civil war, Caesar's dictatorship, the death of Tullia.

4 *your uncle*: the younger Cato, who had committed suicide at Thapsus in Africa in 46, something over a year before.

5 *It was . . . from my earliest years*: C. tells us in the *Brutus* that he studied with philosophers, as a young man in his late twenties on his trip to Greece in 79–78, and in *On Duties* that his success in oratory rested on his philosophical training.

7 *philosophy . . . of recent date*: see Gildenhard 2007, 205. In the preface to Book 4.1–5, C. distinguishes proto-philosophical wisdom from philosophy proper, which began the days of Laelius and Scipio; here C. says it was philosophy in all but name.

the Seven: the usual list of the Seven Sages consisted of Solon, Thales, Pittacus of Mitylene, Bias of Priene, and three of the following: Periander of Corinth, Cleobulus of Rhodes, Chilon of Sparta, and Anacharsis (see n. to 5.90). Only Thales was primarily a thinker and in *On Duties* 3.16 C. denies the Sages were wise in the full philosophical sense.

Lycurgus . . . Homer too lived: Lycurgus was the traditional founder of the Spartan institutions and way of life. His date, like that of Homer, was disputed.

Ulysses and Nestor . . . men of wisdom: the Homeric Odysseus and Nestor are shrewd and wily, eminently practical men.

8 *tradition would not tell . . . fictions of myth*: C. explains myth here as reflecting fame of a more intellectual sort. Atlas was sometimes thought of as an astronomer; Prometheus gave fire and astronomical information to men, but Cepheus, his wife, Cassiope, and son-in-law Perseus are not elsewhere credited with astronomical knowledge.

Heraclides . . . eminent in learning: a philosopher of the fourth century (Diogenes Laertius 5.86–94).

Pythagoras: see n. to 1.38.

reply . . . a philosopher: Pythagoras meant that he had no special area of knowledge or expertise but was a lover of wisdom, pursuing the knowledge of nature (see 5.9).

9 *true independence of spirit*: the Latin *liberalissimum* points to pursuits worthy of a free man as opposed to a slave.

10 *from ancient philosophy . . . Socrates*: like the 'pre-Socratic philosophers', Socrates too began with the study of physical phenomena (Plato, *Phaedo* 96A) but then gave it up.

11 *immortalized in Plato's literary account*: Socrates himself left no writings. C. expresses no doubts about the veracity of Plato's portrait of him.

what was most probable . . . Carneades: head of the Academic School in the second century when it was in its sceptical phase. He did not leave writings himself but was an effective polemicist against the Stoics (*Academic Books* 2.131; *On Ends* 5.20). By using the key word 'probable', C. shows he was actually following Carneades.

12 *thinks it is*: see n. to 5.1.

13 *tasted rather than drunk*: in Greece and Rome it was normal to drink wine diluted with water, drinking undiluted wine being regarded as a barbarian custom. To taste the Stoic notions means here sampling them before they are diluted.

14 *no virtue . . . good sense*: see n. to 2.63. Virtue is based on sound judgement about things good, bad, and indifferent. *Prudentia* is the word for practical wisdom in contrast to *sapientia* for theoretical.

Marcus Aquilius: of the three examples C. gives in chronological order, only the first is a 'good man' in the moral sense. Perhaps C. is using a more commonsensical meaning (as with 'life of happiness' for *beata vita* below), such as 'respectable' or even 'politically sound', or 'undeserving of punishment'. Marcus Atilius Regulus was said to have been tortured to death at Carthage in 250 after he kept his promise to return from Rome if he failed to secure an exchange of prisoners (C., *On Duties* 3.99). Quintus Servilius Caepio was defeated by the Cimbri in 106 and condemned in the courts. He died in exile at Smyrna. That he was Brutus' maternal grandfather may contribute to his sympathetic treatment here. Manius Aquilius was killed by Mithridates in 88 by having molten gold poured down his throat to punish his venality: he had earlier in the 90s been acquitted for extortion, though the evidence was against him (C. *In Defence of Flaccus* 98).

15 *What person . . . be happy*: in the last two sentences of this paragraph C. summarizes the content of the first four books: death (1), pain (2), other negative emotions (3 and 4).

17 *this point . . . mental disturbance*: 'this point' is that those free of fears, desires, and other emotions without struggle are happy; 'the other point' is that virtue of her own power can give one such freedom, as the case of the wise man shows.

18 *latter . . . latter*: Stoicism was regarded as a particularly coherent system, so one could start at any point and the crucial doctrines would follow from one another (see, e.g., 5.21).

19 *proofs and recommendations*: C. reminds us that philosophy is not only a series of doctrines but that those issue in precepts on how to behave.

20 *with what it achieves*: C. finds it hard to believe the Stoic doctrine that virtue on its own can secure happiness, regardless of the blows of fortune.

offered a reward . . . a pleasure that was new: a story told of Persian kings in general and of Xerxes in particular (Valerius Maximus 9.1.3 ext.).

21 *Brutus . . . Aristus and Antiochus*: the last was the founder of the 'Old Academy' and Aristus was his less well-known brother, whose lectures Brutus had attended (C., *On Ends* 5.8). Like the Peripatetics, they held that there were good things other than virtue, which was the supreme good, but they were not necessary to happiness, though they could enhance it (see 5.22; C., *On Ends* 5.71–2).

22 *as 'Imperator'*: as governor of Cilicia in 51–50 C. won a minor victory for which he was hailed by his soldiers as 'Imperator' (commander), a precondition for a triumph, which, however, he never secured owing to the advent of the civil war.

23 *three categories of evils*: those of the soul, those of the body, those inflicted by circumstances. C. assumes that to suffer any evil of the soul rules out happiness (cf. 5.51).

24 *Theophrastus*: of Eresos of Lesbos, *c.*370–285, Aristotle's successor as head of the Peripatetic school. He believed there were goods and evils other than virtue and vice, and, according to some authorities, also regarded the presence of the former and absence of the latter as essential to the perfectly happy life (C., *On Ends* 5.77).

exiles . . . loved ones: the plural 'exiles' barely conceals C.'s personal anguish over his exile in 58, even though it lasted less than a year. The climax of evils, 'loss of loved ones', points to the more recent wound of Tullia's death.

three categories of good things: cf. n. to 23.

that book: see Diogenes Laertius 5.43. The book is frequently mentioned by Cicero, as at *On Ends* 5.85.

25 *in his Callisthenes*: a book subtitled *On Grief* (Diogenes Laertius 5.44), written in memory of Aristotle's nephew Callisthenes, who fought in and wrote about Alexander's campaigns but quarrelled with him and was executed (see 3.21).

26 *Antisthenes*: a follower of Socrates who lived *c.*445–360 and believed that virtue was sufficient for happiness.

27 *Metrodorus*: see n. to 2.8.

Aristo of Chios: see n. to 2.15.

30 *my friend Brutus . . . teachers we shared*: Antiochus of Ascalon and Aristus.

Speusippus, Xenocrates, and Polemo: Plato's successors as heads of the Academy.

32 *novel terminology*: in Book 3, the younger Cato expounds the Stoic system, and, in Book 4, C. presents objections to it, including an attack on the doctrine of indifferents. *On Ends* was finished by June of 45, which supplies a *terminus post quem* for this part of the *Tusculan Disputations*.

33 *I give voice . . . I alone am free*: C.'s summary of the sceptical Academic position evades the question of his own consistency of opinion on any particular issue and puts the stress first on the Stoics' dogmatic consistency over time and then on the logical consistency of their doctrines.

34 *Zeno of Citium . . . the Old Philosophy*: C.'s playful snobbishness brings out the importance of Plato's authority, but also the difficulty of getting a consistent answer from what Plato wrote. The 'Old Philosophy' alludes to the view of Antiochus of Ascalon that all the dogmatic schools from Plato on formed essentially one tradition, which must be rescued from scepticism (C., *Academic Books* 1.13–43).

Plato . . . in his Gorgias: at 470D–471A. C. liked translating Plato, an early work being a translation of the *Timaeus*. He follows Plato closely here, but explains the 'Great King' as the king of Persia and, in condensing the third sentence from the end, fails to make explicit, as Plato does, that not only a good man but also a good woman is happy.

Perdiccas' son Archelaus: king of Macedon, 413–399.

36 *the funeral oration . . . that old proverb*: the passage quoted is *Menexenus* 247E–248A. In the dialogue, Menexenus persuades Socrates to recite a funeral oration, which, he said, was composed by Pericles' mistress, Aspasia. Unlike Plato, C. does not quote the proverb 'Nothing in excess' and he moves the 'in particular' to modify 'children' rather than heeding the proverb, the death of Tullia being much in his thoughts.

37 *to the limit of their natures*: there is a hint here of Aristotle's scale of Nature (*On the Soul* 2.2.413c–414a), in that animals have sensation and mobility, unlike plants, and human beings add a divine soul.

38 *soul of man . . . culled from the divine mind*: for the Stoics, sparks of the divine fire that determines the character of the universe are in human beings as their minds or souls.

39 *I am in agreement with Brutus*: see n. to 5.34 for the 'Old Philosophy' according to Antiochus of Ascalon, whose philosophy Brutus followed.

40 *the man who divides good things into three*: see nn. to 5.23 and 5.24.

42 *Philip*: of Macedon.

43 *anxiety . . . misunderstanding good things*: C. summarizes the four basic passions, according to the Stoics, two (anxiety and ecstatic joy) responding to evils and goods thought to be present, and two (fear and desire) responding to evils and goods expected: the goods and evils are not genuine, since only virtue is good and only vice evil.

    joy: as opposed to 'pleasure', is a good emotion in Stoicism.

44 *these people*: presumably the Peripatetics and those who agree with them on this point.

46 *Anticlea's praise . . . suppleness of body*: the quotation is usually attributed to Pacuvius' play *Niptra*. There is a confusion here between two Homeric figures: Anticleia, who is Odysseus' mother, and his nurse, Eurycleia, who bathes him.

47 *your friends*: see n. to 5.44.

    are called 'high-ranking' or 'preferred' by the Stoics: 'preferred' in the sense of receiving preferment or promotion to high status. Although the Stoics regarded the only good as virtue and the only evil as vice, they allowed that, among things 'indifferent' (see n. to 5.1), some had value and some lacked it, while other things were absolutely indifferent, like the number of hairs on one's head. Those with value were called 'preferred' and were regarded as worthy of choice.

49 *Epaminondas . . . shorn*: for Epaminondas see n. to 2.59. The verse is a Latin translation of the first line of an epigram inscribed on a statue base at Thebes (Pausanias 9.15.4).

    Africanus . . . deeds: the elder Scipio. The elegiac couplet is thought to be from Ennius' epitaph on him.

51 *the celebrated balance of Critolaus*: see n. to 4.5; for the weighing of virtue against other 'goods' see *On Ends* 5.91–2.

    Xenocrates: see n. to 5.30.

52 *Atreus' well-known counsel . . . to be defeated*: Accius wrote a Latin tragedy named after Agamemnon's father, from which this verse may come.

54 *to be consul . . . four times, like Cinna*: Gaius Laelius was consul in 140; Cornelius Cinna, an ally of Gaius Marius, was consul from 87 to 84.

55 *Gnaeus Octavius*: consul 87.

   Publius Crassus: consul 97.

   Lucius Caesar: consul 90.

   in time of peace and of war: they all held the highest magistracy and participated in the Social War.

   Marcus Antonius: consul 99. One of the leading protagonists, along with Lucius Licinius Crassus, in C.'s *On the Orator*.

   Gaius Caesar: brother of Lucius Caesar, who died young. C. often praises his charm and wit (*On the Orator* 2.98, cf. 2.217–89).

56 *Gaius Marius . . . colleague Catulus*: Gaius Marius was consul with Quintus Lutatius Catulus in 102. The next year they defeated the Cimbri, a formidable German tribe.

   resembling Laelius: C. compares Catulus to the loyal friend of Scipio Aemilianus, just as he compared himself to Laelius in a letter to Pompey, another great general (*Letters to his Friends* 5.7.3).

   friends of Catulus . . . 'He must die.': Marius and Cinna, returning to Rome after Sulla had left for the East, brought about the deaths of those mentioned in 5.55 and of Catulus.

   final stages of his life: Marius had been consul in 107 and 104–100 and was in his seventies in 86 when the murders were committed.

57 *Dionysius*: tyrant of Syracuse, 405–367.

58 *He came . . . by different writers*: Isocrates (*To Philip* 73, 75) and Diodorus Siculus (13.96) give him undistinguished origins.

   lovers in the Greek fashion: homosexual relations were not unknown in Roman society, but were morally condemned and technically illegal.

   shut himself up in gaol: cf. Plato *Rep.* 9.579A–C on the 'tyrannical man'.

61 *Damocles*: the story of Damocles in the historian Timaeus is found in Horace (*Odes* 3.1.17) and Persius 3.40.

63 *the case of the two followers of Pythagoras*: the anecdote rests on the tradition of close bonds of friendship between Pythagoreans. It is told more fully by C. in *On Duties* 3.45, where he explains that the condemned man wanted to make arrangements for his family, so needed a friend to go bail for his reappearance.

   a poet . . . consider himself excellent: perhaps Aquinius was the same as the bad poet mentioned by Catullus (14.18).

64 *of Plato or of Archytas*: a distinguished Pythagorean philosopher from Tarentum, whom Plato met in south Italy (C., *On Ends* 5.87).

   a lowly little man . . . Archimedes: for Archimedes see n. to 1.63. C.'s description 'a lowly little man' is clearly ironic, emphasizing the neglect of the memory of 'its most ingenious citizen' (see 5.66) by Syracuse.

   my quaestorship: C. was one of the two quaestors assigned to Sicily in 75 and was based at Lilybaeum.

64 *sphere . . . top of his tomb*: Archimedes wrote an extant mathematical treatise comparing the dimensions of the sphere and the cylinder. Plutarch says that Archimedes himself wanted the discovery of the ratios to be commemorated on his tomb (*Marcellus* 17.7).

66 *So that celebrated Greek city . . . a man of Arpinum*: C. emphasizes the greatness of Syracuse, and hence its negligence, by stressing the undistinguished municipal origin of the discoverer of the tomb.

   compare Democritus, Pythagoras, Anaxagoras: see nn. on 1.22, 1.38, and 1.104. C. chooses philosophers who, like Archimedes, were interested in mathematics and science to compare with Dionysius.

68 *threefold progeny*: C. alludes to the traditional threefold division of philosophy into physics, ethics, and logic.

69 *innumerable stars . . . seven others*: the planets (from the Greek term for 'wanderers')—that is, the Moon, Sun, Mercury, Venus, Mars, Jupiter, and Saturn—do not move with the heavens themselves, as do the 'fixed' stars.

   the earth . . . in equilibrium: the earth was thought to be held in the centre of the universe.

   caverns . . . the seas in place: the caverns are supposed to explain why the sea, as the lighter element, did not float above the earth.

70 *the god at Delphi*: see n. to 1.52.

   imitating . . . eternity: see n. to 1.78. The soul is not eternal, but forgetting that helps it to achieve a sense of proportion about human concerns. This idea links physics and ethics, summarized in 5.71.

71 *discovery . . . utmost in good things*: the subject of C.'s *On Ends*.

   our duties: the subject of C.'s *On Duties*.

72 *channelling . . . his own house*: the metaphor comes from the common illegal practice of diverting water from the public supply into one's home (Frontinus, *On Aqueducts* 2.87–8).

73 *Or will Epicurus*: see n. to 2.17.

   physical sensation . . . smooth or rough: an allusion to the Epicurean idea that pain was produced by contact with rough atoms, pleasure with smooth.

75 *Peripatetics . . . Old Academy*: C. often amalgamates the two schools because the Peripatetics were in the doldrums at this period, and Antiochus of Ascalon had borrowed from them, for his 'Old Academy', the idea that the happy life could be enhanced by gifts of fortune.

   Phalaris' bull: see n. to 2.17.

76 *three kinds of goods*: see n. to 5.23.

   the Stoics' complicated arguments: the Stoics were known for their dry and syllogistic way of arguing. C. is here speaking of their refusal to use the term 'good' for anything but Virtue.

   called 'good' . . . 'to be chosen': see n. to 5.47.

   previous days' discussions: in Books 1–4.

77 *Spartan boys do not groan*: see 2.34.

    casting themselves into the flames: see 2.40 and 2.52.

78 *Never . . . defeated by custom*: C.'s aphorism comes after examples of admirable customs that subdue the natural aversion to pain and is then illustrated by decadent Roman and perverse Egyptian customs, and then by examples of animal endurance before he returns to his argument that the happy life is compatible with experiencing pain.

    Egyptians' custom . . . crocodile: known from earlier times in Herodotus 2.65ff.

82 *any definite school*: C. means dogmatic schools, like the Stoa; see 1.17 and 1.78, and Introduction n. 21.

    a short time ago: at 5.75.

83 *we alone*: adherents of C.'s school, the New Academy.

    virtue . . . for a happy life: the question addressed in this book (see 5.2).

    Carneades: see n. to 5.11.

84 *But let us examine . . . of them all*: C. uses political vocabulary familiar to his readers: 'declaration' (*decretum*) is the term for a senatorial decree and 'views' (*sententiae*) for the opinions senators give when asked by the presiding magistrate.

    Hieronymus' view: see n. to 2.15.

    first goods of nature: the things to which the human being is naturally attracted, including self-preservation (*On Ends* 4.15). Of these, the goods of the mind contain the seeds of the virtues. The doctrine is thought to have arisen in the Academy after Plato.

85 *not much different*: see n. to 5.75.

    Diodorus: of Tyre. He became head of the Peripatetic school after Critolaus in the second century.

    Aristo, Pyrrho: see n. to 2.15.

    Herillus: of Carthage, pupil of Zeno. Like Aristo, he rejected distinctions among 'indifferents' and stressed knowledge rather than virtuous action.

    Theophrastus: see n. to 5.24.

87 *it goes down into the bull*: see n. to 2.17.

    with the approval . . . Polemo: C. lists Academic and Peripatetic philosophers.

88 *the one . . . devoted to pleasure*: Epicurus.

    who calls the day . . . happy: a reference to a letter said to have been written on his death-bed (Diogenes Laertius 10.22).

    For severity . . . in slightness: C. has ridiculed this doctrine at 2.44.

89 *one has said . . . simple lifestyle*: cf. 5.26 and *On Ends* 2.90.

90 *Anacharsis*: a Scythian prince of the sixth century, to whom letters, such as C. quotes, were falsely attributed.

91 *Xenocrates*: see n. to 5.30.

thirty minas: half a talent.

92 *Diogenes, as a Cynic*: the name for the Cynic philosophers comes from the Greek word for 'dog', since they were shameless, despising social conventions, including the concealment of natural functions. Their serious aim was the life of virtue, and, unlike the other philosophical sects, they had no metaphysical or logical doctrines specific to themselves. There were many such anecdotes about Diogenes, whom Plato dubbed a 'mad Socrates'.

93 *Epicurus . . . types of desires*: one of Epicurus' *kuriai doxai* ('sovereign maxims'); see Diogenes Laertius 10.139–54.

94 *indecent pleasures*: these are clearly in the category of natural and not necessary. Epicurus specifically noted that only the ignorant and prejudiced thought that the pleasures of sensuality were indicated by deeming pleasure the goal of life (Diogenes Laetius 10.131).

95 *system of counter-balance . . . greater pleasure*: often called the 'calculus of pleasure'.

97 *Darius*: Darius III, who was defeated by Alexander the Great at Gaugamela in 331.

Ptolemy: it is not clear which Egyptian king is meant.

98 *Dionysius*: the following story is told of Dionysius I of Syracuse, great soldier of the early fourth century.

the Eurotas: see n. to 2.36.

99 *Xenophon says*: in the *Education of Cyrus* 1.2.8.

dryness: as opposed to sweatiness.

100 *Timotheus*: son of the Athenian admiral Conon, who established Athenian supremacy by sea in the 370s.

famous letter . . . elements: Dion was ruler of Syracuse for a short time in the mid-fourth century. He brought Plato to Syracuse, and admired his non-democratic views, which led to his assassination. C. quotes here from the bogus seventh letter of Plato (326B).

101 *Sardanapallus . . . not of a king*: in Herodotus 2.109, Sardanapallus is king of Assyria, often confused with Syria. In *On Ends* 2.106, C. gives only the second part of Aristotle's reply to the last two lines of the epitaph, which had been translated into Greek hexameters.

102 *Those who own them . . . came into their possession*: the possessors of such country estates doubtless acquired these treasures as booty in war or through extortion in administration.

103 *my admired Demosthenes*: the Greek orator whom C. most admired, as he makes clear in *Brutus* 35.

a poor woman . . . in Greece: C. explains that a woman passed by Demosthenes carrying water in a pitcher, perhaps because in Greece the domestic supply usually relied mostly on wells and cisterns, whereas in Rome even the poor could access water through public pipes placed at regular intervals and therefore needed to carry it only trivial distances.

communing . . . with himself: C. probably alludes to the custom of moral self-examination, labelled as Pythagorean in *On Old Age* ¶38, and attributed there to the Elder Cato and in *On Duties* 1.1 to Scipio Africanus the younger. It was taken over by the philosopher Sextius in Seneca's youth (*On Anger* 3.36.1).

104 *Democritus:* see n. to 1.22. The following anecdote is told in fuller form by Diogenes Laertius 9.36. C. lists him last to show contempt for his atomic theory.

105 *Heraclitus:* a sixth-century philosopher from Ephesus.

Hermodorus: later tradition had him go into exile in Italy and help the Roman Decemviri to draft the Twelve Tables.

Aristides . . . with the people: he was ostracized by the citizens of Athens because, according to anecdote, they were tired of hearing him called 'the Just'. C.'s allusion to his own case elides the difference between ostracism, a purely political act of the people, and legal banishment by the popular assembly, though C. left Rome before he could be tried.

107 *most distinguished of philosophers . . . Posidonius:* C. groups them by sect, two from the old Academy, two from the middle Academy, two Peripatetics, two founders of the old Stoa, their two successors, two from the new or sceptical Academy, two from the new Old Academy, and two later Stoics, Posidonius being an older contemporary of C.

108 *Teucer's remark . . . prospers*: possibly from Pacuvius' play *Teucer*.

Socrates . . . 'The world.': the remark is also credited to Diogenes the Cynic (Diogenes Laertius 6.63).

Titus Albucius . . . life of politics: C. elsewhere mentions his earlier stay in Athens (*On Ends* 1.9). He was exiled in 103 for extortion as governor of Sardinia. Epicurus recommended abstention from politics to preserve tranquillity (the famous *lathê biôsas*).

109 *In what way . . . Arcesilas*: Metrodorus was from Lampsacus but came to study with Epicurus, an Athenian citizen resident in Athens. In the following pairs, Xenocrates came from Chalcedon and Arcesilas from Pitane in Aeolia.

111 *some people even argue . . . have perception*: see 1.46 for C.'s own view.

112 *Antipater the Cyrenaic*: a follower of Aristippus, on whom see 2.15.

Appius: Appius Claudius, consul in 306 and 297, after being censor in 312, when he commissioned the building of the Appian Way from Rome to Capua and of the Aqua Appia, the first aqueduct.

Gaius Drusus: brother of Marcus Livius Drusus, who opposed C. Gracchus.

Gnaeus Aufidius: praetor in 108.

113 *Diodotus . . . at my house*: in *Brutus* 309, written in 46, C. mentions Diodotus' death in 59 in C.'s house; he taught C. philosophy and other subjects, logic in particular.

played the lyre . . . the Pythagoreans: see n. to 1.38.

Asclepiades . . . philosopher: belonged to the school of Menedemus of Eretria.

behave as certain Greeks do every day: C. seems to allude to the parasites of Greek New Comedy, who begged for food. He may include Cynic philosophers who begged, if he agreed with Seneca that if one professes poverty one should not beg (*On Benefits* 2.17.2; *On the Happy Life* 18.3).

114 *Democritus lost his eyesight*: on Democritus, see n. to 1.22. In *On Ends* 5.87, C. records but does not vouch for a report that Democritus deliberately blinded himself.

travelled into all infinity: Democritus believed in the infinity of space, a belief that Epicurus took over (Lucretius 1.968–83).

115 *Anaxagoras*: see n. to 1.104.

the prophet Tiresias: a Theban seer, who features in the story of Oedipus.

Polyphemus' case get what it likes: C. misremembers Homer's *Odyssey* 9.447–9, where Polyphemus notes how fast the ram used to move in contrast to its present slowness, which he does not know is actually caused by its carrying Odysseus under its belly.

116 *Marcus Crassus*: see n. to 1.12. C.'s letters show that he actually had no high opinion of him.

followers of Eipcurus are ignorant of Greek: see n. to 1.6.

117 *Lysimachus . . . Spanish fly*: see n. to 1.107. Decoction of Spanish fly (cantharadine) is a deadly poison, though the insect is tiny.

118 *Paullus*: Lucius Aemilius Paullus, as consul, defeated and captured King Perseus of Macedon at Pydna in 168.

Hieronymus: see n. to 2.15.

119 *those philosophers . . . in the soul*: the Epicureans, here contrasted, at the end of the paragraph, with, first, the Peripatetics and then the Stoics.

120 *Carneades*: see n. to 5.11 n.

Stoics regarded as . . . 'goods': the Stoics regarded virtue as the only 'good', and these advantageous things merely as 'positive indifferents'.

121 *this leisure . . . whatever form it will take*: C. hints at the effect of Caesar's dictatorship.

CATO THE ELDER: ON OLD AGE

1 *O Titus . . . night and day*: C. addresses his friend, Titus Pomponius Atticus, with a passage from Ennius' epic about Rome, the *Annals* (10.355f. Skutsch) in which a shepherd from Epirus addresses Titus Quinctius Flamininus

during a campaign against Philip V of Macedon in 198. The quotations enable C. to introduce, in an ironic way, the subject of old age and its problems, topics appropriate to Cicero and his friend Atticus, who was three years his senior.

brought home from Athens: Atticus left Rome to live in Athens in *c.*85, during Sulla's dictatorship, and remained there until the mid-sixties, when he returned to help C.'s campaign for the consulship of 63.

2 *old age . . . advancing upon us*: C. is being tactful to Atticus here, as both were over 60, when old age was usually taken to begin: C. was 62, and Atticus 65.

a philosopher: Atticus was an Epicurean, C. a sceptical Academic, but the common interest in philosophy is here held to unite them. C. never used Atticus as an Epicurean spokesman in his dialogues, perhaps because Atticus, like a good Epicurean, preferred not to be in the limelight.

3 *ascribed . . . as the Cean Aristo did*: Aristo was the head of the Peripatetic school at Athens in the late third century. He apparently wrote a dialogue featuring Tithonus, the mythical character granted immortality but not eternal youth, who would therefore have had exceptional experience of old age.

the elderly Marcus Cato: the dialogue is set in 150, a year before Cato's death, when he was eighty-three years old.

Laelius and Scipio: Gaius Laelius (consul 140) and Publius Cornelius Scipio Aemilianus (consul 147) were both young men, who are shown calling on the venerated older man, a mark of respect remarked on in ¶63.

more learning . . . as is well known: all the testimony we have to Cato's knowledge of learning comes from C. here (¶¶26 and 38) and in the earlier *Academic Books* pref. 2.5, but it is confirmed by his use of unacknowledged quotations from Greek historians and other authors, attested by Plutarch (*Cato Maior* 2) and Pliny the Elder (*Natural History* 29.14).

4 *Etna itself*: in myth, the giant Typhon was underneath Mount Etna and was responsible for its eruptions. His punishment is alluded to in ¶5.

5 *worthy of . . . my surname*: Cato's name was derived, in popular etymology, from *catus* ('clever'). Plutarch *Cato Maior* 1 says that his name was changed from Marcus Porcius Priscus to Marcus Porcius Cato on account of his cleverness.

I follow nature . . . as a god: Cato's formulation suggests the teaching of philosophy, though he is denying any but natural wisdom.

6 *we expect . . . to be old*: both Scipio and Laelius lived for another twenty years. Scipio died in 129 and Laelius at an unknown date after that.

what kind of place . . . you have reached: C. doubtless intended his readers to pick up the echoes of Plato's *Republic* 328D–330A in this passage until the end of ¶8, but Plato only alludes to the proverb C. quotes in ¶7.

7 *those former consuls*: Gaius Livius Salinator was consul in 188 and died in 170; Spurius Albinus in 186 and died in 180. Given their consular dates,

they were probably both younger than Cato when they died—Salinator in his late fifties, Albinus in his early fifties.

7 *pleasures*: C. does not specify sexual ones as Plato does.

8 *Themistocles . . . Athens*: the anecdote about the great Athenian general of the fifth century, victor of the battle of Salamis, is in Herodotus 8.125, and the obscure birthplace is Belbina.

9 *a man's awareness . . . happiness*: cf. ¶71. The sentiment is found in several philosophers and in popular morality. Cato used it in a speech (frag. 17, *Oratorum Romanorum fragmenta*, ed. H. Malcovati, 1955).

10 *Quintus Maximus*: Quintus Fabius Maximus was consul in 233. He is introduced as an example of virtue leading to a pleasant old age, as becomes clear in ¶13. Cato was born the year before.

   consul for the fourth time: in 214.

   Cincian law . . . gifts: passed in 204, it forbade advocates to receive fees or gifts and forbade gifts of any kind above a certain amount, except between relatives.

   My friend Ennius: see nn. to *Tusculan Disputations* 1.3. Cato is said to have brought the poet to Rome from Sardinia (Nepos, *Cato* 1.4).

11 *And as for Tarentum . . . lost it*: Tarentum was taken by Hannibal in 213 and regained by Fabius in 209. The anecdote illustrates the affability mentioned in ¶10.

   while consul . . . against the auspices: the incident dates to 228. The land was taken from the Senones in northern Italy. C. was always against land distribution and interested in augural activity, being an augur himself. He represents Fabius' remark as shocking to Cato, perhaps even to readers of his own day when political manipulation of the auspices was common.

12 *he endured the death of his son*: his son Quintus Fabius Maximus died in 213. C. had collected examples of fathers' bearing the deaths of their sons bravely (*On Friendship* ¶9) in his *Consolation to Himself* on the death of his daughter Tullia in February of 45.

   what philosopher . . . contemptible: Cato was said to distrust philosophers (Plutarch, *Cato Maior* 23). This dialogue demonstrates C.'s view in *Tusculan Disputations* 1.2 that the Roman ancestors had by nature moral qualities that others had to learn from books.

   He had read widely . . . for a Roman: C. is keen to emphasize Cato's appreciation of Greek literature, brought out by his citation of Greek examples in ¶13.

14 *only nineteen years . . . sixty-five years old*: giving the dramatic date of 150 by naming the consuls of the year, C. goes on to date Fabius' death to 169.

   the Voconian law: about inheritances, including restrictions on women being appointed as legal heirs.

15 *four reasons . . . unhappy*: the beginning of the discussion proper, after the extended preface of ¶¶1–15. The first reason is discussed in ¶¶15–26; the

second in ¶¶27–38; the third in ¶¶39–66; the fourth in ¶¶66–84, with ¶85 serving as a conclusion.

Quintus Maximus: his achievements were recounted in ¶¶10–12.

Lucius Paulus . . . my own son: Lucius Aemilius Paulus was Scipio's natural father and victor of the battle of Pydna in 168; his daughter Aemilia married Cato's son.

the other old men . . . Coruncanius: Caius Fabricius Luscinus (consul 282), Manius Curius Dentatus (consul 290), and Tiberius Coruncanius (consul 280), used often by C. as examples of old Roman virtue (cf. ¶43).

16 *making peace . . . Pyrrhus*: Pyrrhus was king of Epirus and, briefly, of Macedonia. Between 280 and 276, when peace negotiations had failed, he won several victories over Rome with the support of the south Italian cities, but he returned home in 275 after heavy losses.

the speech of Appius: C. says in *Brutus* 61 that the speech was preserved in family records.

the seventeenth year . . . consulship: since the second consulship was in 296, this was in 279.

he first held this office: he was censor in 312, and consul in 307 and 296.

18 *commander-in-chief*: the Latin has *consul*, but, as C. is giving his military career, the translation reflects the military role of that office before the first century.

Carthage . . . completely destroyed: that he ended every speech with a warning against Carthage is maintained by Diodorus, Plutarch, and Appian. Cato died in 149, three years before Carthage was finally destroyed by Rome.

19 *He died . . . time as consul*: this places the death of the elder Scipio Africanus in 185, whereas the thirty-three years mentioned before would give 183: there may be a textual error as Powell 1988, Appendix 3e, suggests.

my own time as consul . . . to that office: the election was in 195 for the consulship of 194.

if these qualities . . . the senate: C. alludes to the etymology of *senatus* which is related to *senex* ('old man').

20 *'the elders' . . . actual age*: the Spartan equivalent of the senate was called *gerousia*, related to *gerôn* ('old man') (as with *senatus* and *senex*).

Naevius' The Lydian: Naevius was a dramatic and epic Latin poet, active in the late third century. The title of his play is given in manuscripts as *Ludus*, taken to be a transcription of the Greek *Ludos*.

21 *greeting Aristides as Lysimachus*: the latter being the name of Aristides' father and his son.

in reading . . . lose my memory: a superstition also found in the Babylonian Talmud.

22 *Sophocles . . . extreme old age*: Sophocles was about ninety when he died. The play he was then revising was presumably the *Oedipus Coloneus*.

22 *in our law . . . guilty of mismanagement*: the procedure under Roman law was *interdictio bonorum* (Paulus, *Sentences* 3.4a.7).

23 *the Stoic Diogenes*: one of the three philosophers who came as ambassadors to Rome from Athens in 155. The others were Carneades the Academic and Critolaus the Peripatetic.

24 *Roman farmers from Sabine territory*: Cato owned a farm in Sabine territory (Nepos, *Cato* 1.1), which he mentions in ¶55. His work *On Agriculture* shows a practical knowledge of farming.

25 *Statius*: Caecilius Statius, a Latin playwright who adapted Greek comedies.

26 *learning . . . in my old age*: see n. to ¶3.

    examples: C. has made Cato cite Greek examples in ¶¶13, 21, 22, and 23.

    Socrates . . . in the case of the lyre: see Plato, *Euthydemus* 272c.

    the ancients learned the lyre: it is not clear if by 'the ancients', Cato means both Greeks and Romans, but it is hard to believe that C. had him wanting to learn something eschewed by Roman aristocrats (Nepos, *Lives*, 1.1–3).

27 *the second heading*: see ¶15.

    Milo of Croton: a renowned wrestler of the late sixth century, who was six times an Olympic victor.

    Sextus . . . in the law: examples of jurists of the late third to early second century; see also ¶50.

29 *Gnaeus and Publius [Cornelius] Scipio*: uncle and father of the elder Scipio Africanus.

    your two grandfathers . . . Africanus: Lucius Aemilius Paulus was Scipio Aemilianus' paternal grandfather by birth, Publius Cornelius Scipio Africanus by adoption.

30 *Cyrus . . . Xenophon . . . youth had been*: the passage is *Cyropaedia* 8.7.6, a work C. knew well and which Cato could have known. C. has Cato discuss Xenophon's *On Household Management* at ¶59.

    Lucius . . . twenty-two years: Lucius Caecilius Metellus was consul in 251 and 247 and chief pontiff from 243 until his death in 221.

31 *Nestor . . . his own virtues*: in *Iliad* 1.260, 7.123–60, 11.668ff., 23.629ff.

    as Homer says . . . sweeter than honey: *Iliad* 1.249.

    the famous commander . . . perish soon: *Iliad* 2.369–74.

32 *I am in my eighty-fourth year*: Cato was 83 in 150 when the dialogue is set.

    as a private soldier . . . Glabrio: Cato was a private soldier, then military tribune in 214, quaestor in 204 in Spain, consul in Spain in 195, and military tribune serving under Glabrio in 191.

    the strength of . . . Titus Pontius: centurions were non-commissioned officers known for their toughness and physical strength; this one is mentioned in a fragment of the satirist Lucilius (frag. 89M).

    Milo . . . Pythagoras: for Milo see n. to ¶27; he was traditionally connected with the Pythagoreans.

34 *your grandfather's friend . . . Masinissa*: king of Numidia and a friend of Scipio's grandfather, the elder Africanus.

  extremely dry: freedom from secretions was popularly thought to be a sign of good health (cf. *Tusculan Disputations* 5.99), avoidance of spitting being noted by Pliny *Natural History* 7.22.

  men of my age . . . public services: Elder Seneca, in *Controversies* 1.8.4, gives 65 as the age at which senatorial attendance was no longer required; Seneca, in *On the Shortness of Life* 20.4, gives 60. Possibly there was a change in the first century AD.

35 *Publius*: the father of Scipio Aemilianus, he did not have a public career, but C. says in *Brutus* 77 that he left some short speeches and a history in Greek.

36 *a regimen of health*: ancient medicine could not cure many diseases, but actively promoted preventive measures involving lifestyle, diet, and exercise.

  Caecilius: see n. to ¶24.

37 *Appius . . . four sturdy sons*: Appius Claudius Caecus, consul in 307 and 296. His four sons included the ancestor of the Clodii Pulchri and the ancestor of the Claudian emperors.

38 *seventh book of my Antiquities*: Cato's *Origines*, the first historical work in Latin, started with the foundation of Rome and dealt with the origins of Italian towns before recounting the First Punic War and other wars. The seventh book dealt with his own time, and he was still writing it when he died.

  my speeches: Cato's speeches were extant and esteemed by C. (*Brutus* 63–8).

  I call to mind . . . each day: in *On Anger* 3.36.1, Seneca, not mentioning Pythagoras, ascribes this practice to Sextius, who developed a Roman type of philosophy in Greek during the triumviral period (cf. *Epistles* 59.7).

  I . . . attend the senate: though he was not required to do so at his age (see n. to ¶34).

39 *the third ground . . . lacks pleasures*: the third of the reasons given in ¶15 for why old age is not happy.

  What an outstanding gift . . . our youth!: cf. ¶7 for this point.

  Archytas of Tarentum: mathematician, politician, and Pythagorean philosopher.

  Quintus Maximus: see ¶¶10–11.

40 *indeed rape . . . those of pleasure*: the point was made forcibly by Plato (*Phaedo* 66C).

41 *Nearchus . . . friend of the Roman people*: a detail that could be taken to confirm the existence of Nearchus, who is heard of again only in Plutarch, *Cato Maior* 2–3, probably derived from C.

  the consuls . . . battle of Caudium: trapped by the Samnites in the Caudine Forks, the consuls of 321 made a treaty and then abdicated.

  Plato . . . Claudius: 349, though this visit is not otherwise clearly attested. On the whole episode see Powell 1988, Appendix 3f.

42 *Lucius Flamininus . . . Flaccus and myself*: Lucius Quinctius Flamininus
   was consul in 192 and Cato was censor with Lucius Valerius Flaccus in
   184. His brother Titus Quinctius Flamininus was a successful commander
   who declared the freedom of Greece in 196.

43 *Gaius Fabricius*: he led an embassy in 280–279 to Pyrrhus, king of Epirus,
   on whom see n. to ¶16.

   Manius Curius: Manius Curius Dentatus was consul for the second time
   in 275. He finally defeated Pyrrhus near Malventum; see n. to ¶16.

   Tiberius Coruncanius: see n. to ¶15.

   Publius Decius . . . I have spoken of: he performed the heroic act, or act of
   devotion, mentioned here when he was consul in 295, rushing to meet
   death in battle as an act of self-consecration to the gods; his father, also
   called Publius Decius Mus, had done the same thing before him.

44 *as Plato puts it . . . like fish*: in *Timaeus* 69D.

   Gaius Duilius . . . Carthaginians: as consul in 260, he defeated the
   Carthaginians at Mylae in Sicily. He died in 220 when Cato was 14 and so
   Cato could have seen and remembered him.

   to be preceded . . . his glory gave him: the privilege was granted only to
   magistrates but Gaius Duilius was not prevented from assuming it because
   of his achievement.

45 *the time of my quaestorship*: 204. These ancient institutions, some of which
   were older than the ones Cato is made to mention, were usually religious,
   as here.

   the rites of the Great Mother: Cybele, the mother goddess of Anatolia, was
   brought to Rome, was served by oriental priests in a temple on the Palatine,
   and was honoured with the Megalensian Games.

   convivium . . . in that association: derived from *cum* and *vivere*, unlike the
   Greek *symposium* or *syndeipnon*, for which C. here gives only the Latin
   terms *compotatio* and *concenatio*. He makes the same point in a letter
   (*Letters to his Friends* 9.24.3) written a year later.

46 *'afternoon feasts'*: banquets that began early and lasted longer than the
   afternoon.

   pleasure . . . a certain measure of it: an allusion to Aristotle's 'mean', the
   recommended area of moral choice that displays moderation; cf. *Academic
   Books* 2.135.

   appointing masters . . . ancestors' practice: the master of ceremonies held
   office for a number of banquets, which he organized and over which he
   presided. The 'top' was the left-hand couch, one of the three arranged
   from left to right around three sides of the table.

   cups that are small . . . Xenophon's Symposium: at 2.26.

   the Sabine country: known for simple habits, so luxurious banquets would
   not be expected.

47 *It was a good reply . . . master*: the anecdote is from Plato's *Republic* 1.329b.

48 *Ambivius Turpio*: Lucius Ambivius Turpio was the most famous actor of Cato's day.

49 *the soul . . . lives with itself*: C. has a fuller version in *Tusculan Disputations* 1.75.

Gaius Galus . . . sun and moon: interested in scientific astronomy, Gaius Sulpicius Galus predicted the eclipse of the moon before the battle of Pydna in 168 (C. in *On the Republic* 1.21–3).

50 *Naevius*: see n. to ¶20.

Livius . . . when I was a young man: Andronicus, the oldest of the early Latin poets whom C. names here; the play C. mentions was produced in 240. The other two playwrights lived into the early second century.

Publius Licinius Crassus: see ¶22; he was known especially for his knowledge of pontifical law and was pontifex maximus from 212 to 183.

Publius Scipio: Publius Cornelius Scipio Nasica Corculum, a cousin of Scipio Aemilianus, who became pontifex maximus in 150.

Marcus Cethegus . . . marrow of Persuasion: Marcus Cornelius Cethegus (consul 240). In *Brutus* 57 C. explains that the expression was a Latin translation from the Greek made by Ennius.

as I have said: at ¶26.

51 *the pleasures that farmers know*: to have Cato praise agriculture (¶¶51–3) is appropriate, given his authorship of *On Agriculture*, but C.'s largely aesthetic praise is not inspired by Cato's work, which is, as Powell 1988, 205, says, 'either strictly utilitarian or concerned with the good effects of agriculture on character'. Xenophon's *On Household Management* is more the inspiration. Cato's allusions to what 'the farmer' does (¶¶52 and 54) and his own 'relaxation and delight' (¶52) in his old age show that he does not think of himself as doing the practical work (see P. A. Brunt, *Studies in Stoicism*, Oxford, Oxford University Press, 2013, 155).

the life of the wise man: although the Romans thought agriculture a commendable occupation, and Posidonius (Seneca, *Epistles* 90.21) thought it was developed by a wise man, it is not given as a suitable way of life for the wise man until Musonius Rufus (frag. 11). But Cato's conception might be rather rugged.

an account in earth's bank: the banking metaphor might seem odd since C. represented Cato, in *On Duties* 89, as disapproving of lending money at interest.

54 *usefulness of manuring*: cf. Pliny, *Natural History* 18.174, where Cato is quoted as an expert who makes manuring almost as important as ploughing. Cato discusses it in *On Agriculture* 8, 29, 36–7, 49, 151.2.

Homer, who lived . . . many generations before: C. indicates that the date of Homer was controversial in his day. His contemporary Varro thought Homer and Hesiod were roughly contemporary. The Homeric passage is *Odyssey* 24.226–7 but it does not explicitly mention manuring.

55 *old age . . . wordiness*: cf. Cato's mention of the loquaciousness of old age in ¶31.

Manius Curius: see n. to ¶43.

56 *Samnites brought . . . gold to Curius*: in *On the Republic* 3.40, C. makes clear that this was a gift from clients, not a bribe.

senes or old men: see n. to ¶19.

Lucius Quinctius Cincinnatus . . . a tyranny: tradition has it that he was called from the plough to be dictator in 458 and, as dictator, dealt with Spurius Maelius in 439.

those who summoned . . . viatores or wayfarers: the official messengers of Roman magistrates.

farmers call 'their second flitch': *succidia* is a rustic word found only here and in Cato's own writings (Gellius 13.25.12; *Antiquities* frag. 48, *The Fragments of the Roman Historians*, ed. T. J. Cornell, 2013).

59 *Xenophon . . . carry on reading*: C. not only stresses Cato's intellectual interests in Greek but has him encouraging the young in that direction. C. says in a letter to Quintus (*Letters to his Brother Quintus* 1.1.23) that Scipio was fond of Xenophon's *Cyropaedia*.

that book: the passage is *On Household Management* 4.20, which C. here adapts.

Lysander of Sparta: the Spartan admiral who defeated Athens at Aegospotami in 405, bringing the Peloponnesian War to an end with Persian help under the command of Cyrus, son of the Persian King Darius II.

a certain park . . . planted with care: the Latin makes clear that C. means a *paradeisos*, an ornamental park in the Persian style.

Cyrus the Younger . . . fortunate as well: for the relationship of this scene to the encounter of Lysander and Cyrus in Xenophon's *On Household Management* 4.16–25, see Powell 1988, 229.

60 *Marcus Valerius Corvinus . . . forty-six years*: traditionally, he lived from 372 to 271. His first and sixth consulships were in 348 and 299, but the forty-six-year interval would be accurate from his second consulship of 346. C. or his source is mistaken.

span of life . . . beginning of old age: old age traditionally began at the age of military discharge, though in C.'s own time it began at 65 or 60.

61 *Lucius Caecilius Metellus*: see n. to ¶30.

Aulus Atilius Calatinus: consul 258. His tomb was outside the Porta Capena of Rome.

Publius Crassus: see n. to ¶50.

his successor . . . Marcus Lepidus: Marcus Aemilius Lepidus (consul 187). He was pontifex maximus in 180–152.

Paulus . . . already mentioned: in ¶¶15, 19 and 10–13 respectively.

62 *I once stated*: it is not known where.

63 *when an old man . . . take a seat*: perhaps an incident at the Panathenaic Festival.

64 *your college of augurs*: Scipio and Laelius were both members of the college, as was C. Cato was not, though at ¶38 he is shown studying augural, as well as civil and pontifical, law.

   those who hold the highest offices of all: those with *imperium*—that is, consuls, praetors, censors, and dictators (when there was one).

65 *those brothers in the Adelphi*: 'The Brothers', the last play of the Roman playwright Terence, was commissioned in 160 for the funeral games of Lucius Aemilius Paulus (see n. to ¶29).

66 *miserliness*: as censor in 184, Cato showed himself hard on luxury and extravagance, taxing ornaments, women's clothing, expensive vehicles, and slaves (Plutarch, *Cato Maior* 1.2; Nepos, *Cato* 2.3). He claimed (Plutarch, *Cato Maior* 4.4) that he wore inexpensive clothing, drank the same wine as his slaves, spent little on meat, sold a tapestry he inherited, left his farm buildings unplastered, and limited his expenditure on luxury and on food for slaves.

   journey's end: the metaphorical reference to death makes a neat transfer to the last complaint of the four listed in ¶15—that old age is close to death.

   Plainly it should not . . . where it will exist for ever: the two alternatives often mentioned, going back to Plato, *Apology* 40C.

67 *young men . . . disease more easily*: the old have built up immunity to diseases, aside from the strong constitutions that have allowed them to have a long life. The concept of immunity would not have been understood by ancient medicine.

68 *I lost my excellent son*: the son, Marcus Porcius Cato, died about two years before the date at which the dialogue is set, when he was praetor-elect. Cato returns to his loss at ¶84, a loss that evoked C.'s recent bereavement, the death of his beloved daughter Tullia.

   you, Scipio . . . lost your brothers: C. means Scipio Aemilianus' two natural brothers, also sons of Lucius Aemilius Paulus, one of whom died one day before the other and three days after the father's triumph in 168 for the victory at Pydna. That left another adopted brother, Quintus Fabius Maximus Aemilianus.

69 *as I have seen it recorded*: another allusion to Cato's Greek reading, which Cicero is at pains to emphasize.

   Arganthonius: Herodotus 1.163 reports that a king of Tartessus at the mouth of the Guadalquivir river lived and reigned to these great ages. He welcomed the Phoceans, who sailed west to escape from Persian occupation but returned home.

71 *everything . . . counted as good*: this view is attributed by C., in *On Ends* 5.89–91, to Antiochus of Ascalon, who accepted, against the Stoics, that there were goods other than virtue.

72 *This explains . . . Solon said 'Old age'*: the anecdote is found in Plutarch, *Solon* 31 and *Moralia* 794.

   neither greedily seek . . . without good cause: the Greeks and Romans did not condemn suicide, provided it was rational—that is, done in a calm state of mind and with good cause. Here 'greedily' is the irrational opposite.

73 *And Pythagoras . . . from a god*: see *Phaedo* 61Dff. for the Platonic doctrine and *Apology* 28D for the comparison of life to military service.

   Ennius . . . see me on the bier: for Ennius see nn. to *Tusculan Disputations* 1.3. These lines are about poetic immortality but C. presents them as being about literal immortality. In *Tusculan Disputations* 1.31ff. he fills out the argument by saying that Ennius' desire for glory after death implies the survival of the soul to enjoy it.

75 *Lucius Brutus . . . liberty to his country*: Lucius Junius Brutus was responsible for freeing Rome from the rule of the Etruscan kings in the late sixth century.

   two Decii . . . death they had chosen: see n. to ¶43.

   Marcus Atilius . . . with the enemy: Marcus Atilius Regulus, consul 258, 254, one of C.'s favourite *exempla*. As a captive in 255, he kept his promise to return to Carthage if he did not persuade the Romans to surrender.

   the two Scipios . . . their own bodies: Gnaeus and Publius Cornelius Scipio, on whom see n. to ¶29.

   Lucius Paulus . . . colleague: for Lucius Paulus Aemilius see n. to ¶29. As consul in 216, he was killed fighting Hannibal at Cannae; his colleague was Gaius Terentius Varro, who escaped to Venusia.

   Marcus Marcellus . . . honours of a funeral: Marcus Claudius Marcellus, consul many times, was killed near Venusia by the Carthaginians, and Hannibal sent his ashes back to Rome, according to *Tusculan Disputations* 1.89, though Livy 27.28 has him buried.

   my Antiquities: see n. to ¶38.

77 *I have a clearer understanding . . . the nearer I get to it*: an idea in Plato, *Republic* 330E. The ideas about the immortal heavenly soul that follow feature in Plato.

   the soul is . . . plunged in the earth: the descent of the soul comes from Plato *Timaeus* 41D–E, as does the notion of imitation of the heavenly order (47C).

   the greatest philosophers: here Pythagoras and Plato.

78 *the Pythagoreans . . . fellow countrymen of ours*: the existence of a Pythagorean colony in southern Italy led to Roman claims of this sort; cf. *On Friendship* ¶13 and *Tusculan Disputations* 4.2.

   Socrates . . . wisest of all: from Plato, *Apology* 21a.

79 *the teaching of Plato*: in *Phaedo* 72e ff. and *Meno* 83ff.

   in Xenophon's work: *Cyropaedia* 8.7.17–22, which C. adapts in what follows.

81 *when we are asleep . . . at liberty*: dreams were often thought to be prophetic in the ancient world, though C. himself thought that some were just recycled thoughts of the day (*On the Republic* 6.10.10).

82 *two grandfathers . . . or his uncle*: see n. to ¶29 for these persons.

83 *whom I have . . . written myself*: in his *Antiquities*. See Nepos, *Cato* 3.4, where Cato is said to have omitted the names of generals in his narrative, so his emphasis on affection for individuals here and in ¶84 seems odd.

84 *I shall go to meet . . . my own Cato*: see n. to ¶68.

   his body . . . burned by him: a sentiment already well known from Pericles' funeral oration in Thucydides, and celebrated in epitaphs.

85 *insignificant philosophers . . . no sensation when dead*: principally, the Epicureans who denied immortality.

LAELIUS: ON FRIENDSHIP

1 *the augur Quintus Mucius Scaevola*: Quintus Mucius Scaevola (consul 117), called 'augur' to distinguish him from Quintus Mucius Scaevola pontifex (consul 95), the son of the augur's cousin Publius Mucius Scaevola (consul 175). Both were distinguished jurists.

   Gaius Laelius: the son of a new man who held the consulship in 190, he was consul in 140 and a close friend of Scipio Aemilianus, as his father had been of the elder Scipio Africanus, under whom he served in the Second Punic War. Laelius was the younger Scipio's legate in the Third Punic War. The dialogue is set in 129, the year of this Scipio's death.

   calling him 'the wise': C. held that the epithet, accorded in his lifetime, was for culture and learning (¶6).

   the toga of manhood: coming of age militarily was marked by the swapping of the purple-bordered *toga praetexta* for the plain *toga virilis*. The usual age was 15 or 16, so probably *c.*90 for C.

   Scaevola . . . a sense of what was fair: the word used for 'fairness' is *iustitia*, and C. is alluding to Scaevola's interest in the law.

2 *Publius Sulpicius . . . friendliest terms*: Sulpicius was tribune in 88, when the consuls were Lucius Cornelius Sulla (later dictator) and Quintus Pompeius. His brother Servius was married to Anicia, a cousin of Atticus (Nepos, *Atticus* 2). Sulpicius, having attacked the consuls who left Rome, had the Mithridatic command switched from Sulla to Gaius Marius, the great general in the war against the German tribe the Cimbri, but was declared a public enemy and was killed when Sulla returned to Rome with his army.

3 *the death of Africanus*: in 129. There are several layers of memory here: the discussion, set in 88, takes place over forty years before the date of composition and includes recall of a discourse on friendship over forty years before that.

4 *dialogue of this kind . . . more weight*: C. points to the earlier *On the Republic* and *On Old Age*. In a letter to Quintus (*Letters to his Brother Quintus* 3.5.1)

and in the preface to *On Old Age*, C. notes that weighty speakers from the past lend the dialogues greater authority.

4 *it is Cato, not I, who speaks*: a compliment from C. to himself.

5 *I have written . . . friend to another*: C., at the age of 62, and Atticus, at 65, had been friends since boyhood (Nepos, *Atticus* 1.4).

  you may recognise a portrait of yourself: in the discourse on friendship, not in the figure of Laelius. That would have been tactless, given the reverence with which Scipio is always regarded by Laelius, as portrayed by C., here as in *On the Republic*. In a letter of 62 to Pompey (*Letters to his Friends* 5.7.3), C. had suggested parallels between himself and Laelius, and between Pompey and Scipio.

6 *Lucius Acilius . . . learned in civil law*: Lucius Acilius was a jurist (*On the Laws* 2.59).

  'the wise': C. calls the Elder Cato wise in several places, but the epithet is not attested for him elsewhere.

7 *Seven Wise Men*: see *Tusculan Disputations* n. to 5.7.

  one man at Athens . . . wisest of men: Socrates, according to the Delphic oracle (Plato *Apology* 21A); also in *On Old Age* ¶78.

  Decimus Brutus: the consul of 138.

  the Nones of this month . . . on that day: the Nones of either April or May, so 5 April or 7 May. C., in *On Divination* 1.90, shows that the meetings had ceased by 44. As an augur himself, C. was keen to mention the college whenever possible.

9 *he bore the death of his son*: the younger Marcus Porcius Cato died when praetor-elect *c.*152. C. mentions his death in *On Old Age* ¶¶68 and 84, and *Tusculan Disputations* 3.70. He probably identified Cato's bereavement with his own recent loss of Tullia in early adulthood.

  the case of Paulus: Lucius Aemilius Paulus, the victor of the battle of Pydna, had two of his four sons adopted into other families and then lost his two remaining ones as adolescents (Plutarch, *Aemilius Paulus* 45).

  the behaviour of Galus: Gaius Sulpicius Galus, astronomer. C. lists all these cases in a letter of 45 (*Letters to his Friends* 4.6.1).

10 *that very man . . . wisest of all*: Socrates, as in ¶7.

  I bring myself . . . consolation: C. had written himself a consolation for Tullia's death.

  inconveniences: the Latin word *incommoda* is one that C. often uses for the 'negative indifferents', as the Stoics called misfortunes, holding that they were not bad, just not to be sought after.

11 *was made consul twice . . . almost too late*: Scipio was consul first in 147, at 37, three years before the usual age, so he could take command at Carthage; then again in 134 to finish the war against Numantia in Spain.

  generosity: remarked on by the contemporary historian Polybius 31.26.6; 31.28.8.

a discussion . . . with Scipio and myself: C. refers to *On Old Age*, in which Laelius was a speaker; cf. ¶14, where he recalls the conversation in C.'s *On the Republic*.

12 *It is difficult . . . people's suspicions*: Scipio was found dead in his bed, with no trace of illness the night before. Poisoning by one of his relatives or friends was suspected (Appian, *Civil Wars* 1.19; Livy, *Epitome* 59) and suicide was also mooted, but officially the death was natural, as reflected in Laelius' funeral eulogy.

people of Rome . . . and the Latins: Scipio was opposing the agrarian law of Tiberius Gracchus, which would have distributed to citizens some land that belonged to Rome's allied cities and towns with Latin rights.

13 *those who . . . begun to argue*: C. means the Epicureans, for whom the soul was composed of atoms that dispersed at death. C. is rather tendentious in treating the view as recent, but he is siding with the even earlier ancestral Romans, Pythagoras and Socrates as depicted by Plato. He ignores Socrates' contemporary Democritus, who anticipated Epicurus' view.

those who . . . educated Great Greece: C. harks back to the flourishing of the cities of southern Italy, founded by colonists from Greece in the sixth and fifth centuries but which were now in decay—that is, no longer 'great'.

oracle of Apollo: see n. to ¶7 *one man at Athens . . . wisest of men*.

say sometimes one thing and sometimes another: C. is thinking of Plato's aporetic dialogues, in which Socrates casts doubt on whatever position the speaker espouses (cf. *Tusculan Disputations* 1.99). His belief in immortality is taken from Plato's *Phaedo*.

14 *Philus and Manilius*: Lucius Furius Philus (consul 136) was a friend of Scipio and Laelius and features in C.'s *On the Republic*; Manius Manilius (consul 149) had Scipio serving under him as military tribune in the Third Punic War.

with me, he discussed . . . for three days: C. has Laelius refer to the discussion in *On the Republic*, particularly the *Dream of Scipio*, with which it ends.

nothing good in death . . . nothing bad in it: C. had used these arguments in *On Old Age* ¶¶66, 74, 81, 85, and the *Tusculan Disputations* 1.25–6, 82, 117–18.

15 *complete community . . . opinions*: an anticipation of the definition of friendship at ¶20.

my reputation for wisdom: see ¶¶5–6.

in all the course of history . . . have reached our ears: mythological examples of pairs of friends are Theseus and Pirithous, Orestes and Pylades, and Achilles and Patroclus.

17 *men of learning . . . proposed for debate*: Greek philosophers often asked for a *zêtêma* or puzzle to be proposed and would then lecture impromptu on it (C. *On Ends* 2.1–2; *Letters to his Friends* 9.26, a letter to Papirius Paetus making fun of the practice).

17 *give friendship precedence . . . life of man*: C. does not elevate friendship above virtue but only above good and bad fortune. Friendship fits human nature and garnishes good fortune and mitigates bad.

18 *friendship can exist . . . attained it*: C. accepts the Stoic doctrine (Diogenes Laertius 7.124; Seneca, *Letters* 1.12; Epictetus 2.22) that true friendship can exist only among good men, but argues for a realistic conception of 'good', not demanding full virtue in the Stoic sense. Aristotle accepted several levels and types of friendship (*Nicomachean Ethics* Book 8).

Gaius . . . Coruncanius: for these three see *On Old Age*, n. to 15.

19 *they follow Nature . . . living well*: Greek philosophers assumed that happiness could be attained only by living according to Nature, but they differed as to what that meant.

tie . . . between us all: this is the Stoic doctrine of *oikeiôsis*, which makes us feel akin to other human beings. The Stoics had an elaborate system of concentric circles of attachment moving from oneself outwards to the human race (A. A. Long and D. N. Sedley, eds., *The Hellenistic Philosophers*, Cambridge: Cambridge University Press, 1987, 346–51).

And so . . . that lacks stability: friendship is less stable than kinship in that it dissolves without goodwill, but it is superior in that it implies goodwill. The idea about fellow countrymen being closer than strangers is already in Xenophon, *Education of Cyrus* 8.7.14.

20 *true affection . . . just a few*: C. thinks primarily of friendship between two people (¶15). The treatise is dedicated to Atticus, who was C.'s closest friend, though Atticus himself had many friends, some of whom (e.g. Brutus) may have been as close to him as C.

a shared set of views . . . human and divine: cf. ¶61. Yet C. did not think that Atticus' adherence to Epicureanism, a philosophy of which C. is quite critical, even in this very work, reduced their friendship. In fact, C. had other Epicurean friends, such as Papirius Paetus and Trebatius Testa (J. Barnes and M. Griffin, eds., *Philosophia Togata*, vol. 2: *Plato and Aristotle at Rome*, Oxford: Oxford University Press, 1997, 105–9).

pleasure . . . animals: although C.'s list of candidates for the highest good includes things not recommended by philosophers, here he clearly has the Epicureans in mind.

those who . . . in virtue: the Academics and the Peripatetics thought virtue the highest good, but the Stoics thought it the only good.

without virtue . . . able to exist: see ¶¶27–8, where C. explains this statement.

21 *men like . . . Philus*: see ¶9 for Paulus, Cato, and Galus, and ¶14 for Philus and Manlius.

22 *Ennius' phrase*: for Ennius see *Tusculan Disputations* n. to 1.3 *Livius . . . Naevius*.

someone with whom . . . with yourself: a common conception of friendship (e.g. Seneca, *Epistles* 3.2; Pliny, *Letters* 51.2–3).

commonplace friendship . . . true and perfect friendship: see n. to ¶18.

23 *For the man . . . reflection of himself*: the idea that a true friend is another self is found in Aristotle (*Nicomachean Ethics* 9.1166a) and the Stoics (Diogenes Laertius 7.23).

24 *a certain learned man . . . strife*: Empedocles in his *About Nature*, of which fragments are preserved. 'Friendship' here is the Greek *philotês* often translated as 'love'.

Marcus Pacuvius: Latin tragic playwright, nephew and pupil of Ennius. Laelius was a patron of his.

the king . . . Orestes: in Pacuvius' play *Chryses*, Orestes and Pylades were pursued by the Taurian king Thoas, whom Chryses killed.

those . . . discuss such topics: Laelius contrasts himself with professional philosophers.

25 *politics came under discussion*: in Book 3 of C.'s *On the Republic*, Philus, arguing against Laelius, presents Carneades' view that government involves injustice.

26 *my sons-in-law*: Scaevola had married Laelius' elder daughter; Fannius the younger one.

27 *friendship has its origin . . . in need*: Plato, in *Lysis* 214e–215e, has friendship arise from insufficiency in the parties, and Aristotle, in *Nicomachean Ethics* 9.1157a26–1157b6, regards this as a lower form of friendship than the truest one, which is based on good character. Epicurus found it hard to be consistent in valuing friendship for itself, and not just for its contribution to pleasure in that it enhances security (C., *On Ends* 1.68–9).

certain animals . . . their feelings: humans and animals are often paralleled in ancient philosophy, though animals cannot describe their feelings.

28 *Gaius . . . Curius*: for these two see n. to ¶18.

Spurius Cassius, or Spurius Maelius: two Spurii were said to have attempted to be tyrants in fifth-century Rome and both were killed.

with whom we fought . . . Pyrrhus and Hannibal: put together as hostile invaders of Italy, Hannibal from Carthage, Pyrrhus from Epirus.

29 *born of Poverty and Insufficiency*: the first parent of friendship according to this view comes from Plato's *Symposium* 203C, where love is born of poverty.

31 *for we do not loan . . . within itself*: Aulus Gellius 17.5 defends C.'s use of the parallel with generosity against the criticism that he is taking as agreed what is disputed, by pointing out that C. means true generosity, which can have no ulterior motive.

32 *like beasts . . . refer all things to pleasure*: another hit at the Epicureans, but unlike ¶13 this attacks their ethics, which held that pleasure is the highest good.

real friendships last for ever: the element of instability that comes with the inclusion of goodwill in the concept of friendship (¶19) is removed in real friendship, which is based on nature and is immutable.

32 *I may answer . . . is younger than I*: Roman social conventions obtain even during a philosophical discussion.

33 *Scipio and myself . . . end of one's life*: Laelius is here giving Scipio's rather more worldly wisdom on friendship, beginning with the possibility that the relationship may not last for ever, though Laelius had said (¶32) that true friendships do so last.

toga praetexta: see n. to ¶1 *the toga of manhood*.

34 *glory*: C.'s next work was *On Glory* (*On Duties* 2.31). In *On Duties* 2.43 C. distinguishes true glory, based on the approval of good men, from false glory. He speaks more loosely here and puts the point into the mouth of Scipio, who adopts a commonsensical and worldly point of view, not distinguishing between types of glory or of friendship.

36 *if Coriolanus . . . helped by their friends*: Laelius here introduces the problems that will issue in the first law of friendship in ¶44. Gaius Marcius Coriolanus went into exile when accused of tyrannical conduct and of opposing a grain distribution to the starving populace. He then marched on Rome at the head of their enemies the Volscians, but was persuaded by his mother and his wife to turn back. Vecellinus is taken to be a cognomen of Spurius Cassius. On Spurius Maelius, see n. to ¶28. Aulus Gellius (*Attic Nights* 1.3.19) complains that C.'s advice here not to take up arms against one's country for the sake of a friend is more than obvious.

37 *As for Tiberius Gracchus . . . body politic*: the incident took place in 133, four years before the dramatic date of this dialogue and is a rare piece of auto-biography by Laelius. The main sources are Plutarch, *Tiberius Gracchus*, and Appian, *Civil Wars*, Book 1. The turmoil is the political conflict in which Tiberius Gracchus, who as tribune had proposed an agrarian law to distribute public land to small holders, was killed. Laelius was part of the *consilium* investigating the fracas.

support by . . . Gaius Blossius of Cumae: Gaius Blossius belonged to a distinguished Campanian family. Because Quintus Aelius Tubero (see n. to ¶101) had philosophical interests, and Blossius studied Stoic philosophy with Antipater of Tarsus, philosophical motives have been sought for the Gracchan programme.

Laenas and Rupilius: Publius Popilius Laenas and Publius Rupilius, the consuls of 132.

met with the . . . punishment that the Republic demanded: according to Plutarch, Blossius of Cumae committed suicide when Aristonicus, whose claim to rule Asia he was supporting, was defeated by Rome (*Tiberius Gracchus* 20).

39 *Aemilius Papus . . . Fabricius Luscinus*: the latter is the Gaius Fabricius of ¶18. He and Quintus Aemilius Papus were consuls together in 282 and 278.

Tiberius Coruncanius: see n. to ¶18.

Gaius Carbo: Gaius Papirius Carbo, tribune in 131, was a supporter of Tiberius Gracchus who proposed a law allowing tribunes to be elected for a second term, which would have made Tiberius' attempt at re-election legal. He was a member of the land commission in 130.

Gaius Cato: a grandson of Cato the Elder and a relation of Scipio Aemilianus, he was consul in 114.

his own brother . . . most enthusiastic: in 129, while doing military service in Spain, Gaius Sempronius Gracchus was made a member of the land commission to implement his brother's law. He supported Carbo's law (see n. above).

40 *look far into the future . . . days to come*: Laelius is shown looking ahead to the tribunate of Gaius Gracchus in 123 (see ¶41) and more generally to the civil wars, as is made more explicit in ¶43.

41 *Publius Nasica*: Publius Cornelius Scipio Nasica Serapio, a cousin of Scipio Aemilianus, was the person who actually killed Tiberius Gracchus in 133. For his safety, he was sent by the senate in 132 on an embassy to Pergamum to organize the new province of Asia. C. implies that his death there was not accidental.

In the case of Carbo . . . as best we could: it is not clear what is meant here.

the ballot . . . Cassian law: Laelius refers to the secret ballot applied to elections by a law of 139 passed by the tribune Gabinius; to trials before the people by a law of Lucius Cassius Longinus, tribune in 137; and to legislation by a law passed by Carbo in 131. C. himself proposed to include a modified form of the ballot in his code of laws at *On the Laws* 3.33–9, where Quintus and Atticus give the arguments against it.

42 *a penalty . . . treasonous activity*: Gaius Gracchus' followers were dealt with by action taken under the *senatus consultum ultimum* in use for the first time. The decree required the magistrates to see that the state came to no harm—a kind of martial law.

Themistocles . . . suicide: Themistocles and Coriolanus were often compared as military leaders, both of whom won great victories and then contemplated committing treason (*Letters to Atticus* 9.10.3). In *Brutus* 41–3, 'Cicero' is made to say that the Volscian War and the Persian Wars were virtually contemporary and that both men died similar deaths—that is, by suicide—but Atticus, who had written a chronology of Roman history, which C. used, is made to point out that Thucydides, writing much closer to the events, has Themistocles die a natural death. The story of his drinking bull's blood starts with Aristophanes' *Knights* 83–4, and in *Brutus* 43 Atticus is jokingly made to offer to add that story to Coriolanus' death as well.

43 *a conspiracy . . . one of these days*: Laelius' prophecy would remind C.'s readers of the actions of Sulla and their contemporary Caesar and their followers.

44 *first law of friendship*: this is the conclusion drawn from the discussion that began in ¶36 on how far love should go in friendship.

counsel: C. returns to this topic at ¶88.

45 *the key . . . on behalf of several*: the sentiments here are those of Phaedra's nurse in Euripides' *Hippolytus*, lines 253–62, who claims the support of wise men in her opinion (line 266).

46 *for the sake . . . should be sought*: the view rejected—that friendships are even now desirable as protection—like the view earlier (¶26) that friendship arises from insufficiency, is Epicurean.

   weaker sex: the translation aims to catch the patronizing tone of the Latin diminutive *mulierculae* (literally 'little women').

48 *distress of mind . . . a wise man*: Laelius is made to attack the idea of the Stoic wise man, who is exempt from mental distress.

   as I said before: in ¶27.

49 *to coin a phrase, loving back*: C. is actually coining a word, inventing the Latin term *redamare*: 'to love back'.

52 *men who . . . true understanding*: the target is again the Epicureans.

   life lived by tyrants: the unhappiness and loneliness of tyrants is a common idea in Greece and Rome, developed by C. elsewhere (e.g. *Tusculan Disputations* 5.57–63).

53 *Tarquin*: Tarquinius Superbus (Tarquin the Proud) was the last king of Rome. The Etruscan dynasty was finally expelled by the ancestor of C.'s contemporary Marcus Brutus.

56 *three views . . . puts on himself*: C. rejects all of these views, because they involve a strict rationing of friendly feelings, which might rule out any kind of real generosity or self-sacrifice.

57 *attacking . . . normally use*: C. is probably thinking of advocacy in the courts.

59 *the Seven*: the Seven Sages, see *Tusculan Disputations* n. to 5.7.

61 *even if by some chance . . . does not ensue*: with C.'s concern here over the proper limits of indulgence to a friend's misdemeanours, cf. his correspondence with Matius in this volume (*Letters to his Friends* 11.27–8), which discusses how to apply such general advice to particular cases, something Gellius *Attic Nights* 1.3.13–16 complains that C. omits in the treatise. Dealing with autocracy and civil war led to many compromises with principle in this period. Unfortunately, we cannot date either the treatise or the correspondence with precision, the first being between March and November of 44, the letters within that period at the end of August (Griffin 1997, 89 n. 12).

62 *every man . . . signs and marks*: reports of Scipio's ideas usually mark a practical turn in the conversation (as in ¶33)—here on choosing friends. The remark about goats and sheep is reminiscent of Xenophon *Memorabilia* 2.4.4, where it is horses and oxen that are mentioned.

64 *where would you find a man . . . place of himself*: C. betrays here one reason why he had so many non-senatorial friends, including his closest friend Atticus, Gaius Matius, Papirius Paetus, Volumnius Eutrapelus, and Marcus Marius. Some of these, like Atticus, were Epicureans (see Barnes and Griffin 1997, 105–6).

Ennius . . . fickle: *Scaenica* frag. 210 Vahlen; 185 Jocelyn.

65 *the basis . . . is trustworthiness*: the Latin word is *fides* ('good faith'), a term very important in Roman law, as well as in business and social life.

a good man . . . a wise man: C. refers back to ¶18, where he said that friendship can exist only among good men but defended a commonsensical non-Stoic conception of the good or wise man. Here, his discussion of neces-sary and undiluted virtue suggests a more Stoic view, though he goes on in ¶66 to eschew sternness and strictness, qualities often associated with Stoicism.

67 *the saying . . . friendship's requirements*: C. alters the point of this Greek proverb, which, according to Aristotle (*Nicomachean Ethics* 8.1156B27), means that long association is necessary to know someone properly and test his reliability.

69 *Philus or Rupilius*: see n. to ¶14 and n. to ¶37.

Mummius: Spurius Mummius, the brother of the Mummius who sacked Corinth. C. believed, perhaps mistakenly, that he was a senator like his brother (see T. R. Broughton, *The Magistrates of the Roman Republic*, 2 vols., New York, American Philological Association, 1951–2, i, 468).

Quintus Maximus: Scipio's blood brother, the elder son of Lucius Aemilius Paulus, who was adopted by Quintus Fabius Maximus and hence became Quintus Fabius Maximus Aemilianus (consul 145).

71 *acts to be remembered . . . by the doer*: Nepos (*Atticus* 11.5) says that Atticus remembered kindnesses, but remembered what he gave only as long as the recipient was grateful, cf. Seneca, *On Benefits* 2.10.4, 2.11.

73 *as much as the person . . . is able to take*: Seneca, *On Benefits* 2.15.3–17.2, makes the point about considering what is suitable for oneself to give and recipients to take, but has in mind material things or help. Publius Rupilius (consul 132) was said to have been so grieved when his younger brother Lucius, who had been praetor in 133, was not elected consul (presumably in one of the years 131–129) that he died soon afterwards (*Tusculan Disputations* 4.40).

75 *Lycomedes . . . that journey*: Lycomedes was the maternal grandfather of Neoptolemus, the son of Achilles. He tried to stop Neoptolemus from going to Troy when he was very young but he was important in the sacking of Troy.

76 *friendships of the ordinary kind*: perfect friendships last for life (¶32) but ordinary friendships can end. C. makes this distinction often (e.g. ¶¶22, 33–5, 77, 100).

I have heard Cato say: many wise sayings were credited to the Elder Cato.

77 *Quintus Pompeius . . . Metellus*: Quintus Pompeius was elected consul for 141, having promised Scipio that he would not stand but would support Laelius' candidature. Quintus Metellus Macedonicus (consul 143) is called 'our colleague' because he, like Laelius, was a member of the augural college. In *On Duties* 1.87, as here, C. says that Scipio and he disagreed without

rancour but in *On the Republic* 1.31 he had called Metellus a leader of the 'slanderous enemies of Scipio'.

80 *a true friend . . . another self*: at ¶23 C. had said that one looks on a true friend as a reflection of oneself, but at ¶56 he rejected the idea that one should have the same attitude towards a friend as towards oneself because it ruled out both doing more for a friend and self-sacrifice. The Stoics believed that the attachment to oneself that is evident from infancy was the origin of the sense of mutual attraction that unites human beings as such (*On Ends* 3.59).

81 *plain to see in animals*: see n. to ¶27.

searches for another . . . one out of two: cf. ¶93 where friendship turns many minds to one.

82 *feeling of respect*: the Latin word *verecundia*, etymologically connected with the verb 'to fear', embodies self-restraint and regard for others. See the full discussion of the word in R. A. Kaster, *Emotion, Restraint, and Community in Ancient Rome*, Oxford, Oxford University Press, 2005, chap. 1, esp. 26–7. The Loeb Library translation 'reverence' is not sufficiently egalitarian for friendship between equals, which C. discusses here.

83 *the highest goals . . . virtue in isolation*: not the view of the Stoa, which taught that virtue alone was sufficient for the highest good, happiness. That it was a necessary condition for happiness is stated in ¶84.

85 *one should judge . . . judgement*: C. reproduces a saying of Theophrastus, presumably from his essay on friendship referred to by Seneca (*Epistles* 3.2: 'against the advice of Theophrastus, they exercise judgement when they have loved instead of not loving until they have exercised judgement').

contravening the old proverb: *actum ne agas* ('Don't redo what is done').

86 *to live . . . the life of civilised men*: *liberaliter vivere* means, literally, to live like free men.

87 *Timon of Athens*: a misanthrope mentioned in Aristophanes *Lysistrata* (line 808) and later writers.

88 *Archytas of Tarentum*: a contemporary of Plato.

human nature loves nothing solitary: as in *On Duties* 1.158, C. regards human beings as naturally sociable.

criticism . . . should be taken in good part: cf. ¶44 on the importance of giving good advice in friendship. Here C. explicitly includes criticism.

89 *my good friend . . . hatred*: the Roman comic playwright Terence, contemporary with Scipio and Laelius. C. quotes line 68 of his *Andria*.

we do not live . . . with a friend: C. may be thinking of relations with the recently deceased Julius Caesar after he had become dictator.

90 *Cato . . . witty to say*: see n. to 76.

92 *the effect of friendship . . . become one*: related to the Pythagorean definition of friendship in *On Duties* 1.56: that several be united into one.

93 *Someone says no . . . Gnatho*: a character in Terence's *Eunuchus*; the lines are 252–3.

95 *a demagogue*: the Latin word is *popularis*, which means someone who appeals to the people and supports their power, as opposed to supporting senatorial power; it can be used pejoratively (as here) or favourably.

96 *tribunes . . . be re-elected*: on Carbo's bill, see n. to ¶39.

   a law . . . of the people: C. had achieved the same outcome when, as consul in 63, he spoke successfully against the agrarian law of Servilius Rullus, which would have distributed public land in Italy and the provinces.

   law on priesthoods . . . Crassus: in 145 Crassus as tribune proposed to change the mode of election to priesthoods, previously done by co-optation. C. praises Laelius' successful speech in opposition in *Brutus* 83 and *On the Nature of the Gods* 3.5, 3.43. In 104 a law of Gnaeus Domitius Ahenobarbus had the pontiffs elected by seventeen of the thirty-five tribes, chosen by lot—clearly a compromise.

   the first politician . . . addressing the people: Plutarch says that Gaius Gracchus was the first to do this. When *On Friendship* was written, Julius Caesar had just replaced the old rostra or speaker's platform, which faced away from the forum towards the senate house, with a new one facing towards the forum and away from the senate house.

   praetor, five years . . . consulship: Laelius was praetor in 145 and consul in 140 after more than the minimum interval of two years.

98 *boastful soldiers . . . he says*: both Plautus and Terence satirized such characters as Thraso in Terence's *Eunuchus*. The lines quoted are 391–2. Thais is a courtesan.

99 *Of all . . . me today*: a quotation from a lost play of Caecilius Statius.

100 *the wisdom . . . capable of attaining*: see n. to ¶18n.

101 *Lucius Paulus . . . Galus*: see n. to ¶9.

   Nasica: Publius Cornelius Scipio Nasica Corculum, father of Nasica Serapio (see n. to ¶41).

   Tiberius Gracchus . . . Scipio: father of the tribunes Tiberius and Gaius, and of Sempronia, who married Scipio Aemilianus.

   Lucius Furius . . . Mummius: see n. to ¶69.

   Quintus Tubero: Quintus Aelius Tubero was a nephew of Scipio Aemilianus, his mother being the daughter of Lucius Aemilius Paulus; see also n. to ¶36.

   Publius Rutilius: Publius Rutilius Rufus (consul 105) served under Scipio Aemilianus at Numantia and studied Stoicism with Panaetius. Legate to Quintus Mucius Scaevola (consul 95) when he was proconsul of Asia, he was unjustly condemned for extortion in 92 and thereafter lived as an exile in Asia.

   Aulus Verginius: a lawyer mentioned by Pomponius in *Digest* 1.2.40.

103 *We had one house*: this makes more explicit the 'I associated with him at home' of ¶15 and seems to suggest that Laelius and Scipio shared a household.

104 *leisure time*: C. compares Scipio's leisure activities with his own enforced solitude in *On Duties* 3.1–4.

every trial . . . severe: an Epicurean idea about suffering, used to support the notion that the balance of pleasure over distress is always possible to maintain.

APPENDIX: LETTERS TO FRIENDS

LETTER FROM CICERO TO GAIUS MATIUS
(*LETTERS TO HIS FRIENDS* 11.27)

1 *Trebatius' visit*: Gaius Trebatius Testa, an equestrian lawyer, to whom C. dedicated the *Topics* and whom he recommended to Caesar in Gaul, where he became friendly with Matius.

your complaint: see ¶7.

2 *the difference . . . lifestyles*: Matius remained an *eques*, whereas C. sought and achieved senatorial office and rank.

when Caesar was in Gaul: Caesar was the governor there from 58 until the start of the civil war in 49.

3 *at the outset of the civil war*: on 19 March 49.

the letter you sent me: a letter from Matius and Trebatius, received by C. on 25 March 49 (*Letters to Atticus* 9.15a).

4 *I set out . . . Pompey*: C., after much hesitation, crossed to Greece to join Pompey at the end of June 49 (*Letters to Atticus* 15.25).

I came to Brundisium: C. returned to Italy in October 48 after the Pompeian defeat at the battle of Pharsalus.

5 *began to live . . . in Rome*: in autumn 44, after being well received by Caesar at Tarentum in September.

you urged me . . . ouvrage philosophique: C. credits Brutus, at the end of the *Tusculan Disputations*, with spurring him on to write philosophy. He had by then written the lost *Hortensius*, the *Academic Books*, and *On Ends*.

7 *I now return . . . complaint*: Matius had been told that C. criticized his regret for Caesar's death and his attitude thereafter in supporting a certain law (see next n.) and joining in the management of Octavian's games.

that notorious law: probably not the law of Caesar about debt, mentioned in Matius' reply (*Letters to his Friends* 11.28.2), but one of Antony's laws, perhaps the one of 1 June 44 changing Antony's province to Transalpine and Cisalpine Gauls for five years.

your management of the games: combining victory games and funeral games for Caesar, they were given by Octavian at his own expense in July 44. C. complained to Atticus (*Letters to Atticus* 15.2.3) of Matius' role in giving them.

8 *if Caesar was a king . . . he was*: C. is referring to Caesar's *de facto* autocracy. Caesar himself, in an effort to allay such fears, had refused a diadem offered to him.

LETTER FROM GAIUS MATIUS TO CICERO
(*LETTERS TO HIS FRIENDS* 11.28)

1 *good citizen*: Matius probably uses *bonus* in the sense C. often uses it, to mean 'optimate' or 'conservative'.

could have been persuaded recklessly: perhaps an allusion to C.'s philosophical adherence to Academic scepticism, which favoured caution in assenting to opinions.

you have . . . countered on my behalf: as C. at least claimed to have done (*Letters to his Friends* 11.27.7).

2 *But I shall not resort . . . philosophical level*: Matius decides not to contest the view that Caesar's death was beneficial to the state, whose interests must always be preferred to friendship, but just pleads loyalty to his old friend. In *On Friendship* ¶61 C. allows for supporting a friend to some extent, even in dishonourable things.

the very law . . . their citizenship: C. probably means Caesar's bankruptcy law of 46 or 45, which allowed debtors to hand over their property in settlement and thus avoid *infamia*, which carried the forfeit of some civil rights.

3 *the very same men . . . his death*: C. possibly points to both the Caesarians among the conspirators, who abused their influence with the dictator, and also the conquered Pompeians, whom Caesar pardoned and who then proved ungrateful.

'champions of liberty': as the conspirators like to style themselves.

5 *if you feel . . . right thing*: C. was about to argue, in his work *On Duties*, that the expedient, rightly understood, coincided with the honourable. Matius presumably knew that C. agreed with this Stoic view.

6 *I took responsibility . . . the young Caesar*: C. claims to have defended Matius on this count in *Letters to his Friends* 11.27.7. That politics could be kept separate from private duty in this case is questionable, given that the 'young Caesar' was Caesar's nephew and adopted son Octavian.

7 *Antony the consul*: Marcus Antonius, who had been Caesar's legate in Gaul, became his colleague in the consulship in 44, then colleague to Cornelius Dolabella on Caesar's death.

8 *my life . . . Rhodes*: a favourite place of retreat, contemplated by C. in April of 46 (*Letters to his Friends* 7.3.5), and a good place for exile—it was where Cassius went (*Letters to Atticus* 11.13.1; *Letters to his Friends* 4.7.4, cf. Horace, *Epistles* 1.11.17).

The Oxford World's Classics Website

www.worldsclassics.co.uk

- Browse the full range of Oxford World's Classics online

- Sign up for our monthly e-alert to receive information on new titles

- Read extracts from the Introductions

- Listen to our editors and translators talk about the world's greatest literature with our Oxford World's Classics audio guides

- Join the conversation, follow us on Twitter at OWC_Oxford

- Teachers and lecturers can order inspection copies quickly and simply via our website

www.worldsclassics.co.uk

American Literature

British and Irish Literature

Children's Literature

Classics and Ancient Literature

Colonial Literature

Eastern Literature

European Literature

Gothic Literature

History

Medieval Literature

Oxford English Drama

Philosophy

Poetry

Politics

Religion

The Oxford Shakespeare

A complete list of Oxford World's Classics, including Authors in Context, Oxford English Drama, and the Oxford Shakespeare, is available in the UK from the Marketing Services Department, Oxford University Press, Great Clarendon Street, Oxford OX2 6DP, or visit the website at www.oup.com/uk/worldsclassics.

In the USA, visit www.oup.com/us/owc for a complete title list.

Oxford World's Classics are available from all good bookshops. In case of difficulty, customers in the UK should contact Oxford University Press Bookshop, 116 High Street, Oxford OX1 4BR.

Bhagavad Gita

The Bible Authorized King James Version
With Apocrypha

The Book of Common Prayer

Dhammapada

The Gospels

The Koran

The Pañcatantra

The Sauptikaparvan (from the Mahabharata)

The Tale of Sinuhe and Other Ancient Egyptian Poems

The Qur'an

Upanisads

ANSELM OF CANTERBURY	**The Major Works**
THOMAS AQUINAS	**Selected Philosophical Writings**
AUGUSTINE	**The Confessions** **On Christian Teaching**
BEDE	**The Ecclesiastical History**
KĀLIDĀSA	**The Recognition of Śakuntalā**
LAOZI	**Daodejing**
RUMI	**The Masnavi**
ŚĀNTIDEVA	**The Bodhicaryāvatāra**

An Anthology of Elizabethan Prose
Fiction

Early Modern Women's Writing

Three Early Modern Utopias (Utopia;
New Atlantis; The Isle of Pines)

FRANCIS BACON   Essays
The Major Works

APHRA BEHN   Oroonoko and Other Writings
The Rover and Other Plays

JOHN BUNYAN   Grace Abounding
The Pilgrim's Progress

JOHN DONNE   The Major Works
Selected Poetry

JOHN FOXE   Book of Martyrs

BEN JONSON   The Alchemist and Other Plays
The Devil is an Ass and Other Plays
Five Plays

JOHN MILTON   The Major Works
Paradise Lost
Selected Poetry

EARL OF ROCHESTER   Selected Poems

SIR PHILIP SIDNEY   The Old Arcadia
The Major Works

SIR PHILIP and   The Sidney Psalter
MARY SIDNEY

IZAAK WALTON   The Compleat Angler